D1058561

CORPORATE CULTURE

_____

FROM VICIOUS TO
VIRTUOUS CIRCLES

CORPORATE CULTURE

FROM VICIOUS TO VIRTUOUS CIRCLES

CHARLES HAMPDEN-TURNER

The
Economist
Books

Hutchinson

First published in Great Britain by
Hutchinson Business Books Limited
An imprint of Random Century Limited
Random Century House, 20 Vauxhall Bridge Road,
London SW1V 2SA.

Copyright © 1990 The Economist Books Limited
Text copyright © 1990 Charles Hampden-Turner
Charts and diagrams copyright © 1990 The Economist
Books Limited

All rights reserved under International and Pan-American
Copyright Conventions

No part of this publication may be reproduced or
transmitted in any form or by any means, electronic or
mechanical, including photocopying, recording or any
information storage and retrieval system now known or to
be invented, without permission in writing from the
publisher.

British Library Cataloguing in Publication Data

Hampden-Turner, Charles
    Corporate Culture.
    1. Organisations. Effectiveness. Improvement
    I. Title
    658.314

ISBN 0-09-174665-5

Printed and bound in Great Britain by Butler & Tanner,
Frome, Somerset.

Contents

List of figures

List of tables

Acknowledgements

I am most grateful to the many people who assisted me in this book. Fons Trompenaars has over the years reminded me of the role of culture in management affairs. His contributions to Chapter 2 were invaluable. I learned much from Gareth Morgan, Harrison Owen, Jim Wilk, Ronnie Lessem, David K. Hurst, and Iain Mangham who all attended a culture conference of mine at the London Business School.

Other influences upon me over the years include Ed Schein, Roger Harrison, Peter Senge, Alistair Mant and Charles Handy, whose *Gods of Management* persuaded me that there was a British audience for cultural studies after all.

I am especially grateful to those whose work I describe. Royal Foote, who consulted to Annheuser-Busch, is an old friend from my days at the Wright Institute in Berkeley and Nick Georgiades former human resource director for British Airways, who gave a wonderful presentation at the University of Bath, proved highly informative, as did Luke Mayhew and Mike Bruce.

Anders Lindström, turnround specialist and Goran Carstedt until recently at Volvo showed me just how Swedish managers are admired around the world for their skill and humanity. David K. Hurst of the Federal Metals Group, formerly Russelsteel, is my favourite corporate conceptualizer, a renaissance man of Canadian business. I was extraordinarily impressed by Tom Melohn of North American Tool and Die who took time to show yet one more visitor around and shared with me his humour and commitments. Access would not have been possible but for Tom whose help was deeply appreciated.

To Stephen Haggard of The Economist Intelligence Unit belongs the credit of first seeing the possibility of this book, while Carolyn White my current editor has been a pleasure to work with and an ally from earlier times. Finally Rosemary Epaminondas not only types better than I, but has better grammar, punctuation and critical judgement. Without her word processing skills I'd have despaired while reading my own efforts.

Chapter 1

WHAT *IS* CORPORATE CULTURE?

The culture of an organization defines appropriate behaviour, bonds and motivates individuals and asserts solutions where there is ambiguity. It governs the way a company processes information, its internal relations and its values. It functions at all levels from subconscious to visible. In the world of increasingly "flat" companies and sophisticated "knowledge-based" products, control and understanding of an organization's corporate culture are a key responsibility of leaders, as well as a vital tool for management if it is to encourage high performance and maintain shareholder value.

A corporate culture can be described and mapped out using different categories and classification systems, but all cultures are in fact responses to corporate dilemmas. The role of the corporate leader is to manage conflicting needs in a synergistic way, creating an environment in which opposing forces can be reconciled to create rapid and strong growth.

Culture is used by social scientists to describe a whole way of life, ways of acting, feeling and thinking, which are learned by groups of people rather than being biologically determined. Great variations occur in the behaviour of human groups with similar genetic endowments. Sir Edward Bernard Taylor attributed these to culture, "that complex whole which includes knowledge, belief, art, morals, law, custom and any other capabilities and habits, acquired by man as a member of society".

Corporate culture has been likened to one of those ink blots in which we see what we want to see. In corporations, culture is used to explain why nothing seems to work, or why competitors are so much more successful. Culture is thought to bestow unique competitive advantages and/or dire limitations. Could Westerners be like the Japanese even if they wished to be? Would it mean losing for ever the distinctive aspects of Western culture? This book argues that corporate culture is describable, measurable if necessary and, within limits, alterable.

Corporate cultures and macro-cultures

It is important to distinguish between the culture inside the organization and the broader culture of the nation, economic group or geographical region. The first will be called "corporate cultures" and the second "macro-cultures". The investigation of corporate cultures involves looking at how people in an organization behave; what assumptions govern their behaviour; and what bonds or glue hold the corporation together.

But the macro-culture cannot be ignored because, as we shall see, corporate cultures act out themes and patterns of the wider culture. Corporate cultures are specific episodes of more general national and regional patterns. US corporations, for example, will display particular variations of a larger North American theme. The reason many Japanese corporations are such formidable competitors has a lot to do with Asian culture. Those seeking to mobilize Japanese, French, UK or US staffs by giving meaning and purpose to their corporate culture can help themselves by choosing ideas and themes from the macro-culture in which the organization is embedded. Otherwise they may not be understood.

SOME CHARACTERISTICS OF CORPORATE CULTURE

Individuals make up a culture

Where does a culture come from initially? The answer is that it lies within the potential of an organization's individual members. They use the culture to reinforce ideas, feelings and information which are consistent with their beliefs. The culture discourages, even represses, sentiments and information that are inconsistent.

All cultures exclude something. Otherwise the organization would become simply a confused collection of its members' various desires, and might fail to serve its customers effectively. A culture which admits a wide range of human expression is known as a high-context culture. One that limits this range has low context.

Cultures can be rewarders of excellence

Cultures embody the needs and aspirations of a group's members. This makes the process of culture forming inherently satisfying and a strong source of motivation. All members of a group can strive to create a habitat for their own feelings and ideas. They can help establish the norms and standards by which they will be judged, set up the categories into which their own ideas will fit and create the roles they aspire to fill. Culture, at best, can be an environment for bringing out the potentials of all the group's members and a system for rewarding defined tasks.

Culture confers immense prestige on particular accomplishments. At 3M, for example, the culture contains an organized system for admiring innovative work. National cultures likewise excel at what they most admire. The US admiration for the individual has produced the pioneer, the frontiersman, the mountain men, the robber barons, the grand acquisitors and the junk bond bandits. The relish of the English for their spoken tongue has produced some great literature and theatre, and a modern broadcasting, entertainments and teaching tradition. Switzerland has turned its geographical location into a meeting place for nations and a centre for negotiation, rescue, refuge, healing, medicine and banking. National cultures can be powerful influences.

Culture is a set of affirmations

A culture proves that no group, corporation, tribe or nation can start from nothing. Their members need to be imbued with beliefs and assertions. Some executives will remember training-groups (T-groups) when they were common some 20 years ago, and may have felt at first hand the sheer anxiety of a leaderless, purposeless group without structure or agenda. They may have experienced the eagerness, almost desperation with which the group developed norms, values, procedures, purposes and shared agendas, and the great relief and intensity of mutual feelings which these brought to many group members. Culture, then, is especially strong where people most need reassurance and greater certainty.

Cultural affirmations tend to fulfil themselves

The assertions that create a culture typically take form before that culture creates wealth or value for its customers. Getting together around a belief may help to make that belief come true. At the very least it can be made credible through continual commitments by the group. Thus, if the Macintosh computer is described by its developers in Apple as an "insanely great" product that will "change the world", then Apple employees may expend greater efforts and creativity upon this product than might otherwise be the case. There is also a risk of disappointment and an increase in tension, together with envy from employees working on other products. So culture has consequences, whether for good or ill.

Cultures make sense and have coherent points of view

Even if people do not share the values and the premises of a culture, once they grasp what these are they will see the logic of following the example of true members of the culture. It is impossible to appreciate a corporate culture until it is understood that its actions follow logically from its beliefs and assumptions. The feeling that a culture is illogical is usually the result of people mistaking its premises for their own. For example, the continuous monitoring of employees' work by video cameras is a logical consequence of the assumption that they are naturally lazy and careless unless carefully supervised and corrected. Such assumptions may become self-fulfilling because workers will tend to relax the moment scrutiny is interrupted and they may try to evade the cameras. Such behaviour "proves" to the satisfaction of top managers that it is necessary to continue close control and monitoring.

Cultures provide their members with continuity and identity

Without a shared culture Volvo would not be recognizably Volvo and companies like British Airways could not be distinguished from other carriers in terms of service. Nor would employees seek to identify themselves with these companies. Only if beliefs are shared, affirmed, fulfil themselves and retain distinctive meanings over time despite changing environments can a corporation retain its sense of identity and continuity. Like a ship at sea it will retain its purposes, values and sense of direction, even if it is blown off course, damaged or temporarily disabled. In an emergency everyone will realize that the "ship" needs to be saved and needs to reach its destination by whatever route is possible. The ship analogy facilitates the understanding of two additional elements of corporate culture.

A culture is in a state of balance between reciprocal values

Just as a ship needs to move forwards in order to keep its balance and buffer itself against turbulence, so a corporate culture is a balancing act between turbulence and stability, continuity and change, the course to be steered and the force and direction of wind and tide. It cannot be all change or all continuity. And within the ship's company are many sets of reciprocal roles which must also achieve some kind of balance. One person or group provides the power (shareholders, for example), another steers. One scans the environment and looks to the outside, and others make sure that the ship is in good trim inside. There are leaders and followers, heads and hands, those who send and receive signals and those who respond to them. Any culture is not simply a division of labour but an integration of that labour into a balanced whole.

A corporate culture is a cybernetic system

The word cybernetic is from the Greek *kybernetes,* helmsman. To call a culture cybernetic is to imply that it steers itself and perseveres in the direction it has set itself despite obstacles and interruptions. An automatic compass, for example, indicates which direction a ship must be steered in order to compensate for being blown off course or to divert around an obstacle. A corporate culture may similarly try to penetrate a new market from different directions following a series of frustrations. All cybernetic systems process feedback about changes in the environment and make appropriate course corrections.

British Airways, for example, uses several kinds of feedback to improve its culture of customer service. There is the routine trip report, but there are also "Customer First" teams which meet to consider how service might be improved in the light of their experience in the cabin. Finally there is a Videobox in which customers are filmed making complaints or expressing gratitude (see Chapter 4). These are scrutinized so that the culture can learn. Learning is what it is all about.

Cultures are patterns

A culture is no particular thing or object, but a pattern which appears both through time and across the organization. For example, it was found in a major study of a US bank that the relationship between the bank's service staff and its customers was repeated in the relationship between supervisors and service staff and was repeated in the relationship between top managers and supervisors. It is probable, although the research did not go that far, that the pattern was repeated again between the HQ of the bank and its branches. In fact, culture resembles a hologram in the sense that information is distributed throughout the pattern, and any piece of any pattern contains within it a microcosm of the whole. Hence a skilful and kind encounter between the airline stewardess and a frightened passenger is a microcosm of how that stewardess has herself been treated, which, in turn, is part of a more general attitude towards empowering cabin crews to serve customers better.

Cultures are about communications

It is most important to grasp that many cultures facilitate communication, the sharing of experience and information. They can make their members strongly supportive of each other. Corporations may develop patterns of wishful thinking and mutual reassurance (see Chapter 8 for the interesting range of excuses used by Volvo in France to assure its members that a Swedish car could never appeal to the Latin temperament). The corporate culture was failing, yet mutual affections required that failure be cushioned and excused. However, the affectional systems of cultures are not necessarily barriers to better performance. Work of world-beating quality is performed in North American Tool and Die as acts of friendship for fellow workers and for its founder (see Chapter 9). To win the affection of peers and fellow workers can be the ultimate and most powerful reason for working.

Cultures are more or less synergistic

A subtle, yet vitally important aspect of culture is the synergy among its values. The word synergy is from the Greek *syn-ergo,* "work with", and refers to the extent that different values held within a culture "work well" with each other. Synergy is probably the closest Westerners get to the Asian concept of *wa* (or harmony) in business, a central axiom of Japanese national and corporate culture. Values work with each other if they have been designed to do so.

Synergies can be woven into the elements of corporate culture. For example, corporate creativity is highest not when self-styled geniuses advertise themselves vociferously, but when a flow of original ideas encounters intelligent and constructive feedback, along with people willing to push these ideas through and complete every last detail of their implementation. For Western Oil (see Chapter 3), the highest standards of road safety could, in the end, be pushed through only by truck drivers, but this had to happen in conjunction with a management culture determined to reduce losses through accidents.

Only cultures can learn – and organizations must learn

There was a time when a company simply took whatever knowledge was already available from professional bodies or research departments and put it into production. The learning was "brought in" by hiring experts and then ground out by the factory. Employees learned up to a point, but the organization simply exploited what was known, buying new expertise when appropriate. Today everything is simply moving too fast. The market environments are in ever more rapid evolution, while science develops faster than commercial applications can be generated.

In such circumstances there has to be a network of people who can learn simultaneously from changing markets "outside" and burgeoning technology "inside", and bring to customers the latest satisfactions which new knowledge makes possible. This can only be achieved by a culture that continuously learns from several sources: that is the much discussed "learning organization". Organizations whose business is based on innovative and entrepreneurial individuals with high levels of knowledge have a particular problem. These workers must feel more creative and unrestricted within the organization than they would as solo operators, otherwise they will either leave and set up on their own or fail to create the networks that lead to quality products. Norsk Data, for example, finds that it must offer employees more scope for entrepreneurship than they could possibly have if they set up their own companies.

CULTURE AND LEADERSHIP

A most vital connection exists between culture and leadership. Indeed, the successful leaders described in this book exert their most direct influence upon their companies by using the corporate culture. The leaders help to shape the culture. The culture helps to shape its members. Why is culture needed as an intermediary between leaders and followers? Consider the following situations.

"Flat" organizations

The traditional hierarchy was what supposedly integrated the corporation. If B and C disagreed, both could appeal to A, their superior, who settled it. The "brains" at the top of the organization told "the hands" or manual workers at the bottom what to do, and how and when to do it. Yet the sheer complexity of modern business operations has overwhelmed this system.

The company of the future is often portrayed as "flat", without vertical command chains. The boss, even if there is one, can no longer know what everyone should do. The entire organization is suffused with knowledge. No single head can contain the information and skills which are necessary. It reputedly takes 68 different kinds of engineer to make one lunar-landing module for NASA. Imagine "commanding" this coterie of esoteric experts. It is not possible. All a leader can really do is manage the culture of the place where the work is done, extol the vision of the completed whole and the performance standards needed to attain this, and manage the extremely subtle communications necessary for the working together of all parts of the module.

The whole notion of leaders and followers is increasingly out of date and may even be a source of confusion. Followers "lead" in a variety of ways, using judgement, knowledge, skill and self-management. Leaders may have to spend large amounts of their time "following" what skilled subordinates are trying to tell them. Where traditional views of leadership linger and bosses are seen to possess inalienable forms of superiority in all relationships, independent of their actual knowledge, the whole national economy may suffer (see Chapter 2). The capacity to delegate responsibility to where the knowledge resides is crucial to organizational effectiveness.

The ladder of responsibilities

It is false to believe, however, that "authority is breaking down" because a boss can no longer tell most subordinates exactly what to do. It may break down because leaders fail to manage cultures and do not know how to shape these complex phenomena. This is a soluble problem and a skill that can be mastered. A distinction must be made between behaviours called "hierarchical" – by which the person complaining means that he or she is being ordered around too much and is not being allowed enough discretion – and the existence of a "responsibility hierarchy".

Hierarchical behaviour is becoming less and less appropriate in an environment where employees are required to exercise their own judgement and are being paid to do so. But that does not affect the existence of a responsibility hierarchy in which A is responsible to shareholders for how well B, C and D perform. What needs to happen is that A exerts influence on the conditions, the atmosphere, the working environment and the reward structures in which B, C and D work. While B, C and D perform as well as they can, A defines what good performance is, tells the three subordinates how closely they have approximated to their ideal and creates a workplace in which the particular kind of excellence the company seeks to promote can thrive. Increasingly, the leader may want to seek the help of the subordinates in defining what good performance is.

This concept of levels of responsibility with culture at the top is most important. If A tells B, C and D exactly how they should perform, this inevitably impinges upon their areas of judgement and expertise; but if A tells them what good performance is and then celebrates its attainment or criticizes its non-attainment, then all the responsibility for performing well remains with the subordinates, while A accepts responsibility for creating "a culture of high performance" in the company. Culture, then, stands at the apex of the leader's responsibility hierarchy.

The following chapters portray leaders taking responsibility for the whole culture "game", the complete arena in which all the businesses' activities occur. Colin Marshall of British Airways cannot tell his cabin crews how to care better for passengers, they know more about that than he does. He tells them, however, that they must care; and he provides a culture in which the carers are themselves cared for and are empowered to use their discretion in solving problems for passengers. There will be leaders increasingly behaving like mentors, strategists and coaches to the learning and the performances of their employees – encouraging creativity, for example, as did Anders Lindström at BAHCO, not knowing himself what should be created. If the leaders shape the culture, the employees will shape the ideas and everyone will "lead" at their own level.

The leader as harmonizer of complexity: Ouchi's clan culture

If companies are to learn how to supply highly sophisticated products, often interacting with each other in a system, to different countries, then employees' relationships with fellow experts and with those customers must be of such a quality that subtle communications can flow and elaborate syntheses can be created. Just as "orders from the top" are too simple, so are silly jousts and arguments by which one department "beats" the other politically and enlarges its own "turf". Nothing less than the confluence of all available information and expertise into a totality of far greater value than its separate parts is required. William G. Ouchi has argued that this cannot be done with the "culture of bureaucracy"; it is too segmented to create, too shut away in separate boxes. Nor can it be achieved by the "culture of markets", where information is too superficial, too fleeting and too beguiling. It can only be achieved by the "clan culture" of close cooperation, sharing complex forms of information. Ouchi argues that bureaucratic cultures are stable, with lasting if formal relationships, and are capable of transmitting moderately complex information. However, they are static, segmentalized, rule-based, hierarchical and slow to respond.

The market culture, by contrast, is fluid, kaleidoscopic, flexible and fast, but it transmits only abstract information. The clan culture (and Ouchi uses this word in a somewhat private sense) consists of groups of enthusiasts united around the potentials of a technology, product and/or service. The clan is resilient, with deep, lasting relationships, which are capable of transmitting complex information in many forms. Yet this culture is also fluid, kaleidoscopic, flexible and fast. (Note it is not "clannish" in the sense of deliberately excluding others.) The clan leader then is the harmonizer of complexity, the guarantor of fine synthesis and appropriate combinations.

Ouchi sees Japan as better able to deploy clan cultures because it prefers M-form corporations to H-forms (or multi-divisional companies to holding companies).

The H-form is the classic conglomerate: ITT, Hanson Trust, BTR. These companies own a mixed bag of business units which they manage by creating "internal markets", in which the units compete for corporate investment on the basis of performance and shoot for agreed financial targets.

The M-form organization has multiple divisions organized round a central technological base, for example, Sony, Matsushita, but also IBM, Digital Equipment Co and Apple. Such organizations can enjoy clan cultures integrated by learning and innovation around "dream products". This enthusiasm for the product is in marked contrast to the H-form's near exclusive interest in making money, the one theme common to all its business. Ouchi argues that the M-form learns more profoundly than the H-form how to create value for consumers because its leaders are much closer to the process of creation.

These distinctions are particularly important in a world where total quality is an increasingly urgent demand, and where flexible manufacturing attempts to create variety without increasing costs. High quality is an indivisible value requiring an entire culture to work on hundreds of components with such care and precision that the whole process operates flawlessly.

Motivation and reward

Japanese and other Asian companies pay their top executives roughly one third of top US salaries. Salaries and wages are inevitably reflected in the price of a product. Purchasers of Chrysler cars must pay for what is needed to motivate Lee Iacocca – $17 million at the latest report. Culture may not only motivate more strongly but more cheaply. If people work for a mix of motives, that exact mix can be reflected in the culture. The approbation of peers adds little or nothing to costs. Those using cultures skilfully can price competitors using expensive carrots and crude sticks right out of the market. For example, when Apple employees in the early 1980s took to wearing T-shirts with the slogan "working 70 hours a week and loving it", no one was paying them overtime. They were Prometheans who had "stolen" computers from giant corporations and "given" them to individuals.

It also follows that it may not be in the interest of shareholders to let a corporate culture pass into the hands of someone who neither understands nor appreciates it. Long-term investment is only possible if shareholders are willing to support the development of corporate culture well into the future, rather than demanding in dividends what might better be invested in that culture's human resources for subsequent growth.

A DEFINITION OF CULTURE

All the foregoing can now be assembled into a comprehensive definition of corporate culture, which will be the basis for the rest of this book.

Culture comes from within people and is put together by them to reward the capacities that they have in common. Culture gives continuity and identity to the group. It balances contrasting contributions, and operates as a self-steering system which learns from feedback. It works as a pattern of information and can greatly facilitate the exchange of understanding. The values within a culture are more or less harmonious.

There are of course many other definitions of corporate culture. One practical definition comes from André Laurent of Insead.

"An organization's culture reflects assumptions about clients, employees, mission, products, activities and assumptions that have worked well in the past and which get translated into norms of behaviour, expectations about what is legitimate, desirable ways of thinking and acting. [These] are the locus of its capacity for evolution and change." *

Another useful description of culture is by Ed Schein of MIT.

"A pattern of basic assumptions invented, discovered or developed by a given group as it learns to cope with its problems of external adaptation and internal integration that has worked well enough to be considered valid, and to be taught to new members as the correct way to perceive, think, and feel in relation to these problems."

* *Human Resource Management in International Firms,* P. Evans (ed), London, Macmillan, 1990.

Schein also sees cultures as operating at three levels of more or less visibility, and this model is useful in considering how corporate identity can be used in corporate culture change programmes (see Figure 1.1).

Figure 1.1 **Schein's three levels of culture**

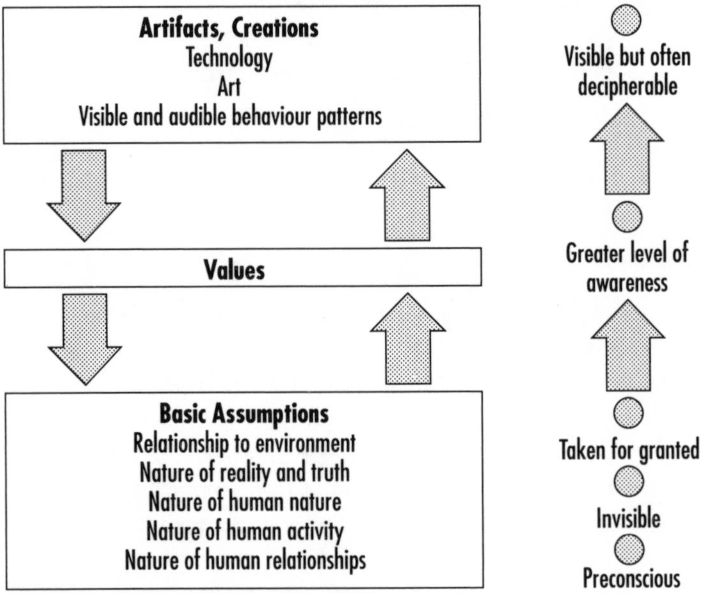

Artifacts, Creations
Technology
Art
Visible and audible behaviour patterns

Visible but often
decipherable

Values

Greater level of
awareness

Basic Assumptions
Relationship to environment
Nature of reality and truth
Nature of human nature
Nature of human activity
Nature of human relationships

Taken for granted

Invisible

Preconscious

Source: E. Schein, "Organisational culture: What it is and how to change it" in *Human Resource Management in International Firms*, P. Evans (ed), Macmillan, 1990.

CLASSIFYING A CULTURE

Is it helpful to fit a culture into a category? Many experts and consultants think that all corporate cultures correspond to a range of ideal types. So a word should be said about diagrams of culture otherwise known as the "quadrants syndrome". Among the more successful of such attempts are those by Terence E. Deal, Allan Kennedy, Roger Harrison and Charles Handy. The last two considerably influenced each other.

Deal and Kennedy model
The quadrant form of analysis looks at two related variables. Consideration, for example, of how big a risk a company must take and how fast the feedback comes as to whether that risk has paid off, produces the quadrants suggested by Deal and Kennedy.

An oil company may risk tens of millions of dollars and not know for 20 years whether this was wise. A film is a notoriously risky venture, but feast or famine come as soon as it is premiered and within months of completion. An insurance company spreads small risks very widely but must wait for years for deaths or accidents; a restaurant, on the other hand, knows in minutes but risks only small amounts (see Figure 1.2).

Figure 1.2 **Simple quadrant by Deal and Kennedy**

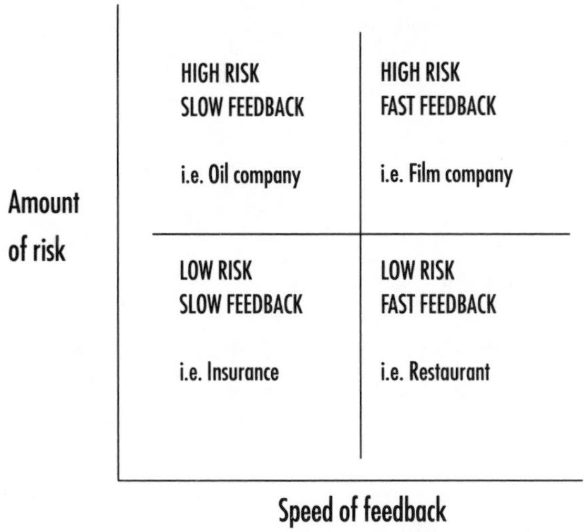

	HIGH RISK SLOW FEEDBACK i.e. Oil company	HIGH RISK FAST FEEDBACK i.e. Film company
Amount of risk	LOW RISK SLOW FEEDBACK i.e. Insurance	LOW RISK FAST FEEDBACK i.e. Restaurant

Speed of feedback

Source: Derived from T. E. Deal and A. A. Kennedy, *Corporate Culture: The Rites and Rituals of Corporate Life*, Addison-Wesley, 1982.

Harrison and Handy model

Roger Harrison, a consultant based in Berkeley, and Charles Handy, adjunct professor at the London Business School, both developed criteria for more complex cultural issues. The ideas are sufficiently similar to be considered together. Harrison conceives of a role culture, which is highly formalized and centrally directed. Handy calls this an Apollo culture after the Greek god. Role and Apollo cultures are bureaucratic or, in the case of the factory, "scientifically" managed by time and motion study and precise mechanical specifications. The power culture (Harrison's term) or Zeus culture (for Handy) is seen as a spider in the centre of a web with informal colleagues "on the same wavelength" as the "old man"; for example, traditional brokerage houses in the City of London, or entrepreneurial companies organized round a brilliant founder. The culture is verbal and intuitive.

Harrison also identifies the task culture with "the matrix" as its sign. Handy calls this an Athena culture. This consists of interdisciplinary project groups organized around the task. For example, a copywriter, visualizer, media buyer, production person and account executive may work together on one advertising campaign which needs them to combine their skills. It is a decentralized way of working but still formalized by the disciplines that must be joined.

Finally, there is the decentralized, informal culture. Harrison calls it atomistic; Handy stresses the fact that bonds of respect and affection often characterize this relationship of free spirits, united by common interests. Hence he calls it Dionysian after the god of wine, passion, theatre and creativity. Such a culture would be typical of independent experts joined together for mutual convenience or stimulation, for example a group practice or a consultancy. The factors determining which category a corporate culture might fall into would be its degree of formalization and centralization (see Figures 1.3 and 1.4).

Hampden-Turner model: culture's main function is to try to mediate dilemmas

The view taken of corporate culture in this book is yet another one, original to this author.

A dilemma is a pair of apparently contradicting statements. Literally, in Greek, it means "two propositions". The everyday issues arising within a corporation take the form of dilemmas: should new products be developed more quickly, to beat competitors on time; or more slowly, to win on quality? The larger strategic issues have the same characteristics: the organization needs to preserve its key continuities, but it also needs periodic change. The whole area of corporate culture is constructed entirely of such dilemmas. As described above, culture originates from elements inside people yet some of these must be registered outside them in remuneration and reward structures that will encourage those capacities most crucial to their shared enterprise. Culture asserts what may or may not be true, yet must live with the consequence of those assertions. Cultures change and yet have continuity; they are balanced between values yet must be able to tilt; they are cybernetic, making errors and corrections; they are wholes, yet each part carries the pattern of that whole; they bond people together, yet each individual has a special role. These differences are more or less synergistic.

Even the ways of classifying cultures are structured around dilemmas. Ideally, the culture should reconcile the dilemma. If big risks are taken

Figure 1.3 **Culture quadrant by Roger Harrison**

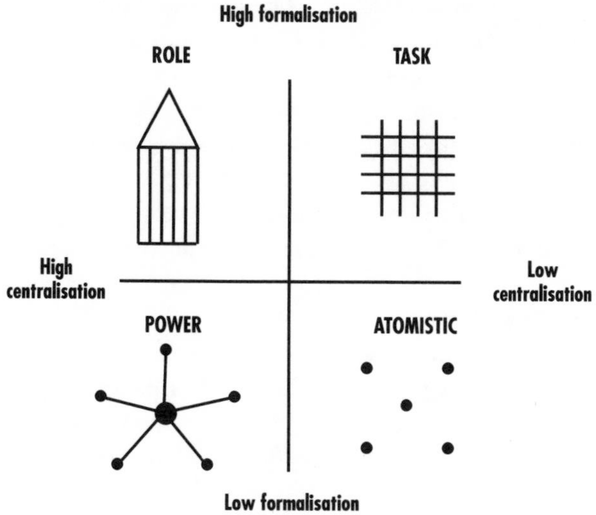

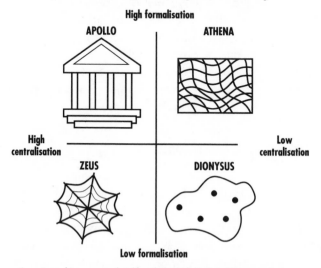

High formalisation

ROLE

TASK

High centralisation

Low centralisation

POWER

ATOMISTIC

Low formalisation

Source: Desmond Graves, *Corporate Culture: Diagrams and Change,* New York,
St. Martin's Press, 1986, adapted from "Understanding Your Organization's Character",
Harvard Business Review, May-June 1972, pp. 119-28.

Figure 1.4 **Culture quadrant by Charles Handy**

High formalisation

APOLLO

ATHENA

High centralisation

Low centralisation

ZEUS

DIONYSUS

Low formalisation

Source: Desmond Graves *op. cit.,* adapted from Charles Handy, *The Gods of Management,* London,
Souvenir Press, 1987, p. 25.

there are ways of getting feedback faster. Informality needs to be recognized and absorbed into more formal understanding so its discoveries are not wasted. The clan culture takes the best from both bureaucracies and markets. There is nothing save skill to prevent a more decentralized organization from also being better coordinated and centralized. But weak culture may only mediate a dilemma in a lopsided way: it may repeatedly overemphasize revenue enhancement at the expense of product satisfaction; or it may allow too much informal networking without directing the results into product development. Such cultures will not last long.

Culture is based on dilemma

Hence the most fundamental characteristic of culture is dilemma itself. Nations and regional groupings have different recurring dilemmas which are likely to show in different ways in their corporations. All corporate cultures take the form of mediated dilemmas, but the form will differ.

This also provides some insight into leadership. People rise to a leadership position because they have a sense of the dilemmas facing the organization and offer to its members a mode of resolution or reconciliation. The culture responds to its leader if he or she can solve its tensions and mediate its dilemmas. Thus James McGregor Burns, the US historian, has contrasted the commonplace transactional leader who gives wages and profits and gets allegiance in exchange, with the rarer, but more inspiring, transformational leader who can sense what is tacit in the needs of the culture and can extract its fullest expression and achievement. Steve Jobs of Apple Computer, for example, sensed that "the corporate computer" was in danger of turning people into punch-cards and created the personal computer as an instrument of self-assertion and liberation, transforming attitudes in the process.

VISUALIZING A CORPORATE CULTURE

Logos

Cultural mediation is often reflected in the logo of a company. Apple, for example, uses the multi-coloured image of the forbidden fruit of Eden, from which a bite has been taken. This symbolizes the birth of new knowledge. Honda uses an H rendered like the *tori* gate at the entrance to Japanese shrines, which supposedly unites earth and sky. Volvo (see Chapter 8) uses the symbol of hands clenching on wrists to promote more cooperative relationships. Tandem Computer uses its name to harness, not just two computers in one, so that each backs up the other, but the many contending viewpoints operating "in tandem".

But it is important not to read into company logos more than is really there or intended. The traditional practice of Western corporations is to sub-contract their image making and advertising to outside experts. Having lent out their "souls", as it were, they should not be surprised to get back the merest artifice. The notion that companies should become known to the public through their authentic culture rather than their carefully contrived manipulation of images is relatively new and important. The best corporate identity programmes now emphasize that the public image should show what the corporation is most proud of. Corporate cultures, then, always have the same form: a set of dilemmas mediated (or not mediated) effectively.

These dilemmas vary considerably in content. What dilemmas your corporate culture mediates is for you to discover. Chapter 10 outlines procedures for detecting this.

Drawing dilemmas

It is helpful to represent the dilemma visually. One way is to think of it as the two horns of a bull: you need to avoid being caught on either one (see Figure 1.5). For example, the need to adapt externally and integrate internally, to which Ed Schein drew attention, and the need for continuity in the midst of change can be seen in this way. Many other examples could be used. Cultures are typically biased in one or the other

Figure 1.5 **Avoid both "horns" of a dilemma**

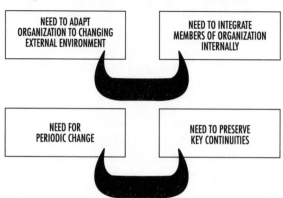

NEED TO ADAPT ORGANIZATION TO CHANGING EXTERNAL ENVIRONMENT

NEED TO INTEGRATE MEMBERS OF ORGANIZATION INTERNALLY

NEED FOR PERIODIC CHANGE

NEED TO PRESERVE KEY CONTINUITIES

direction, but the degree of sustainable bias is limited. After all, a company that maintains a defensive solidarity against external adaptation will, eventually, cease to earn its way and its integration will also founder. A company that changes but loses its sense of continuity will fail to learn from its experience and to sustain itself. A culture's bias is usually its Achilles heel.

But a template is required to quantify a culture's performance between the various extremes of the dilemmas it mediates. For this, it is best to think of the two sides of the dilemma as the axes of a graph. A culture that achieved perfect synergy would be placed with maximum marks on both axes. Lopsided cultures would have a high score on one axis and a low one on the other. It is not enough to have equal scores: that could mean mere compromise, or an adversarial conflict of values. Only synergy is good enough.

How can this be applied to a cultural dilemma? Taking Schein's problem of adaptation and integration, if value A represents adapting to a changing environment and value B represents maintaining and renewing the integration of the organization, then there are a number of contrasting possibilities. The two "horns" of the dilemma – unbalanced excesses – are on the one hand where adaptation is so extensive as to disintegrate the corporation, and on the other where corporate solidity is such as to prevent any adaptation to the changing environment. A number of compromise and conflict options are possible: the two values either weakened and yoked by force, or recognizing each other only through conflict. The point of synergy represents the dilemma of adaptation and integration fully reconciled (see Figures 1.6a and 1.6b).

Cultures exist to cope with dilemmas of this kind. The best will cope by fostering synergy; lesser ones will survive by compromise or conflict. Lopsided solutions threaten the organization's survival. Any corporation can use templates such as these to establish whether its culture mediates dilemmas in a synergistic, compromising or lopsided way. The outstanding leader is ultimately the synergist who so manages cultural values that they are mutually enhancing.

VICIOUS AND VIRTUOUS CIRCLES

There remain two powerful images of how cultures operate which will be followed throughout this book. They can form vicious circles like a cyclone, whirlpool, maelstrom, vortex or regressive spiral, or they can

Figure 1.6a **Basic cultural template**

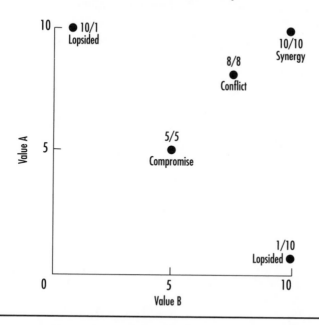

Figure 1.6b **Dilemma of adaptation versus integration**

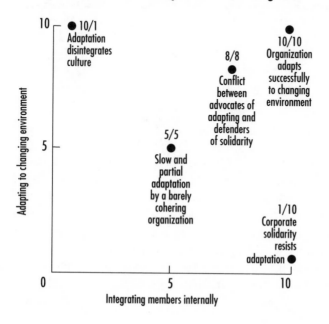

form a virtuous circle, like an upward, developmental spiral or double helix, the structure of life itself. Vicious and virtuous circles can be distinguished by whether the dilemmas or tensions within the circle are unreconciled and fiercely adversarial, or reconciled and synergized.

The vicious circle

This can be illustrated by borrowing two dilemmas or tensions from earlier in this chapter, those of formal versus informal and centralization versus decentralization. These were the axes used to contrast the cultural typologies of Roger Harrison and Charles Handy in Figures 1.3 and 1.4 (see p. 25). Figure 1.7 depicts a "vicious" circle.

Figure 1.7 **The vicious circle**

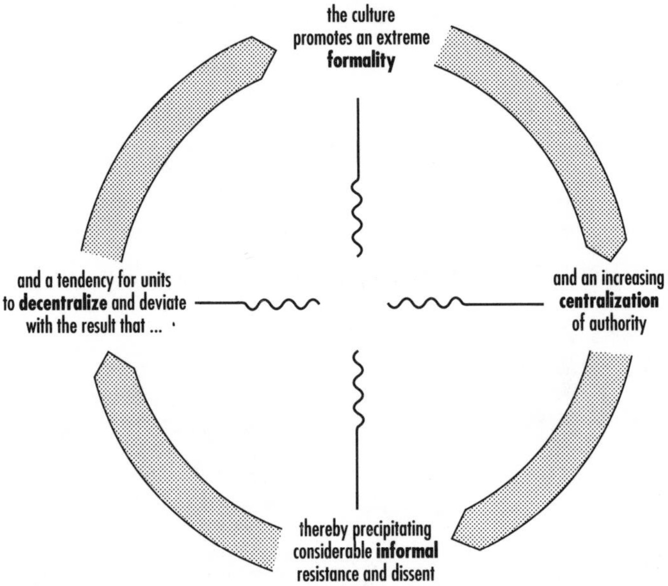

the culture
promotes an extreme
formality

and a tendency for units
to **decentralize** and deviate
with the result that ... ·

and an increasing
centralization
of authority

thereby precipitating
considerable **informal**
resistance and dissent

The cycle is "vicious" because the ropes at the centre have "snapped" and the system is in runaway, its mutual restraints gone. The more top management promotes formality and centralized authority, the more the business units deviate informally and decentralize to escape an influence they dislike. But this only has the effect of increasing attempts to formalize and centralize, which are then resisted in their turn.

Each opposed side of the circle (or "horn" of the dilemma) frustrates the other, contends with it, and contradicts it. Hence the culture as a whole is never effectively formalized, nor does it enjoy opportunities for informal operations without these being fiercely assailed. It is neither well centralized, nor properly decentralized, because of the hostility and mutual impedance among these aims. There may be fierce rhetoric in support of the values involved, but it will not be realized.

The virtuous circle

However, these four values can avoid being split apart, the ropes at the centre can hold together, and the dilemmas can at least be traded off and at best be reconciled. Such reconciliation will create a virtuous circle (see Figure 1.8).

Figure 1.8 **The virtuous circle**

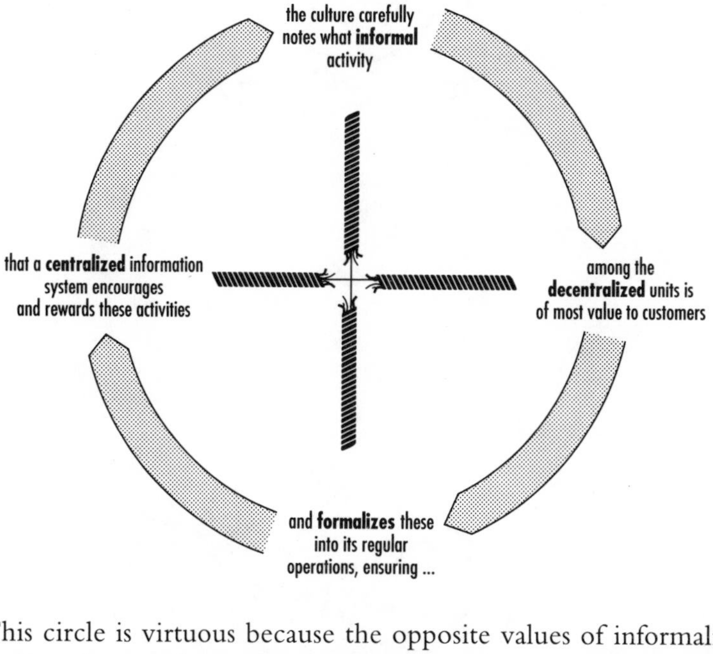

the culture carefully notes what **informal** activity

that a **centralized** information system encourages and rewards these activities

among the **decentralized** units is of most value to customers

and **formalizes** these into its regular operations, ensuring ...

This circle is virtuous because the opposite values of informality–formality, decentralization–centralization remain in creative tension and in mutual restraint. The circle is self-balancing and self-correcting. Those informal activities seen as valuable become integrated into the formal system by official recognition and encouragement. The initiatives of decentralized units are registered at the centre and communicated to other decentralized units for consideration and possible emulation, the centre reserving the right to commend such initiatives or otherwise.

Figure 1.9 **The vicious circle**

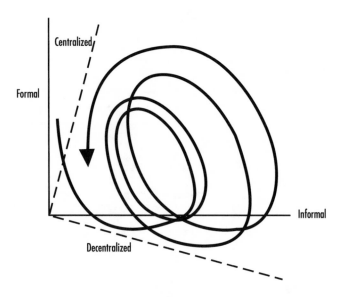

Figure 1.10 **The virtuous circle**

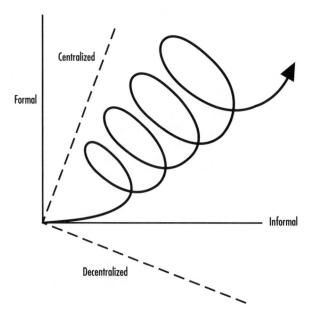

Over time it is likely that the amount of informal activities will increase and the body of formal rules and procedures will grow. The culture will become more decentralized and at the same time better centralized in the sense of guiding and coordinating the autonomous activity of its units. In the event that all four values increase together the whole culture may be said to have developed. Figures 1.9 and 1.10 illustrate this.

Note that the virtuous circle has a harmony, an aesthetic, and a rhythm, what the Japanese call *wa*. The vicious circle excites and savages itself like Uroborus, the self-devouring snake of mythology. The transformation of potentially vicious circles into virtuous ones is what consistently characterizes the leaders examined in this book.

Chapter 2

NATIONAL MACRO-CULTURES:
WHICH NATIONS ARE DEVELOPING AND WHY

All corporate cultures are partly the result of negotiations with the larger cultures in which these are located. It is not possible to start from scratch, although "greenfield sites" can confer some aspects of a fresh start. National cultures still have to be dealt with: Swedish or Canadian, French, English or the "American way", since a culture will already be present among the workforce. Also present are the cultures of finance, R&D, marketing, personnel and so on. Many employees will be more concerned with their profession than with the corporation, or with their independence as sovereign US individualists, than with what their employer might want them to do. Those who would create winning corporate cultures must begin with macro-cultures: social patterns with their own dynamics and their own characteristic opportunities and perils.

This chapter considers four issues which powerfully pattern the economic cultures of different nations so that comparisons leave nations far apart on key axes of these universal dilemmas. The eight case studies of corporate micro-cultures in Chapters 3–9 represent specific answers and resolutions to the dilemmas present within their national cultures. The four macro-cultural issues are as follows.

Manager–worker tensions. How much of the wealth generated jointly by managers and workers belongs to these respective socio-economic groups, and how is the vexed issue of relationships between different classes to be mediated?

Hierarchy or equality in communications. Is it possible to maintain a responsibility hierarchy, while promoting an equality of communication among equals, designed to elicit the best from all concerned?

Analytic or synthetic styles of thinking. Should problems be analysed atomistically into their component parts and only later reassembled, if possible, or should they be configured into wholes before their details are examined?

Individualism and cooperativism. Is capitalism first and foremost a triumph of individualism and personal initiative, as is the fashion in the UK and the USA, or is it predominantly a cooperative and organizational feat as Asians and some Europeans believe?

MANAGER–WORKER TENSIONS

Where does conflict start?

It is hard to think of anything more foolish than for managers to turn their workplaces into arenas of class conflict. Tensions between socio-economic groups of course exist. Typically, unions and working people have appealed to a cooperative ethic (albeit one that excludes management) while managers have favoured an individualistic ethic. Both values have tactical uses for their respective factions and in some cases these roles will even be reversed, with management seeking to create cooperative environments and manual workers preferring individualistic standards of performance. Classically, cooperation by idealizing solidarity enables workers to put collective pressure on management. Individualism defends the existing distribution of resources with the claim that managers have earned their higher rewards, and it can be used to keep workers divided.

The capitalist system has never come up with a general answer as to what is owed to those who supply capital and those who give years, and sometimes their whole lives, to an enterprise. The issue is "negotiated" by a system of organized manoeuvres to withdraw labour or to dismiss and punish workers, and because there is no easy answer the issue is politicized with attacks by each side on the other, retailed by the mass media for dramatic entertainment.

Militancy and productivity are close relations

It has been demonstrated time and again that workers are more productive if their groups are cohesive, and their morale and their social satisfaction high. But there is a good reason why that message may not prove popular. Managers are afraid to make their workforces more cooperative, lest that solidarity be turned against the organization and against management. If the technical and formal systems keep workers alienated and divided, then this may prevent them from organizing themselves to challenge management prerogatives. Yet to keep workers weak and divided will typically reduce not just their potential militancy but also their potential productivity. A culture in fear of its own workers is fatally weakened.

While macro-cultures cannot, in themselves, heal class divides, because this must be done thousands of times *in situ,* they can make this easier or harder. Japanese customs and traditions in their attempts to set wages provide a useful guide to alternative methods.

How do the Japanese do it?

James Abbeglen and George Stalk's book, *Kaisha,** describes how for many years Japanese industry has had an "annual wage round". This is accompanied less by the threat of strikes, followed by a pattern-setting agreement, as in the USA, than by intense public and media discussion of what wage levels would keep industry competitive, while raising domestic purchasing power as high as possible. This is after all an issue in which the whole nation has a stake and many parties make a contribution.

A second major difference between Western and Asian capitalism is that in the West shareholders' interests are deemed sovereign. Senior managers claim to "represent" the interests of shareholders in bargaining with the workforce. Officially appointed shareholders' representatives sit on boards and even hold positions in some companies. The result is that the organization is seen as external to the rights of shareholders and workers, a money-making device which is there to pay each faction its due. These attitudes put the two sides of industry in continual dispute.

In Japan and much of the Pacific Rim not only are dividends to shareholders much smaller proportionately, but shareholders are treated as outside suppliers of capital who must be paid off and paid fairly, even if debt is increased to do this. Then, however, the corporation is "owned" and operated by those who work within it. Their interests are identified with the future of that organization, and all sides of industry are committed long term to its future.

World comparisons on industrial relations

That different nations in the world economy have markedly greater or lesser success in reconciling the interests of managers and workers is evident from Figure 2.1. On the vertical dimension the European Management Forum of nearly 2,000 managers worldwide asked how "constructive and peaceful" were their relationships with their unions on a scale of 1 to 100. None of this means very much unless the unions are also involved in management and participate in making decisions. Otherwise "peaceful" may mean little more than docile or cowed. Hence the estimated degree of union participation has also been registered on the horizontal axis, again on a scale of 1 to 100. The two axes make cross-coordinates possible, and an assessment of degree of success in resolving the management–union dilemma.

---

* New York, Basic Books, 1985.

Figure 2.1 **Constructive relations and union participation in selected countries**

The numbers represent nominal values derived from the range of responses to the questions

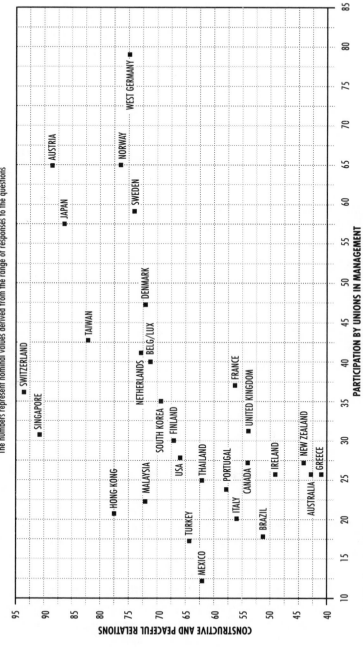

CONSTRUCTIVE AND PEACEFUL RELATIONS

PARTICIPATION BY UNIONS IN MANAGEMENT

Source: EMF Foundation Survey, 1987.

It is interesting to see how poorly the English-speaking economies fare. None of them is in the top ten. This may be partly the result of industrializing early and then trying to limit or cut wages as competitor nations caught up. It may be partly the result of political parties affiliating with the two sides of industry, or partly the penchant for theatricals in front of the media, a habit which usually feeds antagonisms.

Motivation by management

It seems from Figure 2.2 that it takes talented managers to motivate workers and untalented ones to antagonize them. The questions asked were: How great is the sense of drive, responsibility and entrepreneurship among managers of your nationality?; and: How willing to identify with corporate objectives and priorities are the workers of your nationality? There is a fairly strong, consistent correlation between estimates of management talent on the vertical axis and estimates of how motivated workers are on the horizontal axis. The world's stronger manufacturing economies dominate the top right corner, as would be expected.

The North American problem

The North American macro-culture does not come out particularly well of these comparisons. The management–worker dilemma is endemic and stubborn. But this does not mean that specific North American corporate cultures have not produced outstanding examples of resolution. The two case studies in Chapter 3 are examples of how an organized programme of listening and understanding allows a corporation to devise a culture which reconciles conflict between management and workers.

HIERARCHY OR EQUALITY IN COMMUNICATIONS

Every corporation has to integrate itself and, as complexities increase and innovation becomes vital to maintaining a competitive edge, it becomes crucial to ask how this integrity is to be maintained. The traditional way was through hierarchies. Differences between, say, twelve subordinates reporting to a superior were resolved by that superior, who then commanded the subordinates to enact that resolution. Increasingly, the superior will have neither the time nor the knowledge to reconcile these differences. Appealing up a hierarchy is slow and the decision that comes down may not have taken into consideration all the niceties of the twelve positions. It can be far more effective if the twelve can design an

Figure 2.2 Management talent at motivating the workforce in selected countries

The numbers represent nominal values derived from the range of responses to the questions

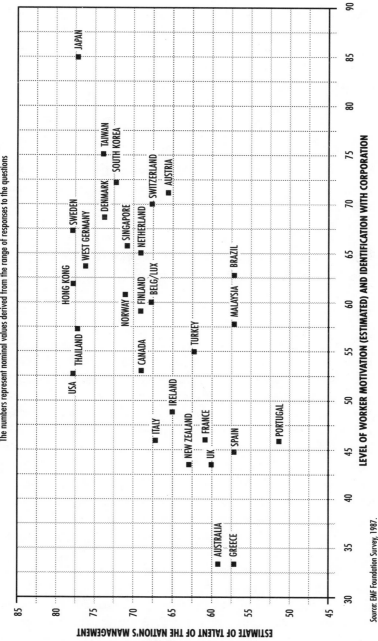

Source: EMF Foundation Survey, 1987.

overall solution which satisfies them all. This may be not only quicker but more subtle and can create a product for the customer in which the many values championed by the subordinates are organized into a larger synthesis. Such mutual cooperation requires communication among equals. "Equal" does not mean "the same", nor a rigid egalitarianism which allows none to rise or fall in influence. People are treated as equals because their relative contributions to a product or service, satisfying to customers, have yet to be discovered, and because that is the style which best facilitates the emergence of their talents and the predisposition to assert their viewpoints.

Do the cultures of different professions and nations have preferences for steeper or flatter hierarchies, depending on the mix of authority and mutual persuasion used to reconcile differences and integrate organizations? There are remarkable differences.

Professional disciplines tend to have their own cultures

First, how do professional and departmental cultures differ? To answer this question administration, general (or more senior) management, marketing and sales, personnel, R&D, finance and control, technical and manufacturing/production have been examined separately to see with what degree of hierarchy or lateral influence they customarily work. The research was conducted by Fons Trompenaars for the Centre for International Business studies in Amsterdam. Most professional/departmental comparisons used in this study came from Dutch executives in the energy business. Hence national differences were eliminated in order to focus on those who play different professional roles in the division of labour. The results are set out in Table 2.1, together with the five hierarchies on a continuum from flatness to steepness. Fons Trompenaars asked his sample of Dutch employees: "Think of the company you work for in terms of a triangle. Which one of the following triangles best represents your company?" Responses were grouped under three heads: triangles a & b, c, and d & e. The functions are listed in order of the flatness of their hierarchy.

The most dramatic finding is that the higher people are in an organization, the more they experience it as flat. In all probability this is because differences at the top have to be negotiated. A major irony of organizations is that the more formal authority people have, the less they can use it simply to get their way. Their peers are mostly "powerful" too and they have to reconcile differences, not throw their weight around.

Of the functions with equal authority, marketing is flattest by far. As the closest department to customers, its service-level staff are the ones who first discover what the customer wants; if these employees are subordinated, so, in effect, are messages coming from the customer. Moreover, these messages are often contrary to the corporation's interior logics. What customers want, they want, never mind whether manufacturing wants to give it to them or R&D has developed it. Marketing, therefore, has information about outside preferences and, unless these are given equal billing with inside preferences, the corporation will respond slowly and poorly to changing patterns of demand. The case studies in this book show a significant change in corporate cultures achieved by raising the influence of those in contact with customers *vis-à-vis* other functions, whether car dealers, cabin service personnel, delivery staff or sales people.

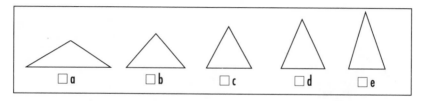

Table 2.1 **The attachment of different functions to hierarchy**

	a & b	c	d & e
General management (senior managers)	66	30	4
Marketing and sales	58	32	10 .
Administration	56	24	20
Personal	52	30	18
Technical, manufacturing and production	46	35	19
Finance	43	33	24
R & D	38	29	33

Technical and finance departments are most hierarchical

Hierarchy relates to how functions deal with the more palpable inputs of the corporation. Administration and personnel remain relatively flat, but technical, manufacturing, finance and R&D have steepening hierarchies, perhaps because of the authority of science, accountancy and engineering which informs their work.

The hierarchical nature of finance could be of particular concern. The trends towards agglomeration and takeover during the last 20 years have placed more and more companies under the control of financial and legal experts. As Robert Reich points out in *Tales of a New America,* [*] fewer people from manufacturing or marketing are reaching the top of major US corporations. The dominant style in the West, much criticized by the Japanese, is to try to make money from the manipulation of money, as opposed to providing novel satisfactions to customers. A hierarchical relationship with manipulated objects is preferred to a more equal partnership with customers and colleagues.

A 1989 study of declining US competitiveness by a specially appointed commission of MIT industrial and management professors identified many social and cultural changes necessary throughout US society before boardrooms and shop floors could effectively focus on regaining competitive edge. Among specific recommendations was a new balance between cooperative business effort and individualism. Lack of team skills was crippling US design quality, the MIT panel discovered: businesses supplying tools and high specification products were failing to establish the sort of cumulative relationships that allow knowledge to become embedded in a product.

Nations have different attachments to hierarchy

The five triangles were also shown by Trompenaars to representatives of twelve national macro-cultures. The same "triangle question" was put to them, and their answers are set out in Table 2.2 in order of flatness. There are few surprises here. The five largely Protestant countries − Sweden, the USA, the UK, West Germany and the Netherlands − have flatter hierarchies than Greece and the three Catholic countries. Japan is anomalous, being seen as both less hierarchical by some Japanese, yet more by others. Despite being an extremely successful economy, Singapore is quite hierarchical, but then hierarchy has a different meaning in Asia, as will be seen. Generally speaking, within Europe and the Americas, stronger economies have flatter hierarchies. France is surprisingly hierarchical, a phenomenon further discussed in Chapter 8 in observations by André Laurent of Insead.

One good test of whether or not authority had been reconciled with a willingness to empower subordinates would be the extent to which

[*] New York, Times Books, 1987.

Table 2.2 **National attachment to hierarchy**

	a & b	c	d & e
Japan[a]	54	13	33
Sweden	50	20	30
USA	47	39	14
UK	46	29	25
West Germany	41	50	9
Netherlands	41	38	21
Singapore	24	30	46
France	22	43	35
Greece	21	51	28
Italy	15	65	20
Spain	11	43	46
Venezuela	9	44	47

[a] Japan's score is somewhat anomalous. The more senior the manager, the flatter he regarded the hierarchy. Junior managers experienced subordination.

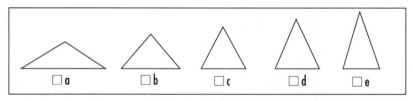

managers in different cultures were willing to delegate authority. Those who delegate cannot thereby escape from responsibility. Delegation involves trusting a subordinate sufficiently to let him or her discharge the manager's own responsibility; the manager substitutes judgement about the character and capacity of a subordinate for the judgement needed to do the job him or herself. Such judgement can only be based on personal knowledge of another and as such is facilitated by communication among equals. In any event, Figure 2.3 (see p. 44), which tests the willingness of managers in several macro-cultures to delegate authority, has results partly confirming Trompenaars' work. Sweden and the USA are again near the top with Japan; the Netherlands scores well; the UK and West Germany fall back a bit; France is again a laggard; and Roman Catholic southern Europe is still unwilling to let its hierarchies go.

The case studies in Chapters 4, 5 and 6 are striking examples of how a system where employees from different levels communicate as equals can bring life, energy and profit to a flagging organization. Both British Airways, Saratoga Systems and BAHCO were stifled by arcane and

Figure 2.3 **Willingness of managers to delegate authority in selected countries**

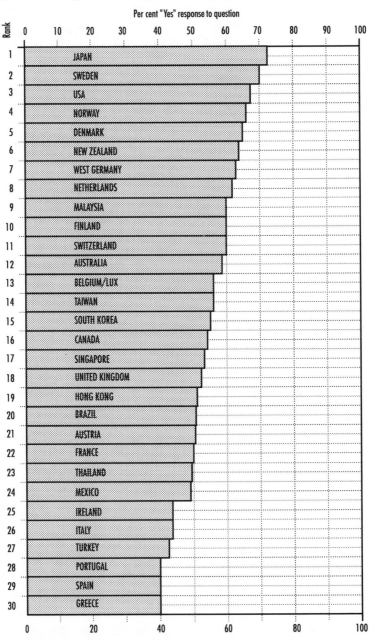

Per cent "Yes" response to question

Rank	Country
1	JAPAN
2	SWEDEN
3	USA
4	NORWAY
5	DENMARK
6	NEW ZEALAND
7	WEST GERMANY
8	NETHERLANDS
9	MALAYSIA
10	FINLAND
11	SWITZERLAND
12	AUSTRALIA
13	BELGIUM/LUX
14	TAIWAN
15	SOUTH KOREA
16	CANADA
17	SINGAPORE
18	UNITED KINGDOM
19	HONG KONG
20	BRAZIL
21	AUSTRIA
22	FRANCE
23	THAILAND
24	MEXICO
25	IRELAND
26	ITALY
27	TURKEY
28	PORTUGAL
29	SPAIN
30	GREECE

Source: EMF Foundation Survey, 1987.

indirect communications that severely hampered their ability to communicate with and serve their customers. Three inspired leaders were able or preparing to break through the barriers of the old closeted corporate culture and create an open organization where people responded to each other and the company responded to its markets.

ANALYTIC OR SYNTHETIC STYLES OF THINKING

Left brain and right brain

A major distinction between cultures concerns the question of whether they think rationally or intuitively. This is often seen as a question of hemispheral dominance. The left and right hemispheres of the human brain are divided in the neocortex, although joined by a bundle of nerves at the base of the brain. Psychologists and neurologists argue that at an early age the hemispheres begin to specialize in contrasting mental processes. The result of this is that phenomena can be seen in different

Table 2.3 **Left and right brain characteristics**

Left brain/right hand	Right brain/left hand
verbal	non-verbal
analytic	synthetic
reductive into parts	holistic
sequential	visuo-spatial
rational	intuitive
time-oriented	timeless
discontinuous	diffuse

ways: there is no absolutely correct way. In many respects this divergence of functions within the human mind is the origin of dilemmas.

Broadly, there are two complementary modes of thought: the first initially analyses and reduces information and events to bits and pieces; the second begins by relating, connecting and synthesizing information into wholes. Analysing phenomena into components is often described as a left hemisphere function; synthesizing elements into wholes is a right hemisphere function. This distinction is sometimes presented as atomism versus holism. Research on brain functions has suggested that the left brain, controlling the right hand and right side of the body, thinks verbally, analytically, reductively, rationally and in discontinuous time segments. The right brain, controlling the left hand and left side of the body, thinks tacitly, holistically, synthetically, visuo-spatially and in timeless and diffuse ways. (The brain cortex has a cross-over point which means that one side of the body is controlled by the opposite side of the brain.) It is not the quality of this research which is of interest here, but its implications for cultural categories.

Naturally all macro-cultures use both left brain and right brain to some degree. The danger for a corporate culture is an excess either way. Those who can only analyse will produce rubble. Those who can only synthesize will produce over-elaborate and unwieldy configurations. Bias in either direction could make it harder for the organization to function. The sort of synergy needed to reconcile corporate dilemmas is a feat requiring both hemispheres.

The US macro-culture is overwhelmingly left brain

Consider the initial states of the two companies described in Chapter 3, Western Oil and Annheuser-Busch. Each one was faced with a macro-culture that was overwhelmingly left brain, relentlessly individualistic, oriented to hard, countable things and suspicious of relationships. Both were over-differentiated and under-integrated to a highly dysfunctional degree, prone to conflict between factions, fragmented by incompatible aims and using "individual responsibility" to pin blame upon each other. In both cases improvements included right hemisphere processes, a stress upon enhancing the whole, building relationships and creating syntheses.

The same sorts of bias are also manifest in larger social institutions: the separation of church and state, the balance of power and the independent judiciary. The USA – and indeed all the English-speaking cultures – places consistent stress upon analysis, separation and isolation of elements from each other. This is far removed from the Asian view. The contrast is made clear in Richard Pascale and Anthony Athos's study, *The Art of Japanese Management,* in a sharp comparison between the corporate cultures of ITT under Harold T. Geneen and Matsushita.

"In Harold T. Geneen's two decades at ITT he was lauded by many as the master corporate manager. His personality dominated the company. Like General Patton 'he wore two pistols' and 'would let people know who was boss by calling them up at odd hours to query item 3 in their report'.

"Geneen put his faith in unshakeable facts. His legendary speed reading, photographic memory and large staff department made him the 'king of the numbers'. In his view an unshakeable fact was something hard and indisputable. 'If you offered Geneen an opinion based on feeling, you were dead.' One of Geneen's greatest secrets was that he got you to put your neck on the line saying 'If we do this, we'll increase our business by 25 per cent and our profits by 12 per cent'. Then he kept track of how you were progressing ...

"Geneen kept ITT on its toes for 20 years, but after his retirement it went into rapid decline because its presiding genius was gone and was irreplaceable – the circus was without its ring-master and his whip ...

"Matsushita is also concerned with numbers, but puts a different meaning on them. Market share shows what the company has done for others. The growth of employees through life-term service will generate profits over the longer term. All leaders of product groups have two bosses, a 'mother and father', with ties to decentralized and to centralized activities.

"Instead of making 'facts' the final arbiter of worth, Matsushita concentrates on superordinate goals which managers fulfil in the way best suited to their capacities. National Service through Industry, Fairness, Harmony and Cooperation, Adjustment and Assimilation are among these 'spiritual values' comprising the larger whole."

Modern business requires a right brain capability ...

The English-speaking preference for individualism and analytical thinking gives advantages in the early stages of industrial development. Moreover, analysis is the best way of understanding simple mechanisms: it reveals their working by dissection when their function is essentially a sum of parts put to a purpose. But the advantage of this style of thinking diminishes when organizations grow large and products constitute complex wholes which encompass many satisfactions. Analysis is of less value when the focus shifts from machines to human systems and social teams because here nothing is gained from dividing the whole into its parts. What a group knows and discovers is potentially more than can be carried away in the heads of its separate members.

Is there any hard evidence that true distinctions help to define the various national cultures? In the Fons Trompenaars studies, managers from different countries were presented with a series of dilemmas. In some cases the managers had a choice of separating themselves from the problem so that they could better solve (or evade) it, or attaching themselves to those immersed in the problem so that the group or person could better solve (or evade) it. In other cases managers had to choose between one piece of unambiguous evidence, and that same piece embedded in a far wider context which qualified it. In yet other cases they could choose to focus on things and persons as a way of improving relationships, or on relationships as a way of improving things and persons. The results are shown in Table 2.4.

The figures show the location of the managers of each country on the continuum between left and right hemispheres. For example, 56 per cent of US managers would blame an individual for an incidence of negligence; only 15 per cent of Italian managers would do so.

... which is not found in the USA ...
Note that the USA, which more than any other nation has influenced the teaching of business administration and theories of management practice, is quite untypical of the rest of the world. At the opposite end of the continuum is Singapore, an outstandingly successful Asian economy which has been growing at a rate 3–4 times that of the USA and the UK for the last 15 years. Only a slight majority of US managers reject profitability or "the bottom line" as the sole criterion of business success (47 per cent believe this), while most other nations reject this proposition by large margins, the Japanese by 96 per cent and managers from Singapore by 89 per cent. Almost three times as many US managers, compared with those from Singapore, would dismiss an employee for poor performance and ignore their 15-year history with the company or whatever mistakes the company has made towards them. Again, Americans are much more insistent on higher income and greater personal responsibility and are little attracted by working with new groups. They are the only nation included here with a majority preference for being individually responsible.

... or in finance
The left and right brain distinction strongly characterizes different functions. Fons Trompenaars applied his method to different job types (see Table 2.5, p. 50). The figures show the location of different job functions on the continuum between left and right hemispheres.

People whose job it is to count numbers develop strong left hemisphere biases. Finance managers, for example, not only focus on isolated

Table 2.4 **Left and right hemisphere managers** (Figures in %)

1. Should the individual or the whole team of which s/he is a member be held responsible for an incidence of negligence at work?

Left brain	USA	SP	UK	WG	NL	G	SW	VEN	JAP	SIN	FRA	IT	Right brain
"the individual"	56	46	44	43	38	36	29	29	28	23	17	15	"the team"

2. Is the only real goal of a company to make a profit or should the well-being of the various stakeholders be taken into account?

Left brain	USA	NL	ITA	SW	WG	UK	SP	GE	FRA	VEN	SIN	JAP	Right brain
"profit"	47	38	30	28	25	22	22	14	17	12	11	4	"stakeholders"

3. Do you see a company as a system designed to perform functions and tasks efficiently with people hired to fit these tasks and functions, or is a company a group of people, the quality of whose relationships make these functions effective.

Left brain	USA	NL	SW	UK	ITA	WG	VEN	SP	JAP	SIN	GR	FRA	Right brain
"tasks"	72	65	55	45	44	42	41	39	36	37	34	29	"relationships"

4. Should the poor job performance of an employee remain the criterion for dismissing him regardless of age or previous records or should management take into consideration his 15-year history with the company and its responsibilities for his life?

Left brain	USA	UK	JAP	NL	SW	SP	GR	WG	IT	SIN	FRA	VEN	Right brain
"single criterion"	61	39	36	25	24	24	22	20	18	18	14	3	"historical context"

5. Are you more likely to value promotion because you will have greater responsibility and a higher income, or because you will be working with a new group of people?

Left brain	USA	WG	FRA	GR	NL	ITA	UK	JAP	SW	SP	VEN	SIN	Right brain
"income responsibility"	89	86	75	70	70	69	65	58	49	48	48	46	"new group"

6. Do you prefer to work on your own, be your own boss, take care of yourself and not expect others to look out for you, or do you like to work with others, share in making decisions and count for help on each other?

Left brain	WG	USA	FRA	UK	SW	GR	SP	NL	JAP	VEN	ITA	SIN	Right brain
"on your own"	80	79	72	71	56	40	40	38	34	29	23	20	"together"

Source: Fons Trompenaars, "The organization of meaning and the meaning of organization", dissertation, The Wharton School, University of Pennsylvania.

Table 2.5 **Left and right hemisphere job function** (Figures in %)

1. Should the individual or the whole team of which s/he is a member be held responsible for an incident of negligence at work?

Left brain	Finance	General	Technical	R&Ds	Marktg. sales	Manuf. prod.	Personnel	Admin	Right brain
"the individual"	75	57	47	46	44	43	41	18	"the team"

2. Is the only real goal of a company to make a profit or should the well-being of various stakeholders be taken into account?

Left brain	Finance	Manuf. prod.	Technical	Personnel	R&D	Admin	Gen	Marktg. sales	Right brain
"profit"	42	36	33	25	21	20	17	12	"relationships"

3. Do you see your company as a system designed to perform functions and tasks efficiently with people hired to fix these tasks and functions, or is a company a group of people, the quality of whose relationships makes these functions effective?

Left brain	Finance	Technical	Manuf. prod.	Admin	R&D	Marktg. sales	Gen	Personnel	Right brain
"tasks"	67	65	63	56	51	46	44	33	"relationships"

4. Should the poor job performance of an employee remain the criterion for dismissing him regardless of age or previous records, or should management take into consideration his 15-year history with the company and its responsibilities for his life?

Left brain	Finance	R&D	Technical	Personnel	Manuf. prod.	Gen	Admin	Marktg. sales	Right brain
"single criterion"	52	50	47	47	31	29	22	22	"historical context"

5. Are you more likely to value promotion because you will have greater responsibility and a higher income or because you will be working with a new group of people?

Left brain	Technical	Admin	Finance	Personnel	Manuf. prod.	Gen	R&D	Marktg. sales	Right brain
"income responsibility"	76	74	70	65	64	57	50	47	"new group"

6. Do you prefer to work on your own, be your own boss, take care of yourself and not expect others to look out for you, or do you like to work with others, share in making decisions and count for help on each other?

Left brain	Finance	R&D	Personnel	Technical	Marktg. sales	Manuf. prod.	Gen	Admin	Right brain
"on you own"	98	93	92	88	77	63	60	56	"together"

Source: Fons Trompenaars, "The organization of meaning and the meaning of organization", dissertation, The Wharton School, University of Pennsylvania.

figures but are the most inclined to single out individuals for blame, to say that profit is the company's only real goal, to fire an older, once competent worker no longer pulling his weight and to work solo, relying on no one else to help them. In contrast, marketing and sales are towards the right brain end on all six questions, giving further evidence that the higher people climb in the organization, outside a purely financial function, the more holistic their orientation. The more senior general managers are to the right brain side on all questions save the first on personal responsibility, where their responses probably reflect the fact that they are and must be personally responsible as top managers. The results show clearly that finance people are not typical of business at all, being narrower, tougher and much more individualistic.

Left brain dominance in UK corporate cultures

That British business culture might be biased towards "the right hand" was a hypothesis recently tested by Professor Peter Doyle of Warwick University. Doyle noted that successes since 1980 were mostly those of the left hemisphere, through rationalization, strong profitability and cash-flow, cost reductions often achieved by lay-offs and the achievement of largly financial objectives.

What was lacking was the right hemisphere marketing emphasis. Market share, that is relationships with customers, had seriously eroded, while 74 per cent of the sample of companies surveyed were stuck in mature or declining markets. Right brain companies are typically Japanese: Hitachi, Komatsu, Toshiba and Sanyo. Doyle blames "the constraints of the City" and the short-termism of financial institutions: 89 per cent of his sample had a finance director on the main board, only 49 per cent had a marketing director. Because the UK did not institute business education until the 1960s, the majority of its professionally qualified business employees aged over 40 are still accountants. The UK's record profitability combined with a growing deficit in world trade could be one result of these preferences.

Left/right brains and advertising

A good test of whether a culture thinks in wholes or in parts is the issue of advertising a product, pushing it strongly at customers, and leaving the customer with a feeling of total satisfaction and trust for the corporation that supplied the product. A "left brain" atomistic culture will tend to think of a "great" advertising feat as persuading customers to buy a product even if it is worthless. Indeed, its worthlessness testifies to the brilliance of the initial persuasion. A star salesperson could sell refrigerators to Eskimos. For Asian cultures, especially the Japanese, it is shameful to push a product that does not live up to its billing when it is ultimately received. Advertising, selling and producing are to be judged as processes by their *wa,* or harmony.

Does this matter? Figure 2.4 and Figure 2.5 (see p. 54), from the European Management Forum survey of managers, suggest that it does. The charts examine the dilemma that those who push the products too hard may lose credibility, so they must push harder, only to lose more credibility, and not just for themselves but for business in general.

While the USA is near the top in sales orientation, the vertical axis, it falls to 14th in the credibility to the public of its corporations while Japan creates that harmony which its culture so values. The same pattern emerges if "the push" is compared with "the product". The USA pushes among the hardest but again drops to 14th in its reputation for the quality of actual product delivered. Japan, Scandinavia, Switzerland and West Germany more nearly keep the promise of that original push.

The problem of synthesizing these two aspects of culture – the left and right brain – to create a more robust organization is one considered by David Hurst of Russelsteel in Chapter 7, and his efforts with corporate culture are recorded in the case study. He took an overwhelmingly left brain company from an unprofitable and unproductive path of merger and acquisition to a rejuvenated market and consumer oriented one.

INDIVIDUALISM OR COOPERATIVISM: TWO VISIONS OF CAPITALISM

The difference between Asia and the West

This section will examine a major cleavage in Western capitalism by asking whether a competitive or a cooperative ethic is best suited to rapid economic development and wealth creation. The evidence from business worldwide, and particularly in the expanding Asian economies, is that the current climate permits the cooperative ethos to work more effectively. Is it then possible for the typically individualistic cultures of corporations in Western nations to benefit from a more cooperative orientation? Chapter 8 examines the attempts of a Swedish company, Volvo, to operate on a cooperative basis in a hierarchical and individualist context, and Chapter 9 looks at a path-breaking US job-shop in Silicon Valley, North American Tool and Die.

Figure 2.4 **How credible are corporations ?**

The numbers represent nominal values derived from the range of responses to the questions

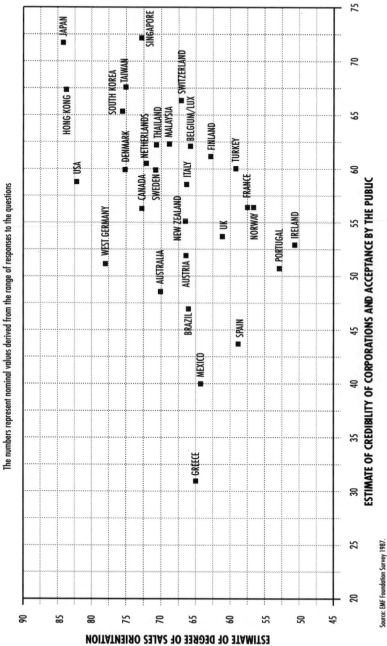

ESTIMATE OF CREDIBILITY OF CORPORATIONS AND ACCEPTANCE BY THE PUBLIC

ESTIMATE OF DEGREE OF SALES ORIENTATION

Source: EMF Foundation Survey 1987.

Figure 2.5 **The push and the product**

The numbers represent nominal values derived from the range of responses to the questions

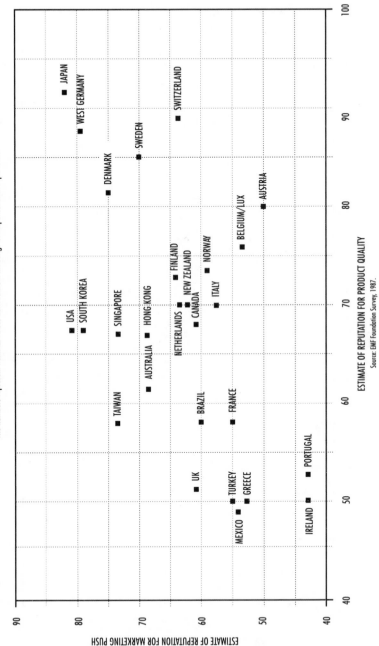

ESTIMATE OF REPUTATION FOR PRODUCT QUALITY

Source: EMF Foundation Survey, 1987.

ESTIMATE OF REPUTATION FOR MARKETING PUSH

The left or right brain distinction is very important to this issue. The approach of the nations that experienced early industrialization, with hostility to strong government, has culminated in a generally left brain, individualistic vision of capitalism. The right hemisphere synthetic approach combined with later industrialism and the more tolerant attitude toward strong governments seen in the Asian Newly Industrialized Countries (Nics) has culminated in a cooperative vision of capitalism.

An interesting global example of this dichotomy is described by Geert Hofstede, who examined the cultures of IBM companies worldwide in his book *Culture's Consequences.** His method had the virtue of holding the influence of IBM's legendary strong corporate culture constant, while examining the differences made by national macro-cultures. On the vertical axis of Figure 2.6 (see p. 56) the degrees of cooperative orientation are ranked according to the assessments of IBM executives in each country. On the horizontal axis are the different rates of economic growth in each nation over the previous decade. Japan, Malaysia, South Korea, Hong Kong and Singapore had been growing at between 4.0 and 9.0 per cent per annum between 1973 and 1984 and all are very high in cooperatism. The three nations highest in individualism, the UK, the USA and Australia, experienced relatively slow growth over the same period.

However, cooperative ethic is a necessary but not sufficient condition for economic growth. Venezuela is almost off the scale in its cooperative enthusiasm and in its allegiance to the right hemisphere, yet it grows very slowly, as do Greece, India and Spain. Cooperation and the maintenance of relationships can also be mobilized for or against capitalist economic development. The Asian five harnessed their cooperative orientation to free enterprise. Rates of growth have altered since this study, but the general point is not affected by growth changes after 1984.

Does the West need individualism to survive?

Surely Western-style individualism is crucial to any organization that seeks to be profitable, creative and innovative? Asian social harmony may be effective at implementing what has already been invented in the West, but somewhere, somehow, there has to be a creative, committed individual willing to defy the opinions of the group. It takes more than ant-like conformity to organizational strategy to create new products.

* Beverly Hills, Sage Publications, 1980.

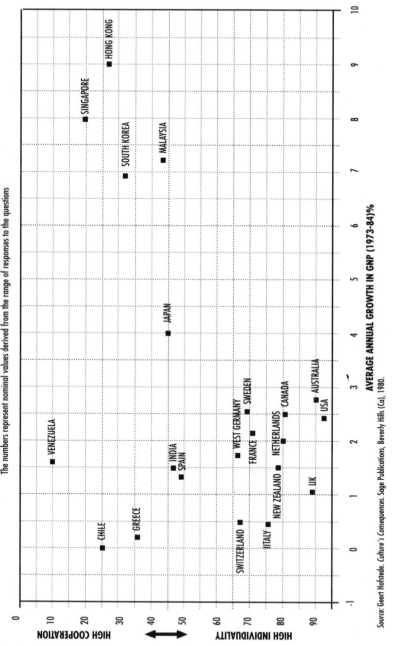

Figure 2.6 **Collaborative values (in IBM executives) and economic growth**

The numbers represent nominal values derived from the range of responses to the questions

Source: Geert Hofstede. *Culture's Consequences.* Sage Publications, Beverly Hills (Ca), 1980.

Such sentiments are particularly powerful in the West, yet they may have to be re-examined. One error is to confuse flamboyant individualism with genuine creativity. It has been well said that "an artistic temperament is an affliction of amateurs". The notion of the creative individual as an isolated individual who flouts convention is a popular Western stereotype, but it may be neither necessary nor desirable. Nor does it follow that groups gang up on heroic individualists.

The alleged non-creativity of the Japanese because of their restricted individualism is a delusion. The West is left at the starting gate in the race towards technological creativity. The Japanese are registering double the number of patents per head of population compared with the USA (see Figure 2.7, p. 58). Moreover, their corporations are extremely willing to take these innovations on board. Compare this with the UK, where cultural resistance to exploiting innovation remains high. The stereotype of the "lone creator" comes from this clash of creative persons with organized resistance. It is a cultural adaptation to frustration and, of course, the more resistant the corporate culture becomes, the more individualism is lauded.

Individualism and corporate restructuring

The surviving ethic of capitalism as individualistic perhaps explains why the USA, the UK, Canada and Australia are the world's leading practitioners of takeovers.

Of course, hostile takeovers and acquisitions find the justification in classical economics that resources are being reallocated to those who can use them more profitably. In an individualist culture corporate managers may run the company for their own personal benefit, unless or until a predator offers to serve shareholders better. This threat will arguably keep managers on their toes and imbue a "concern" for shareholders not otherwise manifest.

But this view also misses much. When Lord Hanson took over Ever Ready, was he wise to sell its R&D facilities to its chief rival Duracel, which not unsurprisingly paid dearly for the "soul" of its competitor? Doubtless shareholder value was much increased in the short term, but can Ever Ready as a culture prosper with its inventiveness torn out of it? It is because such questions are almost unanswerable that individualist–analytical cultures price the pieces, while collectivist–holistic cultures try to develop wholes. If cultures are becoming delicate skeins of learning and information, can their pieces be auctioned off without

Figure 2.7 **Technology, creativity and corporate willingness to exploit innovation**

The numbers represent nominal values derived from the range of responses to the questions

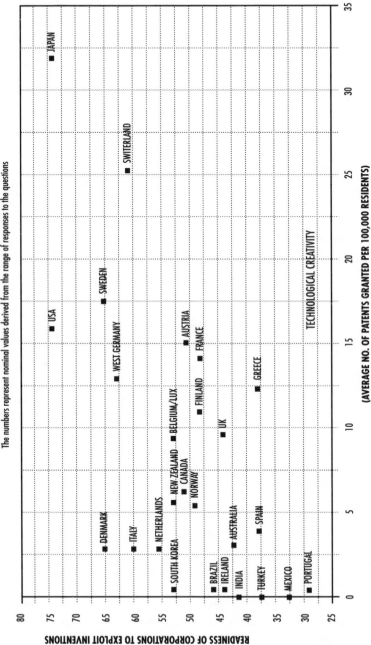

READINESS OF CORPORATIONS TO EXPLOIT INVENTIONS

(AVERAGE NO. OF PATENTS GRANTED PER 100,000 RESIDENTS)

TECHNOLOGICAL CREATIVITY

Source: EMF Foundation Survey, 1987.

trauma? Does the holistic concept explain why hostile takeovers are rare or unknown in many countries, notably West Germany, Scandinavia and Japan?

MACRO-CULTURES AND ADVANCED MANUFACTURING

As the world enters the information age of complex systems and subtle communications, only teams working together in intimate face-to-face settings may be capable of learning and disseminating intricate forms of knowledge. Just as it took a dauntless individualist like Andrew Carnegie to build the USA's steel industry, it may take the interpersonal delicacy of a butterfly's wing for a team to design a fifth generation computer. The mental processes necessary to economic success vary from one era to another.

So far it has been assumed that the four macro-cultural issues examined above are separate from each other but, of course, they interweave to create unexpected combinations and meanings. How, for example, can Asian capitalist countries like Singapore and Hong Kong develop so rapidly and still have far steeper hierarchies than Western economies? Would it not be expected, other things being equal, that steeper hierarchies would slow economies down in the race to develop? The answer may lie in combining Asian holism and right-brain configuration with its greater deference to authority.

If a leader or authority figure gives a broad, diffuse, holistic vision of the future of the company, then hundreds of subordinates can participate in providing the atoms, facts, specifics and analyses that would fulfil that vision. But if, as often happens in the West, a leader issues detailed and specific orders and precise instructions, then subordinates tend either to obey and lose their personal discretion, or to deviate and subvert the leader's intentions. In short, the diffuse holistic style of leadership preferred in Asia permits far wider degrees of participation and interpretation by subordinates. The leader creates a frame which others fill. Hierarchies only become lethal when orders are specified precisely. This point is important because in all the case histories that follow, successful Western leaders gave broad, synthetic visions to their employees, not detailed instructions. In that respect they differed from more common cultural practices around them.

Chapter 3

CONFLICT IN THE WORKPLACE: OIL, BEER AND UNIONS

This chapter includes two cases in which US corporations faced a formidable adversary, the Teamsters Union, not a group to be easily won over by appeals to the brotherhood of man. This union has a long and rather chequered history in the annals of US labour relations, being frequently accused of corruption, violence and organized crime. Its leader, Jimmy Hoffa, disappeared and was assumed murdered only a few years before these two cases began.

This is not to allege any wrong-doing among union locals described here, only to emphasize that the Teamsters have a reputation for toughness second to none, and that they are no soft touch for believers in a kinder culture. The first case concerns the brewing, bottling and distribution of beer; the second one concerns the drivers of oil tanker trucks. Another characteristic shared by both these cases is the use of outside consultants.

ANNHEUSER-BUSCH: A DECADE OF CULTURAL IMPROVEMENT THROUGH COMMUNICATION

Summary

Annheuser-Busch is one of the largest brewers and distributors of beer in the American continent. This case study concerns its plant at Fairfield in Northern California, which suffered from corrosive management–worker conflict at all levels. A cultural enrichment programme, run by the Berkeley consultants Meridian, was based on an extensive interviewing programme. Over a decade a culture of cooperation was created.

It is axiomatic in the literature on high tech that complex and subtle products can only be made out of complex and subtle human relationships. Brewing, canning and transporting beer would not seem to be a task requiring elegant sensibilities or sensitive social intercourse. The beer is made and shipped, and attempts to make something so basic into a silk purse are surely doomed, a needless elaboration on "belting out the beer". Yet Annheuser-Busch faced serious problems at its Fairfield plant within a few weeks of opening in 1976.

Great technology, ghastly problems with people

The technology was not complex. Water, grain, yeast and hops are brewed, put in bottles, kegs and cans and shipped throughout the region. Because the product is bulky, shipment is the major task. Partly for this reason all the company's eleven plants are organized by the Teamsters Union. A strike had hit all eleven North American plants 19 weeks before the Meridian consultants' arrival. The dispute was not simply between the union and management, but between the Teamsters and the older craft union tradition of metal workers (who made the cans), brewers and bottlers. The Teamsters had fought for and won a single-status workforce but the bitterness was considerable. The brewing workers especially felt deprived of their traditional skills and designations. Moreover, the new contract failed to remove an ancient enmity between the plant manager and the brewmaster, an enmity common to all eleven US plants. The first was identified with the bottling process, a machine-timed, high-volume activity of "belting out the beer". The second was identified with the quality of the brew, a somewhat esoteric and aesthetic responsibility surrounded by some mystery, and, in the eyes of the plant manager, leisurely styles of work with much sampling of the merchandise.

Although in theory there had been an opportunity to make a fresh start at a new site with workers who were untouched by ancient enmities, this was not realized in practice. The Teamsters' blanket contract to organize new sites and new workers gave them access to Teamster members who were already living in California. To be even more sure of their grip the union transferred workers from other plants, so that 25 per cent of workers at Fairfield were old union hands from existing company plants.

Organized go-slow

Because their technology was the latest and the plant was brand new, management tried to enforce much higher production targets than the workforce was accustomed to. The goals were theoretically achievable, given willingness to use the new tools effectively, but the result was an organized go-slow. Early production figures were a fraction of these targets. The workforce was sullen and suspicious. In next to no time positions were entrenched.

That was the situation when the Berkeley, California, based Meridian consultants were called in. The union protested at having to talk to them at all. "You won't last the year," they were told. They were seen as called in by management to "cool out" the workforce and subvert its solidarity. That was in 1976. Today Meridian is still employed in one of the longest, most sustained and most successful change programmes in labour relations history. The story remains noteworthy because the intervention, although extraordinarily successful, did not correspond with the presuppositions of union, management or their respective national organizations.

Building up the cultural context

The word context comes from the Latin *contextere,* "to weave together". It follows that a low-context culture has little information, and what information it does have is rather poorly organized. High-context cultures are rich with the feelings, beliefs, ideas and experiences of their members and these are intensively and meaningfully woven into their shared culture. Meridian's standard procedure, and the one that was employed with Annheuser-Busch, is, in some respects, absurdly simple although nothing like as easy to achieve as to conceptualize. It consists of an elaborate process of interviewing by more senior managers of their subordinates, so that information about the experience of employees is drawn up through the organization step by step, enriching it with knowledge about its members. "The interview" is the centre of the Meridian consulting technique and the chief means of projecting the group's values. They start with the top managers but, even as they talk to them, the consultants are modelling the way in which they want all levels of management to behave towards subordinates. The interview is a "miniature drama" which can vary from an interrogation to a mutual discovery.

The senior managers at Annheuser-Busch's Fairfield plant interviewed their immediate subordinates, who then interviewed their own immediate subordinates, who then interviewed the level below them and so on to the foremen and unionized hourly workers, in this way drawing upwards information about employees into the body of the organization. The process continues with monthly interviews even to this day. The longer this continues, and in the Fairfield plant of Annheuser-Busch it has continued for over a decade, the more productivity rises and all manner of activities, seemingly but not in actual fact remote from the interviewing process, continuously improve and break records.

Interview technique

Royal Foote, the partner of the Meridian Group interviewed for this book, said:

> "What we emphasize in the interviews is the whole person. This means much more than that person's role (a professional, an observer, a manager, a superior, or a subordinate or whatever). Of course, people have always known this, so our job is to help them to unlearn narrow, fixed ways of behaving by giving permission for a genuine meeting to take place. So we prepare a place that's neutral, no desk, no trappings of authority, and we teach managers all the way down to foremen how to interview in a sharing and receptive way."

Meridian encourages interviewers to use narrative to let a person's experience unfold. They suggest, for example, concentrating early in the interview on the employee's entry into the culture. This is a period when experiences are novel and most intense, and when aspirations are likely to have collided with unanticipated realities. It highlights the border between "inside" and "outside" and the differences encountered.

Experience suggests that the lowest levels of supervision need the most help with interviewing skills. Foremen are shown how to put workers at ease, how to be worker-centred by following his or her train of thought, how to withold negative evaluations, how to respond to feelings so as to elicit more. There is no obligation on the foreman to "do something about" what he hears. The interview is a moratorium for both in which they learn more about each other.

Teaching managers to be receptive and responsive is no easier, Foote argues.

> "They think these traits are feminine. They've had their asses kicked and names taken, so they believe that promotion gives them the right to do this to others. It only works because we start at the top. Middle managers who are listened to with respect and interviewed responsively by top management can pass this behaviour on down the line. We stress the improvement of corporate culture which we define as the weaving together of all relationships."

According to systems theory, interventions in a work relationship should start one level above the point of the problem. Say, for example, the goal is to improve productivity. An intervention at shopfloor level will probably meet with resistance. Even if achieved, it will cause an unanticipated disturbance in another part of the system. Management will sub-optimize, artificially massaging the productivity figures and wrecking relationships in the process. For example, direct pressure to cut down "tin wastage" (the amount of metal scrap from making cans) will typically cause problems elsewhere. Operators get jumpy, the number of accidents increase, productivity slows down, scrap is hidden. But the indirect approach of improving relationships between the cannery and the quality control departments will allow new methods of cutting and handling to emerge as part of a deeper knowledge by employees of each other.

The interview process

Foote describes how the cultural enrichment programme worked.

"The first few relationships were built personally among the top managers. Each one was interviewed privately and then we discussed as a group the themes that emerged. For example, on one occasion we began by discussing whether computers and information are not being misused in a system that reports the levels of tin wastage in canning beer to St Louis, Missouri, before the manager of the California plant is even awake. A genuine open dialogue revealed that the canning supervisor feels controlled and spied upon."

Once that issue had been raised, subsequent discussions explored why someone who is worth $60,000 a year to a company requires the additional costs of continuous monitoring. Is he or she not being paid to use his or her discretion? Why pay for the discretion and then pay again to undermine it with centralized scrutiny? Only a group willing to discuss the value of trust can save the expenses of distrust. But managers are trained to collect facts, to flee relationships and to take shelter in a calculative mould.

After clarifying some of the issues raised at this level, the interview process moves on: managers interview subordinates in the same way they have been interviewed by the Meridian consultants. Here the aim is to explore and to defuse management–union conflict. But all this must be achieved indirectly. No conscious attempt is made by anyone in authority to surface "the computer issue" or focus on specific conflicts. It is assumed that it is such points of focus which narrow the culture and confine it to official business. If an issue arises spontaneously it is not avoided, but broadened (not narrowed) by discussion.

Management–workforce dialogue

The greatest hidden cost to an organization is conflict and tension. This all too easily gets institutionalized and politicized. Even here the enrichment technique seems to be effective. Participants discover they can get much more for the people they represent by cooperating with management than by threatening and creating adversarial relationships. What regularly emerges is that, if subordinates sense that management is genuinely trying to discover their opinions and develop their experience, then any number of mistakes will readily be forgiven. This openness filters down through the organization. When the Teamsters see their bosses making even a stumbling effort then they in turn will risk making asses of themselves, too, with their subordinates. At this point the truth about avoidable mistakes begins to emerge. The drivers will disclose how crates of beer go missing on delivery; the tricks by which high-school kids divert their attention; the bribes they receive to look the other way. None of this comes out in relationships of mutual opposition and self-justification. It arises only when people communicate openly and admit their errors.

One problem in the Fairfield plant was cynicism: "Do those damn interviews and then get on with your work". "Okay, asshole, I have to spend a few minutes 'listening' to you, but I'm damned if it'll make any difference!" What matters most is how the interviews are done. If it is in a way that enriches relationships and culture then there is nothing to lose: if people are right, they are right, and if they are wrong they learn from the experience. And it is the social learning of a high-context culture which achieves results.

Results

Today the entire Annheuser–Busch company is alive with EPGs (employee participation groups) but it has happened from local initiatives in different plants. The elegant working model designed for the Fairfield plant by Meridian was not consciously copied, a reminder of the fact that it is impossible for people to recognize the value of phenomena which are culturally unfamiliar even when these are under their noses. Participation is typically seen as one more technique that hits or misses, not as an integral part of cultural enrichment. Hence the *ad hoc* approaches in which each Annheuser–Busch plant, in the time-honoured US way, "did its thing". The Japanese were taught about quality circles and self-managing work teams by US consultants, who could not get US corporations to "see" their effectiveness until Asian competition was breathing down their necks.

Creating dialogue and understanding in the Fairfield plant achieved a great deal. The company's advanced systems for measuring output, quality and other indices of organizational functioning showed that between the late 1970s, when Meridian started work at the plant, and 1986 ratios such as man-hours per 1,000 barrels and tin wastage improved dramatically as did beer quality, plant safety, and control of flies, bugs and mould. An annual taste test conducted by Booz Allen gave better ratings each year, customer complaints plummeted, and even measures of environmental impact showed qualitative and quantitative improvement. The management system showed strong improvement on 24 different counts. Things like absenteeism, walkouts, turnover and grievances were among the first to fall to rock-bottom levels, and have stayed that way. Although the Annheuser-Busch group has reported poor results in 1988/89, the Fairfield plant continues to be profitable.

Good hard results can have a downside, however. In 1986 Fairfield was chosen as the company's preferred site for new products and experimental brews. It was a tribute to the strong quality ratings, which had been the best in the company for several years in succession. Unfortunately, brewing new products plays havoc with indicators like man-hours per barrel, because it has to be done carefully, slowly and in small batches with different features. Since man-hours per barrel is the most highly weighted indicator in the Annheuser-Busch productivity measurement system, Fairfield has not been able to head the league since taking over this role.

Superstructure and infrastructure

Meridian's interviewing process is the delivery vehicle for a highly elaborate theory of corporate culture in which balance must be attained between opposing values. This is used both to attract clients in the first place, and to help them account for the cultural changes which the interviewing programme begins.

Meridian discerns two aspects to a living organizational system: the operational part and the human part. Modern management is hugely over-invested in the operational aspect to the neglect of the human side, which it tries to narrow and control by a logic based on operations. This effectively requires it to be impatient and to concentrate on what the anthropologist Marvin Harris calls the infrastructure (operations) to the neglect of the superstructure of values and ideas. The Marxist axiom is that if the infrastructure is changed, the superstructure of ideals will follow. Meridian believes just the opposite. Because the domain of values and relationships is so poorly understood, and because the operational infrastructure is saturated with pushing and shoving, fantastic amounts of leverage are possible through superstructure changes. What people do, and what this means to the culture of the company, are the areas in which the greatest corporate transformations can occur.

Intervention tools

Three tools used by Meridian for intervening to build up the superstructure of an organization are worth mentioning: the four-step problem-solving process (see Figure 3.1), the culture checklist and the rock and whirlpool concept.

Figure 3.1 indicates how meetings can be conducted "cybernetically", making as many passes or iterations around the issue as are needed to achieve group consensus. The culture checklist (see Table 3.1, p. 68) allows managers to assess what is unsatisfactory and needs improvement.

Figure 3.1 **The four-step problem-solving process**

SOMETHING CONCRETE HAPPENS

4 WHO WILL DO WHAT?

CONTROL RESULTS

DO IT

ACT & TEST

SELECT SOLUTION

EVALUATE ALTERNATIVES

3 HOW SHOULD WE CHOOSE ?

DISCUSS PROBLEM

DEFINE PROBLEM

1 WHAT'S THE REAL PROBLEM?

REFLECT & OBSERVE

ANALYSE PROBLEM

ALTERNATIVE SOLUTIONS

UNDERSTAND & DESCRIBE THE SITUATION

2 WHAT CAN WE DO ?

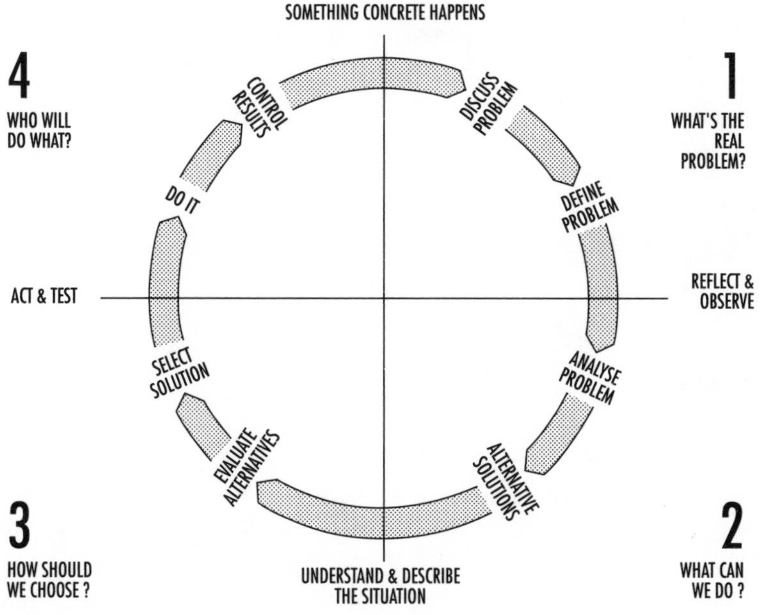

Source: Meridian Consulting Group

Table 3.1 **Culture checklist used by Meridian at Annheuser-Busch**

How do you see your organization's culture? Here are some elements in your company: which are you satisfied with?

Feature	Satisfactory	Needs improvement
How do you work for:		
A productive environment ...		
that is mature and responsible ...		
and has good values such as:		
Caring		
Loyalty		
Understanding		
Commitment		
Trust		
You motivate people through:		
Rituals		
Awards		
Ceremonies		
Making a hero		
Rewards		
Recognition		
Celebration		
And you demonstrate:		
Dialogue		
Cooperation		
Delegation		
Participation		
Involvement		
Responsiveness		
"Walking round"		
The whole company manages:		
Operations/actions		
Decision processes		
Meetings		
"Contexting" (ie interviewing)		
Quality circles		
Assessment circles		

The rock and the whirlpool complementarities, used to help clients achieve better balance, come from the Greek myth about the two dangers which mariners had to navigate: Scylla and Charybdis. Meridian use it to distinguish two orders of reality, one hard, definite, objective, solid, definable, verifiable; the other soft, indefinite, interactive, liquid, indefinable and very difficult to verify (see Table 3.2).

Table 3.2 **The rock and the whirlpool**

Rock	Whirlpool
Hard	Soft
Body	Mind
Masculine	Feminine
Rigid	Flexible
Structure	Process
Closed	Open
Organizational	Institutional
Infrastructure	Superstructure
Controlled	Permissive
Task	People
(Scylla)	(Charybdis)

They argue that in order to create a productive, mature and responsible company that elicits from its members understanding, commitment, trust and loyalty, it is essential to strike a reasonable balance between the infrastructure (Scylla) and the superstructure (Charybdis). This means that actions, plans and resource allocations must be seen in terms of their effect on people. Actions should be connected to the kinds of values, traditions and attitudes that bring out the highest quality of individual experience in the enterprise.

What the interviewing process does is to build up the superstructure. It keeps reminding those who pass orders down the infrastructure what effect this is having on the superstructure. If the interview is a genuine dialogue, values will be balanced in part because the superior is listening, and in part because softer, interactive values are legitimized by the interview setting. Such interviews are the conceptual forerunner of "management by walking round".

The very success of Annheuser-Busch's Fairfield plant is a reminder, ironically, of how important it is to tackle these problems of mentality, approach and balance between different orders of reality. It is, in the end, genuinely difficult for hard-nosed US management to understand the participative patterns which create a rich, high-context culture. Year after year the Fairfield plant of Annheuser-Busch was registering a far superior performance to any other of its many plants. Absenteeism, grievances, turnover, lost days, were all lower by far. All measures of productivity and effectiveness showed superior performance.

Eventually, the company's top management came west from St Louis to award prizes to its best plant and to celebrate almost a decade of rising performance. The puzzled president had grasped that it all had to do with "participation", this latest technique. His speech of congratulation revealed, however, that "rocks" still cannot conceive of "whirlpools": "So we see that participation really is superior to adversary relationships. Wherever we find adversary relationships we must stamp them out …"

The unreconstructed "toughness" of the CEO was matched by that of the Teamsters' HQ. What was this disquietingly "cosy" relationship at Fairfield? Why was not the union doing its job of opposing management? This question was asked by three successive "business agents" (the regionally elected officers approved by the Teamsters' HQ who do the bargaining). The Fairfield plant constitutes only 25 per cent of the region's electorate, so it cannot pick its own agent. The first agent was so supportive of the cultural changes at Fairfield that the larger constituency voted him out. The second agent fell out with the Teamsters' hierarchy when he supported a faction seeking greater democracy in the union. The third agent, a former worker at Fairfield, is again supportive. The International Teamsters met at the Fairfield plant in 1984. They voted overwhelmingly against EPGs in their birthplace. But the elected shop-stewards and the local agent continued as before. Fairfield keeps prospering, much to the puzzlement of the power structures at national levels.

WESTERN OIL: A CULTURE FOR SAFETY

Summary

The author of this book was involved in a project which led to a complete turnround in the attitudes of oil company workers to safety. Initially safety was totally at odds with the main cultural values of productivity (management's interests) and maintenance of a macho image (the workers' culture). A series of initiatives succeeded in reframing these values to reconcile them with safety values. The company concerned is California based and a major energy concern. In the wake of the Exxon Valdez disaster, oil companies' safety records suddenly became a crucial issue. As this company wishes to remain anonymous, it will be called Western Oil.

Western Oil had a culture which put safety in conflict with other corporate values. By analysing the dilemmas which marginalized safety, a consultancy team put together a strategy using teams, worker advice, and intelligent bonus packages for reorienting the anti-safety values to reconcile them with concern for safety. The example emphasizes that the negative values of a culture cannot be eliminated, but they can be turned to the benefit of the corporation and society as a whole.

Safety at work – a difficult value to maintain

The consultants reported to Rick Crosby, an ex-director of safety from a major chemical company, who had been brought out of retirement, following a major explosion at the Louisiana terminal of one of Western's subsidiaries. "We have a few months to get things done," he said. "Right now safety is high on everyone's agenda, but it doesn't last. I've seen it before. It's in the aftermath of a shock like this that changes can be instituted." It was decided to establish a pilot programme starting a week later, and extend it throughout the company thereafter.

Western Oil's patchy record

Western Oil's safety record, although not bad by industry standards, was certainly patchy, and worst in the area of distributing gasoline by truck. Following the principle that no value can ever really be isolated and must always be in tension with others, the consultants started by interviewing the drivers to discover the value dilemmas at large in the company. They looked for values which would be in conflict with safety.

The drivers, who were organized by the local Teamsters, had a long list of complaints.

- The new exhaust systems fitted to the gasoline trucks were leaking fumes into the cabs, making the drivers nauseous.
- Several major highways in California and elsewhere were not safe for the transport of so combustible a cargo as gasoline.
- Productivity bonuses for delivering to more customers per day were unfairly calculated.
- On-site facilities in gas stations to which they delivered were not safely maintained, and station owners or franchisees were absent, contemptuous or even abusive when this was pointed out to them.
- The sales department added to this dangerous clutter by selling more products than the site could safely store.
- Safety regulations were so numerous and petty as to be a joke, and following them literally would make normal delivery schedules impossible to meet.

The evident purpose of the safety manuals was not to assist the drivers to do a good job, but to use against them in the event of an accident. The requirement that they sign to say that they had read and understood the manual was particularly resented, since it was virtually unreadable. A driver said, "They tell you to work fast and to work safe and simply ignore the fact that these goals are not compatible. If they catch you cutting corners you're in trouble, but if you don't make your quota of deliveries you're in trouble, too." Given this dilemma, or "double bind", the consultants did not have much difficulty predicting what would happen. Drivers could go for weeks or months without anyone reporting them for unsafe practices, but if they did not meet their delivery schedules would show up the same day and affect their pay. Hence, deliveries were being made on schedule, even if safety suffered.

Management had seized on the issue of nausea and the "faulty" exhaust system to discredit most of the rest of the drivers' complaints. They were a "bunch of neurotics", the consultants were told. The tankers had all been retro-fitted with the same exhaust system, yet the nausea was confined to drivers in the Sonoma Valley area; a curious case of local malady affecting even those driving newer trucks that had been factory-fitted with the new-style exhaust systems. The drivers were furious.

The trucking culture

A word should be said about the culture of trucking in the USA. It is lonely work on account of the long distances travelled and the late hours. Family life typically suffers and is often non-existent. The image of the driver is macho, self-reliant, tough and individualistic. Truckers often use their CB radios to defeat efforts by law-enforcement officers to police them. There are "truck details" which play cat and mouse games with truckers, who retaliate in various ways, sometimes interfering with police radio frequencies.

While oil companies pick their drivers with far greater care than most other hauliers, and there are periodic checks to control the use of benzedrene and alcohol, driving excessive hours is hard to stop, especially when it appears to benefit the company in the short term. The image of prudence, safety, caution and obedience to the company's regulations does not fit in with this cowboy stereotype at all. The "knights of the road", as many popular movies depict them, are fearless pioneers of the unconventional lifestyle. "Be more careful, boys!" is hardly a plea likely to go down well with this particular group.

The gas-station owners and franchisees are no easier to discipline. They are generally proud of their independence and do not take orders readily. Those in the study were also under pressure from oil companies to keep open late at night and over holidays, so that the owner was not always present.

No one was in the mood to report the breaking of safety rules to managers. Rather, drivers, station personnel and crews at depots tended to stick together against interference from above. Informal norms grew up about what was permissible in the circumstances, and, since circumstances themselves varied widely, the latitude was correspondingly wider – people did not snitch on each other.

From interviews with the line managers, gas station proprietors, gasoline truck drivers and depot crews, safety department personnel and others, the consultants discovered that safety in the culture was in conflict with other values, also central to this culture. Safety was important to nearly everyone, but so were other key values.

Operation Integrity

Five dilemmas within the culture were concentrated on.
1. Safety first versus macho-individualism.
2. Safety everywhere versus safety specialists.
3. Safety as cost versus productivity as a benefit.
4. Long-term safety versus short-term steering.
5. Personal responsibility versus collective protection.

The consultants concluded that if the corporate culture of Western Oil could learn to mediate these dilemmas so that both sets of values now in tension were reconciled, then safety would, among other values, be much improved. They called this "Operation Integrity", the purpose being to integrate the values and to create harmony among them, using myths, symbols, images and metaphors. In order to achieve this, dilemmas 1–5 had each to be reconciled.

1. Safety first versus macho-individualism

It is a great mistake to pretend that a cultural trend can ever be blunted, much less halted. At best it can be used, deflected and its meaning qualified. If Californian truck drivers see themselves as a cross between the Incredible Hulk and Smokey and the Bandit, then the persuasions of their employees are unlikely to stop this. What it can do is "reframe" the heroism and give a new significance to the detached view of the outsider.

It was recommended that all drivers and key personnel in terminals became consultants on safety on the roads, or helped redesign depots for safer operations.

From drivers to consultants. Instead of asking them to drive safely on the road system as it was, or to behave predictably in accordance with the regulations in force at that time, the drivers' advice was sought on the improvement of state and federal highways, together with their contribution to road safety initiatives being undertaken by the Department of Transportation in Washington. Their services would be paid for by Western Oil as part of its contribution to US society.

The rationale was that here were men carrying loads that could burn down a small town or incinerate 50 vehicles in a major accident. When gasoline spills from an overturned tanker, it flows into cellars and, ignited by pilot lights on domestic heaters, can literally blow a house to pieces. Since it is truly an awesome responsibility to drive such vehicles, the men who do this should be listened to with care. Who, after all, are more likely to have intimations of possible disasters? Who, as they go about their work, have more time to reflect on what might go wrong, or greater opportunities to anticipate looming dangers?

Criticizing the system. By making drivers critics of the system, their roles as outsiders were preserved and promoted. The drivers reported, for example, that there were at least four entry ramps on the Nimitz Freeway (the one which collapsed in the 1989 San Francisco earthquake) where a fully loaded tanker, with the accelerator pedal flat to the floor, could reach only about 45 mph as it joined the traffic going 55–60 mph. The ramps were too short to get up sufficient speed and it was dangerous to everyone concerned to try edging into a traffic stream going that much faster. It was only a matter of time before a serious accident occurred. There were also a dozen steep hills in the state with inadequate turn-outs for trucks whose brakes failed on descent. Typically, these escape roads are filled with soft sand to stop a careering truck, but several roads were too short, or the sand had hardened, so that the truck would simply mount them and be launched into space.

It was recommended that drivers should assist in making videos of the most common hazards encountered on their journeys, that these be professionally edited in-house and be offered to local TV stations and the appropriate highway authorities. It was also suggested that the drivers should publish their own safety newsletter, warning each other of hazards like short ramps, mis-labelled gas tanks and rogue customers.

Enthusiasm for CB radios should be turned to the advantage of the company and the public, with a "driver alert" system that warned not simply other Western truck drivers, but all other drivers using the same bands. The consultants suggested that drivers be encouraged to use police frequencies in emergencies, when an accident had been spotted, or in a dangerous situation likely to cause one at any moment.

The company should publicly honour any of its Citizens Band users who gave warnings and possibly saved lives. Drivers should feel within reason that they were deputies in the effort to keep roads safe. Friendly contacts between police and Western Oil drivers should encourage compliance with the law by the drivers themselves.

A new culture of heroism. The consultants were trying to create "knights of the road" in a more chivalrous sense, men pledged to maintain an order based on respect for the public. These were not men who did precisely what they were told from motives of fear or timidity, but men with the capacity to foresee dangers and act decisively to protect the public. They urged that drivers carry emergency telephone numbers for every part of their routes and that the new phone-in-the-cab being installed be used to summon aid, so that Western drivers would become a potential resource for the travelling public. Such services could not be offered as a matter of routine – there was other work to do – but as a recourse in emergencies. After all, no tanker truck was safe while the roads themselves were hazardous or being misused.

The drivers were being offered a different kind of heroism, a plan enthusiastically endorsed and interpreted by Rick Crosby:

"In the final reel of great US movies the real heroes always come to the aid of their communities. Rhett Butler in *Gone with the Wind* finally joins the Confederate armies; Han Solo in *Star Wars* decides to help in the attack on the Death Star; and Rick in *Casablanca,* played by Humphrey Bogart, gives up his love affair because there's a cause more important than his personal happiness. That's how I want our drivers to be. Sure they're loners, they couldn't do the job otherwise. But when the public's in danger they go into action. They foresee dangers, they warn and if necessary they rescue, and we're going to celebrate any of you guys that head off or help in emergencies."

The Teamsters looked a bit sceptical, but Crosby's enthusiasm was all a consultant could ask for. He meant it.

2. Safety everywhere versus safety specialists

Where is safety? Is it distributed throughout the organization in patterns? Is safety a specialism, another contending source of authority within the company? The division of labour is a great convenience. Adam Smith taught that the more labours were divided, the greater would the wealth of nations grow. Yet this is true only of some goals and values, not of others. Say, for example, the object is to increase quality. Organizations are discovering that this needs to be everyone's affair. Hiring more inspectors or beefing up the quality department may not work. Reject too many parts and someone lets your tyres down in the car park. There is only so much an inspector can do, faced by a push for quantity regardless of quality. Safety, like quality, must be everywhere.

While a safety department can provide valuable information and resources, safety must, in the end, be a line responsibility. Western was warned that one danger of making safety one department's speciality is that other departments will believe the issue belongs elsewhere. Another danger is that it can lead people to sub-optimize if it is hyped by just one department; since some safety is good, more is presumably better and total safety is simply sublime. Give safety that kind of hard sell and sales resistance will only increase.

The introduction of cross-functional safety teams in the manner of quality circles was recommended. Their job was to criticize and improve the layout of, say, depots and loading procedures, in the light of safety considerations. These teams pointed out that it should be possible, mechanically, to prevent the fuel flowing into the tanker until the hose was safely inside, and that any spillage of product on the floor must be cleared up at once or others could slip on it. They said that the men would not jump down from their cabs so readily if the steps unfolded faster and that a simple device to earth the truck as it entered the depot could reduce the build-up of static electricity.

Rewriting the rules. The consultants suggested that teams could rewrite the regulations to make them useful on the job. Previously, the rule book had served only to cover the posterior of the safety and legal departments by making certain no "legal accident" could ever occur: it would always be the fault of individuals. Teams of drivers and sales personnel could ensure that gasoline stations were not inundated with more products than they could safely store, that safety equipment be among the lines the company supplied, and that sales play its part by ensuring that the stations had the correct labels, insignia and colours on its different tanks so that these were filled with the right product. Drivers were concerned that if they were ill their substitutes could make serious errors in a station unfamiliar to them.

The slogan "Seamless Safety" was proposed. Safety is not just everyone's business, with safety specialists providing expert advice; it demands that no gaps be left between departmental responsibilities. Just as it cannot be said that "safe roads are the responsibility of the highway department", nor can safety equipment in stations be left solely to their owners, or to sales, or to drivers. Everyone has to contribute. It could save Western Oil millions of dollars to discount safety equipment to garages if that meant more was used. After all, those injured would not sue the station owner, they would sue the wealthy oil company. It follows that, unless the company seized that responsibility, it would certainly be penalized for the oversight of others.

3. Safety as cost versus productivity as benefit

There was a serious, potentially lethal, conflict between safe operations and high productivity. If the drivers raced from station to station to win their bonus, accidents were bound to occur. The consultants discovered that, in fact, the safety engineers rarely spoke to the line managers in charge of the delivery schedules. The unreconciled dilemma between safety and productivity had been evaded at management level, and passed down the hierarchy until the drivers were subjected to two incompatible injunctions, work fast and work safely. This, in the consultants' view, was responsible for the feelings of nausea and stress, and the epithets about "neuroses" added insult to a "double bind".

Dangerous benefits and safety pay-outs. The image of "safe productivity" was suggested: only deliveries safely made should count towards a bonus. It was recommended that the proportion of bonus to basic pay be reduced and be calculated on the number of miles covered rather than destinations reached, since some stations were more scattered than others. There should be a "safety bonus" at year-end, based on spot checks and the recommendations of the safety teams. Such a bonus must be at least as large as those based on productivity, so that the two values were balanced and not skewed by the reward system.

The same principle was, wherever possible, applied to sales. It must pay to sell safety equipment to station owners or managers, so that safety would become a benefit and not simply a cost of doing business. Bonuses paid to sales personnel could give extra weight to time spent on safety checks and better storage. All products sold had to be accompanied by the means of storing and managing them safely. And it should become the salesman's job to maintain this balance.

4. Long-term safety versus short-term steering

There remained the major problem that accidents come too rarely to be instructive and are too appalling in the pain and suffering they inflict. Some means has to be found of learning before it is too late, that is, creating a steeper learning curve. Experience is indeed the best teacher, but the "school fees" can be crushing.

So the device of counting and controlling "unsafe acts" was adopted. Jumping from the cab on to the greasy floor, breaking the terminal's 5 mph speed limit, allowing gasoline vapours to escape during loading and not holding the handrail – these were all "unsafe acts", and it was the job of cross-functional teams to count them, discuss them with those responsible and find ways of reducing them.

It was by such devices that the consultants aimed to create the many minor mistakes from which an organization can progressively learn. A bucket and mop left on the ground where someone could fall over them was an incident noted and reported. Teams could monitor their effectiveness as the number of such incidents dropped week by week and as potential sources of accidents were steadily reduced. Such methods operate like the whiskers on a cat; people learn to blink before a branch takes out their eye. The corrective feedback loop is triggered not by the accident itself, but by its imminence. One stupid act can kill everyone.

5. Personal responsibility versus collective protection

Finally, the pattern by which employees in various functions protected each other from sanction by management for their unsafe conduct had to be broken. It is, anyway, a spurious "protection" that allows an individual to continue endangering all colleagues who work nearby. The consultants believed that the safety teams would provide some of the necessary peer pressure, but it was essential that management ceased to be seen as "them policing us". Moreover, the habit of "blaming the victim" after the accident, with the manuals left at bedsides, had to stop.

A scheme was proposed where any employee reporting another for an unsafe act to the safety team thereby protected that person from official sanction by management. This held unless the safety team, consisting of his peers, regarded the breach as so serious that they must seek sanction. In other words, all workers were primarily responsible to fellow workers, who could, after all, be injured or killed by their carelessness.

The first judgement about the seriousness of any infringement would come from them. In most cases, the individual who acted unsafely would have to appear before a committee of his peers to apologize or explain. The decreasing number of unsafe acts recorded every week would be prominently displayed around the terminal. Publicity on safety should be directed at the social consequences of individual errors: "One stupid act can kill us all", "Unsafe roads make you the hostage".

Success or failure?

Although the consultant, Rick Crosby, has now returned to his retirement, the success of the programme is clear: there have been no accidents requiring hospitalization since its inception, and the monthly record of "unsafe acts" has declined sharply.

The Teamsters themselves, in addition to warmly supporting a party to mark Crosby's departure, have presented him with a silver steering wheel as a mark of their respect, an almost unheard-of honour for an outsider to their union.

A DIAGRAMMATIC SUMMARY

To help make sense of this last case the concepts are presented in Figure 3.2 (see p. 80). The consultants found five dilemmas whose "horns" are represented by dual axes.

In each dilemma Western Oil was badly skewed towards the bottom on each of the five axes.

1. Macho-individualism dominated safety.
2. Safety as a specialist concern eclipsed safety everywhere and for everybody.
3. "Productivity", that is driving fast and hurrying, was emphasized above the time taken to be careful and safer.
4. Short-term gains from taking risks outweighed the long delayed penalties for carelessness which stunned employees rather than educated them.
5. Workers protected each other from management sanction by not reporting and not reducing breaches of personal responsibility.

For each dilemma X marks the lopsided condition of the company. The system was unstable, for when an accident occurred cultural opinion would oscillate to the opposite extreme O, but only for a few weeks before settling back.

The top right-hand corners of each dilemma show the reconciliations which were designed.

Figure 3.2 **Western Oil's five major dilemmas**

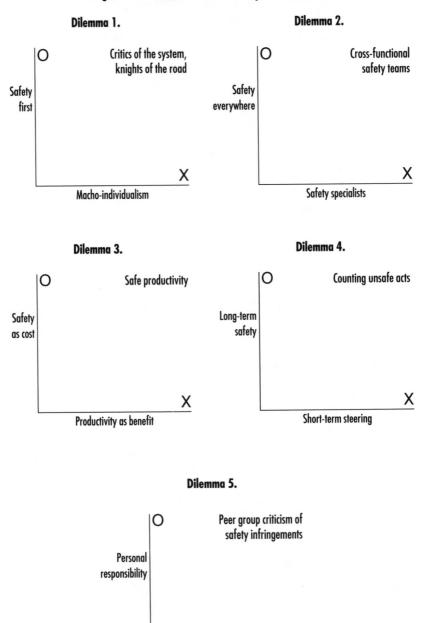

1. Making drivers critics of the system and "knights of the road" combined individuality with serving the community safely.
2. Cross-functional safety teams made sure that specialists in safety suffused the whole environment with their expertise.
3. The rewarding of safe productivity balanced the two objectives of safety and productivity more evenly than before.
4. Counting unsafe acts created a short-term feedback loop for longer-term dangers.
5. Peer group criticism of lapses of personal responsibility, which protected the worker concerned from management sanction, made personal care consistent with peer group loyalty.

A self-perpetuating vicious circle

The unsafe conditions found at Western Oil can also be represented as a self-perpetuating vicious circle. In order to keep its operation simple only three dilemmas have been picked but it could have been written with any three or all of them. Figure 3.3 shows dilemmas 1, 3 and 5.

Figure 3.3 Western Oil: a vicious circle

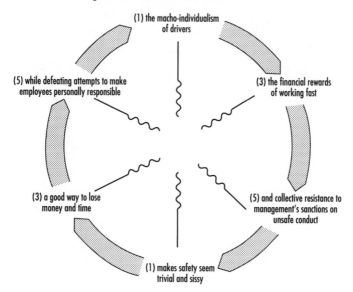

(1) the macho-individualism of drivers

(3) the financial rewards of working fast

(5) while defeating attempts to make employees personally responsible

(5) and collective resistance to management's sanctions on unsafe conduct

(3) a good way to lose money and time

(1) makes safety seem trivial and sissy

Creating a virtuous circle

The reconciliations of dilemmas 1, 3 and 5 are used to "reattach the snapped ropes". The virtuous circle so formed is shown in Figure 3.4.

Figure 3.4 **Western Oil: a virtuous circle**

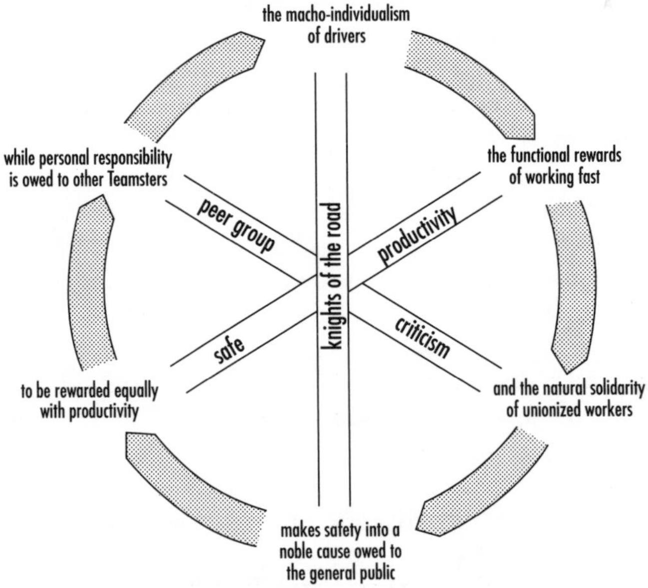

the macho-individualism
of drivers

the functional rewards
of working fast

while personal responsibility
is owed to other Teamsters

peer group

knights of the road

productivity

criticism

safe

to be rewarded equally
with productivity

and the natural solidarity
of unionized workers

makes safety into a
noble cause owed to
the general public

So long as the opposite sides of the loop stay joined a "developmental helix" will be generated. The drivers feel more individualistic and more public spirited, they will work with more dispatch and more safely, and they will show greater solidarity with fellow workers by making sure that each exercises responsibility for the safety of all.

Chapter 4

THE ASCENT OF BRITISH AIRWAYS

SUMMARY

The story of British Airways' culture change is well known. But the success of that change leaves important questions unanswered. Where next? How to keep up with the momentum of change? Between 1982 and 1988 British Airways went from being "Airline of the Last Resort", with year-end losses of around £100 million, to "Business Carrier of Preference", with profits of £320 million. It learned to respond to customers requirements and to act on individuals' initiatives. By learning to care for its own staff, BA generated the pattern of a more caring culture for the enjoyment of its passengers and the profit of the airline. But the goal of widespread cultural change has yet to be realized. Middle management is still ruled by separate functions rather than by a cooperative ethic. At the top all the weight goes on the individualist functions of high finance and clever takeover battles. Will the changes wrought at the grass roots repeat themselves up the scale, or be suffocated by pressure from above?

THE STUDY

Few turnrounds have been more impressive or so extensive as that of British Airways. The airline was a massive loss-maker. In September 1981 its chairman and chief executive, Roy Watts, said in a special Bulletin to staff: "British Airways is facing the worst crisis in its history … we are heading for a loss of at least £100 million in the current financial year. We face the prospect that, by next April, we shall have piled up losses of close to £250 million in two years."

The airline was grossly overmanned, unpunctual and strike-prone, with a very special disdain for passengers. In the words of Nick Georgiades, its fomer head of human resources, "It was a civil aviation dinosaur, the airline of last resort." Executives would say to their secretaries, "Get me there any way you can – but not by BA."

Today BA is not simply the world's largest carrier, but, of those which combine short-haul with long-haul, it is the most profitable. (Small, exclusive long-haul carriers like Singapore Airlines and Cathay Pacific are the most profitable.) BA is easily strongest across the Atlantic where it was the "Business Carrier of Preference" by a wide margin for several years in succession, with the greatest revenues. (Virgin has won the competition recently but is a minor carrier concentrating on a few routes.) In the much contested "resurgence" of British enterprise BA stands out as one success that cannot be doubted and which surely demands an explanation. Since much of the improvement came before privatization, and since SAS, still a publicly owned airline, was the model for many changes BA introduced, the privatization issue is not a sufficient cause. Rather BA changed its culture radically, with almost immediate effect.

How BA thinks of culture

Nick Georgiades introduces the subject of culture with one of his favourite quotes: "The society that scorns excellence in plumbing because it is a humble activity and tolerates shoddiness in philosophy because it is an exalted activity will have neither good philosophy nor good plumbing; neither its pipes nor its theories will hold water."

The challenge faced by those who would shape an effective corporate culture is to develop a coherent philosophy of how the customer can best be served, using that "plumbing". Such philosophy is crucial because, unlike specific programmes, it has sufficient generality to apply to many varying situations. Nick defines corporate culture as "the shared patterns in the organization, in so far as these arise from shared beliefs, values and norms, which themselves arise in part from the history and tradition of the organization, as modified by contemporary events". This culture is not inscribed in any one place and cannot be located in any specific department. It is the spoken and unspoken assumptions about "how people do things around here". Luke Mayhew, the current human resources general manager, puts it in another way: "Cultures are about how people feel, what they value and how they behave." Both agree that it is necessary to understand BA's history.

BA's historical development

"After the war [Nick explains] BA had its pick of the best pilots, navigators, flight engineers ... They came in droves. They had run logistics and transport systems. Our present safety director flew in the Berlin airlift. They were not only damned good, they were victorious over the *Luftwaffe*. It was 'Biggles joins BA'. And the attitudes were military. 'Don't do as I do. Do as I say.' We had more job titles that ended in the word 'officer' than you'd believe. And on the fourth floor of Speedbird House was – you've guessed it – the Senior Managers' Mess. When we abolished that a few years ago, the reverberations could be heard to the ends of the runways. Even today there is a group of men who meet secretly on the fourth Thursday of every month to relive the vanished glories of the Senior Managers' Mess.

"The closest I came to industrial action with the Transport and General Workers Union was when we introduced the new livery. No longer would people walk about in navy blue uniforms with patterns of scrambled egg indicating their rank and role. We abolished military markings. The TGWU stormed into my office. 'How will we recognize our supervisors?' We all thought hard. 'By the way they behave?' I suggested, 'by what they actually do?' I don't think the irony was appreciated. It's still on the agenda.

"We had to make concessions to the pilots who absolutely insisted on their markings and looked to me like refugees from an Argentine military coup. Employees felt they were arriving because they got another ring on their uniform, not because they were treated differently, had accomplished more, or had more responsibility. The symbols had become substitutes for real achievement.

"I remember some years ago, before I joined the company, when BEA and BOAC were still separate, I was invited to the office of the head of engineering at BEA. It had windows down both sides. He was staring from his windows and beckoned me to join him. It was 6.30 p.m. in the evening and there, lined up across the tarmac, wingtip to wingtip, was BEA's entire operational fleet. 'What a sight!' enthused my host. 'Suppose I'm a businessman and want to get back from Zürich this evening?' I asked. He frowned. 'You fly Swissair.' One of our aircraft was not missing. We'd counted our boys back home. You see, the culture was so strong because it had worked. They remembered the Second World War and they wouldn't let it go."

From military to marketing

But if employees felt that this was a culture shock, the privatization-induced changes of 1983 must have sent them reeling. In 1981 Sir John (now Lord) King took over the presidency of BA and in January 1983 Colin Marshall became chief executive. In the months immediately before and after his appointment, BA shed some 20,000 employees, and a score of international passenger routes. Concern with their survival made all the remaining employees hyper-alert. Marshall began sending out some clear signals. First, he wanted people to make decisions. If they made mistakes that was more forgivable than not deciding in the first place. Second, they must start to face outwards, towards customers. Marshall wrote of this period:

> "It was ... obvious to me that the organization was extremely introverted, had really no grasp of what the market place wanted, what the customer wanted – that the organization was almost totally lacking in marketing ... There wasn't anyone in the company with that word in their title ... I believed that the most critical thing was for us to address the issue of customer service. In so doing, we recognized the need to create some motivational vehicle with the employees, so that we had a better prospect of raising their morale and, in turn, seeing better customer service flow."

Hiding within titles

Third, Marshall wanted no one to hide behind titles or job descriptions. A story that was circulating at that time had considerable influence. Mike Bruce of the human resources department, interviewed for this book, explained:

> "It had been the tradition in BA to call the chief executive 'CX'. It was part of the game of military titles. Someone at a meeting chaired by Colin used the word, and he fixed the miscreant with a gimlet eye. 'My name is Colin Marshall. I'd like you all to remember that,' he said.
>
> "The story was repeated everywhere I went, and then, without – as far as I know – any direct orders, the titles began to disappear from people's doors and their names were going up instead. I'm not sure that people saw the human meaning in this at the time. Perhaps they were just trying to survive, but they see it now."

Fourth, Marshall disliked large committees and the time groups took to make decisions. He set up small *ad hoc* groups in parallel, charging them with responsibilities that cut across different functions or, in some cases, duplicated those functions. He liked to work one-on-one, delegating responsibility directly to key individuals. Finally, he was also impatient

with hierarchy and sought to reduce the number of levels. Those dealing directly with customers must have room for discretion and personal
initiative.

These five messages were crucial to the cultural changes that followed. Curiously the actual cultural transformation was much, much
more than Marshall had asked for. It was qualified by research from customers and new insights from human resource management, strongly
supported by marketing and customer services, and modelled after the
success of Scandinavian Airlines (SAS) – all creative additions and inter-
pretations of what the chief executive had initially demanded.

Initial cultural research

Marshall had instigated a major research study into customer attitudes
towards BA. The line of enquiry followed that of SAS under the leadership of Jan Carlson. Carlson had discovered that the reputation of SAS
rested not so much on the products provided, the safety of planes, the
convenience of schedules and so on, than on millions of "moments of
truth", that is, verbal encounters between airline staff and passengers,
most lasting less than 30 seconds. BA, with its 20 million passengers a
year interacting 7.5 times per journey, could expect 150 million of such
moments.

Crucial to customers' satisfaction was not what they thought but how
they felt. Their intuitive reaction was not to any product, but to an
ambience, environment or culture within the cabin and at the check-in
desk. The research findings showed that customers found BA staff to be
professional and competent but "cold, aloof, uncaring and bureaucratic"
in their responses to customers. Respondents suggested many physical
improvements but replied that BA, although not the best, was not the
worst either in this regard. Even if all the physical problems, like smelly
toilets, were taken care of, the response to how the service was given
would remain. The "how" was 50 per cent more important than the
"what" as a source of satisfaction, and 100 per cent more important than
the "what" as a source of dissatisfaction.

Culture in the service industries

Luke Mayhew, human resources general manager, whose earlier experience at Thomas Cook was in marketing, argues that in a service industry
like BA marketing fuses with the highly visible corporate culture experienced by passengers.

"The culture is really what customers buy. It is a larger pattern in which the physical features, such as seating and food, are embedded. Product innovations can be rapidly imitated. Six months after we installed our wide recliner seats for long-haul flights, Qantas did the same. But culture cannot be easily copied. It has to be learned. Develop an effective service culture and you not only move ahead of your competitors, you stay ahead. If they try to fake it they'll fail. We know that. Before we got that right, we used to have an ad of a stewardess helping a little old granny on her first trip to Australia to see her married daughter. Our staff laughed in our face.

"They told us, in effect, 'Don't pretend we can be that good, when the wheels come off the trolleys and the galleys are in disrepair. Give us better support.' So we learned not to over-promise and then under-deliver. We learned that, if you raise customers' expectations too high with your commercials, you will only lay the foundations for disappointing and offending them. We have to learn to be internally consistent in everything we do, so that service is a seamless whole, not a boast belied by realities. Once you develop a credibility gap it's hard to erase it. It's very hard to win back those you've disillusioned."

Nick Georgiades agrees that the plastic smile and the "have a nice day" and "y'all come back now" is counter-productive. The worst cases of burn-out and mental breakdown among staff come when behaviour is artificial, smiles begin to crack and the customers recognize rote greetings and discount them.

Passengers resent behaviour they feel is designed to "cool out" their wrath and weariness. They are angered by standard expressions in non-standard circumstances, and air travel, owing to crowded skies, airport controllers going slow and general congestion, is becoming less and less standardized.

Managing emotional labour

Georgiades speaks of "three industrial revolutions" since the original one. The first of the three, starting from the middle of the nineteenth century, shifted the employment contract from muscle to brain. The second revolution digitalized business with skilled, manipulative fingers, starting with typewriters and culminating in word processors, computers and digitally-controlled machine tools. The third revolution is that of the emotional labourers, those whose prime responsibility is to make those they serve feel good and emotionally satisfied. "We have not realized what this sort of labour costs those who do it for a living."

The more technical aspects of jobs performed by customer service staff are being de-skilled.

"The computer system is so user-friendly that a small child can learn it in a few hours. But dealing with people face-to-face in a highly confined space 37,000 feet in the air is a challenge which still takes an immense amount of energy and skill. It is difficult to get staff to call passengers by their names, particularly check-in staff. The name is on the ticket. Yet resistance is strong and stubborn. We use impersonality to buffer ourselves from the clamour of people's needs. Using names would invite personal requests, idiosyncratic wants, desires for reassurance. And yet it's vital that an airline gives such service. It would really make the difference in terms of quality and reputation.

"What makes it emotionally difficult for cabin staff is that the content of their work varies so much. They don't know what kind of emotional response will be called for: problems can range from Australian cricketers vying for the record of drinking 46 cans of Fosters between Melbourne and London to passengers who want to be left alone, yet the child next to them wants to be talked to and shown the cockpit."

Research into "emotional labour" cultures

In order to illuminate the problems of emotional workers, the human resources department looked at hospices and hospital wards for distressing conditions, and studied social workers as part of a 1983 research programme. It noted three things. First, the best workers were in excellent physical and mental shape. Second, they had close group bonds for sharing each other's grief and pain. You cannot cry in front of the kids in the leukaemia ward, but you can in the arms of others who feel like you do. In the Sloan Kettering Memorial Hospital they are organized into mutual support groups, nurses, orderlies, even cleaners who see the children one day and find the beds empty the next. Third, those who cared best were best cared for by their supervisors. The culture was one in which people passed on to others the quality of the care they received.

A published research project to do with customers' perception of the quality of care received by banking staff in 375 branches showed high and consistent correlations between the quality of the supervisor–supervisee relationship and the quality of the service given by different supervisees to customers. "In a way it's so obvious, it's banal," protests Georgiades, "and yet I have to turn feelings into facts before I can get people to acknowledge what intuitively they have always known."

The other important finding was that the best carers had been given maximum discretion in solving their customers' problems. The supervisors gave them the tools – their trust, their support and their advice – and then left them free to use their judgement.

Much work in the service industries and especially the work in cabins and on counters is not personally fulfilling. People do not get to know customers enough for their efforts to win due gratitude and friendship. If employees are to be convinced that their efforts are worthwhile, then that confirmation must come from colleagues and supervisors and must be an attribute of the culture.

Changing the culture through training programmes

The "handles" on culture are many, and all need pulling to create a coherent effect. Several training programmes were organized by the human resources department. The first, from 1983 to 1987, was called "Putting People First" (PPF). It was designed by Time Manager International, the Scandinavian consultants who had helped SAS. The programme communicated and put into practice the discoveries of the 1983 research with customers. Staff were encouraged to utilize delays, bad weather, running out of preferred food, lost baggage and so on, to show their own ingenuity and concern in the shape of personal initiatives designed to compensate for such difficulties.

Mike Bruce, of the human resources department, explained:

"You free the cabin staff to give the best service they can, on the assumption that this is what they really want. It's a question of empowerment and the capacity for improvisation. With set procedures and standard techniques you actually force them to give bad service – not tailored to the person, not responsive to unforeseen events. We had to build up their confidence that they could make decisions and could use flexible and ingenious means to fulfil the superordinate goal of satisfying customers. We had them express feelings about their jobs, set personal goals and re-examine all their relationships so that they would be seen as whole people, not just roles."

A particularly important aspect of the PPF sessions was the attendance of Colin Marshall at 97 per cent of all the gatherings. He appealed directly and personally to the cabin staff, arguing that the company was wholly dependent upon their ideas, experience and reflections. He asked them to contribute their abilities in specially set up "Customer First" teams. Over 100 quality team circles were started. At the last count 75 were still operating. That is a pretty good record for quality circles – they do not last if they cannot make a difference. After each training session, Colin Marshall would stand in the bar, listening to groups that formed around him and proving the old adage about why we have two ears and one mouth. Seven hundred improvements were generated from the teams formed following those events.

Extending change throughout the organization: down ...
The research had clearly shown that it would not be enough to galvanize the ground staff and the cabin crews alone.

Eight weeks into the PPF programme a deputation of employees from non–customer interface jobs – the backroom staff – came to Marshall having noted the recognition he was giving to the front-line people, and asking for equal recognition.

So PPF was extended to non–customer contact staff. The purpose was to close all the seams between the different functions and departments. Cabin crew heard from the baggage handlers and from the safety engineers on pre-flight checks, and from those who traced lost luggage and serviced the planes. The idea was that everyone would see how their efforts came together and how the remaining gaps could be closed.

... and up
The carers would not be cared for until there was a major change of management style. The traditional style in BA had been bureaucratic, distancing, highly segmented between functions and characterized by low personal feedback, neglect of subordinates, depersonalization and hierarchy.

Georgiades designed and introduced "Managing People First" (MPF), a five-day residential programme specifically for the 1,400 BA managers. (Marshall had fired 66 senior managers in 1983.) Managers were shown how to coach, train and support their subordinates. Progress in doing this could be gauged by how much responsibility was delegated, and whether the subordinate could be trusted to use judgement and discretion. Responsibility remained with those who delegated it to others.

Managers were also trained to create a vision for the whole organization, so that they could identify with their top management group, followed by a vision for the group they managed. This vision had then to be translated into a mission statement, containing key result areas by which organizational effectiveness could be estimated. They were shown how to build a support system, so that managers could get help from one another outside the formal structure and across functions. Subordinates needed to be shown how their job contributed to the larger whole. They were not cutting stone, they were helping to build a cathedral. Urgency must come from the leader, not from events, and every leader was responsible for keeping promises and cultivating trust. Managers must expect their people to do well and catch them doing it.

Evaluation and rewards schemes

All such inspiration might have remained locked up within training sessions, had not Georgiades made it clear that each manager's performance would be appraised on the basis of BA's new culture. He devised a two-dimensional evaluation system, with twin criteria designed to check up on each other's validity. Managers would be judged on what they had achieved against goals set in part by themselves, but also on how they had achieved it.

The "what" could include the average number of rings before a telephone was answered, the time taken to get baggage to passengers, the punctuality of planes and so on. The "how" would require the judgements of subordinates on what it was like to be led by their supervisor. Was he or she caring for the carers, or achieving results by the tactics of Genghis Khan? The results of this appraisal were tied to a cash bonus system, which directly rewarded high combinations of "what" and "how".

The watchword at BA is "feedback" – from customer to staff to managers. A "Videobox" has now been installed at several major locations. Customers come into the box and make their complaints on camera and these are screened by marketing, customer services and human resources. The ideal is fast response.

Management theory can be applied to real management

Luke Mayhew proves that good use can be made of the seven "S" diagram, first introduced by Richard Pascale and Tony Athos in *The Art of*

Japanese Management. * (See Appendix I for more on this diagram and the theory behind it.) The seven Ss include Staff, Skills, Style, Shared Values, Systems and Structure, all mobilized by an overall Strategy. Those who would evolve a culture that can pursue such a strategy effectively, must:

- hire the right Staff (i.e. service oriented);
- train them in the right Skills (i.e. emotional labour);
- manage them in the Style required (i.e. trust, expectation);
- select values to Share with them (i.e. customers first);
- install the right Systems (i.e. performance appraisal);
- improve the Structure (i.e. less hierarchy, more cross-functional teams).

Only where all these six points on the hexagon have been dealt with can they help mobilize a coherent strategy (see Figure 4.1).

Figure 4.1 **BA's version of the seven "S" diagram**

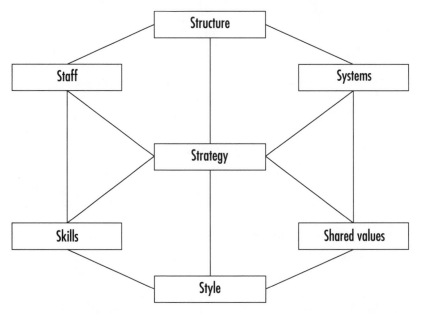

It is by such models that culture and strategy are joined in a seamless whole. Luke Mayhew doubts that enough has been done to improve these systems. There are still many holdovers from more bureaucratic days.

* New York, Simon and Schuster, 1981.

BA's latest cultural challenges

That BA has turned itself round and has registered a greatly improved performance is not in doubt. The changes described so far have been widely published elsewhere, and are summarized here only because they have now become something of a touchstone for the cultural change issue. How can the company continue to meet its challenges after such success? Some of the managers interviewed describe a pause, as if the corporation was searching for the next crisis to help pull its efforts together. Mike Bruce put it well:

"Brits are individualists to the point of anarchy. We need something akin to Dunkirk to get us to pull together and share values. Colin Marshall knows this and he's been good at pulling timely crises out of his hat. It was 'heads down' over privatization and our appalling reputation with customers; then 'heads down' again in the crash merger with British Caledonian; then 'heads down' again over joining Galileo [the multi-airline CRS or customer reservation system]; and now security is the latest focus.

"What concerns me is that we have difficulty in harmonizing our efforts and behaving as a team, without a crisis. Yet it's the best way to work and live. We've been outstandingly successful, but we are still not a reflective organization and I'm not convinced we yet know why we succeeded and how we can repeat that experience.

"When Marshall first routed the committee structures that were sitting on decisions and hiding from personal responsibility, he was correct in his action, but it's left an ambivalent attitude to teamwork. What we've got to build is the kind of groups that nurture individuality and the kind of individuals that can sustain and develop groups. We shouldn't be making invidious distinctions."

There are still dilemmas that the culture must reconcile

Mike Bruce, when introduced to the central proposal of this book (that a corporate culture should mediate dilemmas), volunteered several dilemmas which, in his view, BA was going to have to solve to sustain its present momentum.

One is a "lean and mean" versus "fat and happy" dilemma. "Lean and mean" represents minimal group cohesion, with everyone struggling to outperform as individuals. "Fat and happy", the opposite pole, describes an organization where groups are so cohesive that there is no individual motivation.

"Do we have to get mean with each other and yell 'crisis' to stop happy people getting fat? Haven't the cabin crews shown us that serving the customer 300 per cent better is that much better fun? We 'know' that's true, but I sometimes think we cannot yet believe it. We still need 'bombs', and live in a kind of mental Anderson shelter waiting for the warden to blow the whistle. It really should be possible to be lean and happy, shouldn't it? Anyway, I'd like to combine individual responsibility with group cohesion." (See Figure 4.2.)

Figure 4.2 **BA's "lean and mean" or "fat and happy" dilemma**

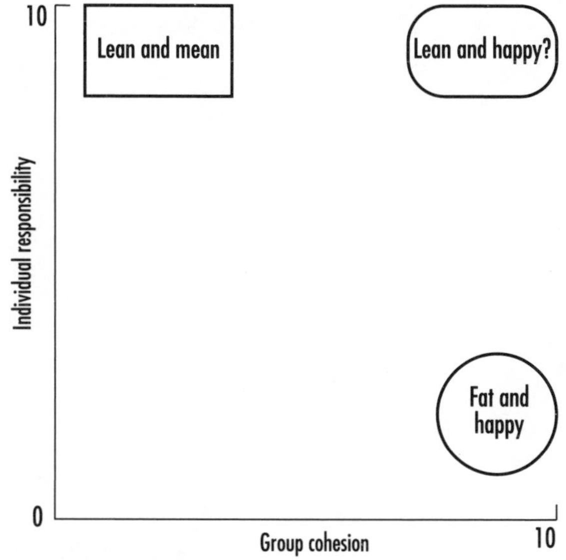

The middle management dilemma

BA, according to Mike Bruce, faces another dilemma in a situation developing with middle management. Could they be expected to care for their subordinates who interfaced with customers, if the company was not caring for them?

"It's been announced that 10 per cent of management is to go. That's not as traumatic as it sounds. They are given a lot of help to get new employment, and redundancy payments are generous. But still it's not good news. They're expected to commit to subordinates, yet they do not feel any strong commitment to them from higher up ... We are not too imaginative in the way we handle people. We do need to cut costs and a layer less of management could help, but we need to be much more flexible in the way we deploy management.

"Rather than create rigid, top-heavy structures, why not point the people concerned at the particular business and other problems and ask them to help solve these? I'm not convinced that people yet understand the indivisibility of culture – that caring either repeats itself like ripples patterning water all through BA, or it's blocked and can't spread. What I fear is a withdrawal of middle management's concern for subordinates as a consequence of feeling abandoned themselves." (See Figure 4.3.)

Figure 4.3 **Caring for middle management**

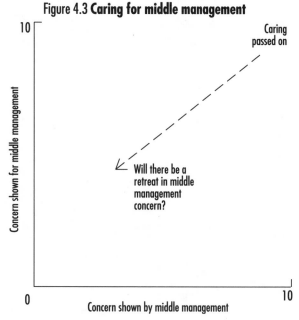

Specialists versus generalists

"Then there are other dilemmas. Where do we cooperate and where do we compete? It's not really clear to many people. And what's the role of specialists *vis-à-vis* generalists? BA is a hugely functional organization and contains a lot of specialists, trained in the sciences rather than the arts. One thing we noticed when we took over British Caledonian was that they had far more generalists than us, far fewer who needed and wanted to stay within their own speciality or function.

"And it's not clear to many of us how the opposing streams are supposed to integrate. We have a world organized around customers and their needs, championed by marketing, to which Marshall has given primacy of emphasis and influence, and a world organized around logistics – that is planning, engineering, the hardware, the schedules, safety and so on. These converge upon each other and clash, and the trade-offs appear to most of us to be political, deals made at the top of the organization by a process largely mysterious to most of us." (See Figure 4.4.)

Figure 4.4 **Political deal-making**

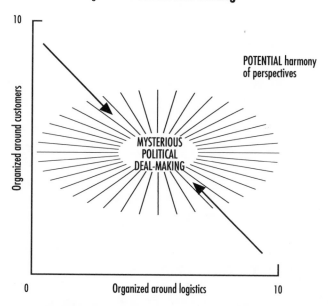

A struggle for the soul of BA ...

"A struggle for the soul of BA, for an integrated, coherent identity that is not yet resolved – this is what is taking place. There is a split between two worlds. The first of these is the 'real world', which is 'hard', authoritarian, robotic, strict/safe, instrumental and traditional. BA is seen in primarily operational terms: as a physical system. This is the familiar world of BA's military, bureaucratic and civil service past. These people are technically trained and see themselves as the instruments of a purpose supplied by the hierarchy in which they have their place.

"Then there is another rhetorical or service world, which is exemplified by the transformation in the culture of our customer service personnel. This is 'soft', people-oriented, humanist, flexible, caring, oriented-to-feeling, innovative and fun. It sees the organization as a 'social system'. These people are oriented to forming relationships and need freedom from hierarchical control to do this job properly."

Table 4.1 "Real" and "rhetorical" worlds in BA

The real world	The rhetorical world
"hard"	"soft"
authoritarian	people-oriented
strict/safe	flexible
threatening	comfortable/lax
unfamiliar	familiar
instrumental, operational values	putting people first

Source: "Moving into the mainstream", *Managment Education and Development*, Vol. 19, Part 3, 1988.

"The difficulty arises from the perception that these polarities are incompatible; that you either have to live in the 'hard' world of the operation or the 'softer' world of relationships. Our passengers don't see it that way. They want both safe, comfortable, punctual aircraft and to be treated as people, individuals whose cares and concerns matter.

"The problem for us is how to integrate the two worlds – to move from an 'either/or' to a 'both/and' perspective."

... and a major dilemma for the leadership: politics or business?

"This is a key challenge for the leadership of the company. They too have a dilemma, for they have to face two ways at once. Internally, they have to reconcile the functional and ideological perspectives through developing team work in addressing customer needs. Externally, they have to search for opportunities to build a global business in a tough, combative world that is intensely political. My fear is that the cultural change will not spread far beyond the cabin crew and other service personnel because the people at the top will only be able to look in one direction – at the hard-nosed struggle for power.

"And, of course, the world at the top of BA is political. Lord King and Sir Colin Marshall have been extraordinarily successful at international political deal-making and working with the Thatcher government. The challenges were enormous. The Laker creditors had to be satisifed before privatization could go forward. We acquired British Caledonian despite the challenge from SAS. In a brilliant coup we have bought 20 per cent of Sabena with KLM owning another 20 per cent. That's pure politics and exceedingly smart, because the Belgians have historically turned to Britain when squeezed between France and West Germany. And it's strategically vital because it will give us access to continental Europe.

"We have agreements with United in the USA, while SAS has had to fall back on Continental, and we've taken a leading part in forming Galileo, the customer reservation system, which is now very well positioned to compete with Sabre, Amadeus, Apollo and the other CRSs. The future belongs to the more comprehensive electronic distribution systems, which can book you from San Francisco to Tokyo via Brussels and Helsinki and provide hotels, limousines and tickets for major events along the route – all from a single reservation system. I can safely say of our leaders that they do not miss a trick."

Management must transfer to a new paradigm

"But I still worry as to whether we can make a permanent switch to a new epistemology or paradigm. Our first efforts have succeeded brilliantly. But can an organization built on analysis grasp the importance of synthesis? This is more than a science versus arts dispute and more than specialists versus generalists; science itself is changing its paradigm. The world of Descartes and the vision of the universe as a Newtonian machine is slipping away. In subatomic physics we find objectivity vanishing; the electron does not have objective properties independent of the mind of the investigator. We find the same in biology, where living creatures are indissolubly related to their environment.

"And the future of management is surely similar. We need to be held together by clearly visualized ends and use opportunistic and improvised means of getting there. This direction is founded on the concept of the organization as a living whole, joined to its environment – not a machine and not a political power match.

"One of the metaphors of BA's internal functional divisions is that of a collection of smoke stacks. The base of the building is joined, then separate smoke stacks stretch upwards and finally the tops of the chimneys are joined by gyre wires. There is more co-operation at the very top and the bottom than in the middle, where the separate functions still rule. My anxiety is that this somewhat rickety structure will prevent us from making an effective competitive response in our increasingly competitive environment."

What next for the BA culture?

"So the ultimate question is what will BA learn from its transformation in the quality of customer service? One choice is for BA to decide that this is a one-off success for people whose job is to be nice, but that the rest of them live in the real world of functional specialization, reliable machinery and politics. Or it could learn that the relationships created in the cabins and the counters are a prototype for the way all of us can work together better. The management at all levels needs to work on this constantly – if they don't set a positive example it pervades the organization.

"The analytically trained, super-intelligent recruits of the last 30 years are not going to give up their professional paradigms. Thank goodness for that, because a plane is either safe or unsafe, mechanically sound or otherwise. Prediction and control has its crucial place in mechanical disciplines. But the kind of synthesis that we in human resources are looking for is the kind that joins the arts to the sciences, the specialists to the generalists and makes a synthesis among analysts themselves. We seek not to shut them out but to include them in cross-functional networks that respond swiftly to the environment.

"In the next few months we are going to discover what has been learned. There are negotiations going on with the British Airports Authority about chronic congestion and a fifth terminal, with Sabena and the Belgians, within the Galileo reservation system about how different airlines can work with each other, with hotels, car-hire, travel agents, etc, and somehow we have to make security an integral part of BA and not an afterthought or a fierce appendage, hired to prowl among passengers.

"In each one of these cases we can concentrate on building mutually responsive relationships, modelled on those created with customers. Or we can stick to our separate functions, strike political deals and hope that our energy does not leak away between the cracks and gaps that open up between us. My own mission is to humanize BA."

New strategic directions

There was a sense of uncertainty around BA at the time of going to press. With the of Nick Georgiades retirement for health reasons, the human resources vacancy on the board remained unfilled. New initiatives from this direction were unlikely to come soon. A new initiative may be afoot in BA's acquisition of a piece of United Airlines, a carrier much envied for its creation of the software packages that can tilt reservations in favour of UAL rather than its strategic partners or competitors. Whether BA has also acquired this key resource remains to be seen. Software "wizards" are an esoteric brotherhood not always in control of all the partners they serve. Don Burr, the late president of People Express, blames his demise on "software shenanigans". "Can't control those fellas!" he was told when he called to protest about what was being done to him. Another type of initiative may come from "theme flights" into London, which engage tourists in British holiday delights while they are still airborne and put content into the customer reservation system with BA as the "hub" of planned vacations. This strategy is still being mooted.

A DIAGRAMMATIC SUMMARY

BA was, until the early 1980s, military and technological in its cultural orientation. Towards its customers, according to a survey, it was "cold, aloof, uncaring and bureaucratic".

A vicious circle, including much of what was reported earlier in the chapter, might read as Figure 4.5 (see p. 102).

The blocking of feedback from customers only perpetuated techno-military "coldness". The vicious cycle was "stuck" and unable to develop. "Snapped ropes" mean adversarial relationships perpetuating the opposition of technical versus human power (dilemma 1), cold bureaucracy versus the potential for warm relationships (dilemma 2) and top–down roles/ranks versus bottom–up needs (dilemma 3).

The cultural interventions accomplished several ends. They emphasized the three subordinated segments of the circle from 6 to 10 o'clock:

- the highlighting of "moments of truth";

Figure 4.5 **British Airways: a vicious circle**

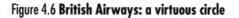

(1) a strong, techno-
military tradition

(3) so that bottom—up feedback
on customers' needs was blocked

(2) a "cold", specialized
bureaucracy

(2) who passed on to
passengers the lack
of warmth received

(3) in which ranks
and roles gave
top—down orders

(1) subordinated and
disempowered
cabin staff

Figure 4.6 **British Airways: a virtuous circle**

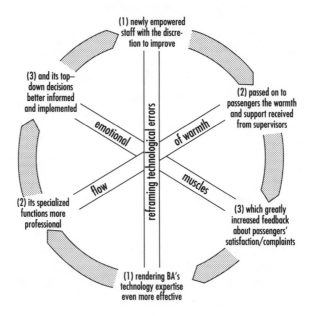

(1) newly empowered
staff with the discre-
tion to improve

(3) and its top—
down decisions
better informed
and implemented

(2) passed on to
passengers the warmth
and support received
from supervisors

emotional

of warmth

reframing technological errors

flow

muscles

(2) its specialized
functions more
professional

(3) which greatly
increased feedback
about passengers'
satisfaction/complaints

(1) rendering BA's
technology expertise
even more effective

- the empowering of staff to use discretion in helping customers;
- treating staff with far greater warmth and respect so that they would pass these on to passengers;
- evaluating managers on how they treated their subordinates.

Whereas feedback from passengers "up" through BA's hierarchy had earlier been blocked, new "Customer First" teams and Videoboxes got the message through.

The cultural interventions also reintegrated the "snapped ropes". The concept of improvised services making up for delays and technical hitches turned cabin staff into people who reframed technological errors. The notion of the flow of warmth from supervisors through cabin staff to passengers reconnected senior specialists to passengers. The idea of developing emotional muscles showed that those who had to mediate top–down orders and bottom–up complaints and requests were people doing work of heroic difficulty and tension. The "rope repairers" deserved BA's utmost respect. The virtuous circle, learning from the experience of serving customers and so able to develop, could read as Figure 4.6.

It is vital to give status and support to people "in the middle". This enables all elements in the circle to learn and develop (see Figure 4.7).

Figure 4.7 **British Airways: a development helix**

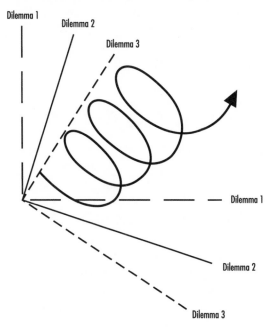

Chapter 5

GETTING ICs FASTER TO MARKET: WHAT AMERICANS LEARNED FROM THEIR JAPANESE PARTNERS

SUMMARY

Saratoga Systems is a medium-sized designer of integrated circuits based in California, just south of San Francisco on the edge of "Silicon Valley", but with fabrication plants in Mexico and the Philippines. The company has five divisions, dispersed geographically, and a highly decentralized administration. This case concerns the Advanced Sensors Division located at Rogue River Valley in Oregon which specializes in circuits which monitor machinery.

In March 1987 Saratoga was approached by Kano Electronics (KE) of Osaka, Japan, with a view to a joint venture. (At the request of the principals all names and places, but not countries of origin, are disguised.) KE is about the same size as Saratoga and designs advanced semiconductors with a strong penetration into Japan's automobile industry. Among its products were accelerometers, tiny sensors which opened airbags and unlocked car doors within a fraction of a second following collisions. KE was especially proud of a sensor that prevented a car being driven off without a matching signal known only to the car's owner. It would replace ignition and could not be "hot wired" by thieves. As car theft is far more common in the USA, KE was looking for partners to exploit the US market.

KE already monitored industrial robots and supplied several Japanese manufacturers based in the USA, but was now under pressure to put "local content" into its manufacturing. It hoped to continue supplying them through the Advanced Sensors Division of Saratoga. In return Saratoga products would be sold by KE to customers in Japan, and there would be a pooling of knowledge and expertise.

KE had followed the strategy of penetrating key industries: automobiles, robot users, nuclear power generators, aircraft and plastics, and especially film. These were all cases where a breakdown in machinery or malfunction could cause major losses. The joint venture gave Saratoga an opportunity to learn how to build competitive edge by relating to its customers in depth, sharing their concerns and designing solutions.

It was also an opportunity Saratoga could not afford to miss: it had chosen to do its own manufacturing and to grow; that meant becoming a $1 billion company, or doubling its size, by 1995. "If you want to stay at the leading edge there's about a $200 million market in really innovative stuff. That's all," remarked Jeff Runcorn, director of Saratoga's joint venture management team. It was essential, therefore, that Saratoga Systems mature with its hugely proliferating market. "We have to change, or the Japanese will get it all." Moreover, it was doubtful if the company could stay small and innovative, even if it wanted to. Small, creative start-ups were popping up on all sides. "Those guys work ten years for someone else, then quit when they have their best idea. There's no way you can compete with free riders."

The story of their venture, derived from interviews with Jeff Runcorn, illustrates some of the fundamental differences in national cultures discussed in Chapter 2, and gives some pointers as to how such dilemmas can be reconciled.

THE LEARNING PROCESS

Jeff Runcorn had maintained for many years that the only way to learn from the Japanese was to work with them on a joint venture to find out how they performed and why. He believed it held the clue to the decline of Silicon Valley. In his view, Americans excelled at start-ups, but were very weak at making the transition from start-up to maturity. As the market proliferated into niches, and customers gained the upper hand and variety increased, the Japanese could supply this diversity at far lower cost with extraordinary levels of quality. It had now happened in product after product and could not be a coincidence. "We keep talking about 'level playing fields' and say the Japanese 'cheat'. In my view they are playing a different game, and we're so busy playing at referee that we haven't noticed."

However, despite Saratoga's best intentions, one problem Runcorn soon identified was that Americans found it hard to learn: they tended to "shoot off their mouths". "We have the verbal initiative, but we noticed that the KE people seemed to be learning more from us than we did from them." Throughout their relationship, KE employees repeatedly asked how they could do better, and again and again Runcorn found himself preaching at them, only to bite his tongue when he witnessed their actual performance. "They all try to speak English, giving you the impression that you're teaching them something, but we're the ones who need to learn from them."

Somehow, Saratoga needed to instil some of this attitude into its employees, as when it had to produce ICs (integrated circuits) in quantity, on schedule, to exact specifications and in the shortest possible time, they behaved as if the fun had gone out of their lives. They dreaded becoming "bureaucrats" or "organization men". "Everyone harks back to when Hank made a $12 million IC in his outhouse and we built the lab on the proceeds." Runcorn believed it was a failure to grow up. "We want to be whizz-kids forever."

Arrival of the Japanese team

Takeo Kano and 26 colleagues arrived in November 1987. Fortunately, Saratoga had had the forethought to hire an adviser, Yuki, to brief it on Japanese business methods. "Thank God we did," says Runcorn. "'Put them up in your homes, not in a hotel', we were advised, and we did, and it was a great success. 'Do not talk business till they do', and we didn't and it took three days before they asked to see the plant."

Ritual greetings

When Runcorn showed his visitors around the plant they became extremely animated, taking extensive notes and many photographs. That evening they invited senior Saratoga staff to a Japanese restaurant in Portland and they had their first experience of the formality of Japanese business customs. For almost half an hour after the soup there was a ritual exchange of toasts and what Runcorn called "vacuous greetings". Yuki acted as an interpreter. Initially, the Japanese greeting lasted about three minutes: "The employees of Kano Electronics give greeting to their gracious American hosts and celebrate this joyful opportunity for deepened understanding with the illustrious Saratoga Systems Company, and its famed Advanced Sensors Division ..." The Americans, acting on Yuki's advice, responded in kind: "We must have gone back and forward about four times, but Yuki had warned us not to look bored and not to laugh, and we didn't."

The negotiation sessions

Runcorn spent the following week at a negotiation session with a team of 14 representatives from KE, while the remainder left on a tour of customers and competitors around the USA. It was a puzzling experience.

KE's negotiators were not its leaders. Indeed, Takeo Kano himself was mostly absent, and everything they promised was contingent on his agreement. This allowed them to withdraw any proposals about which they had second thoughts and make "concessions" first, which would be withdrawn later if Saratoga did not at once reciprocate.

KE had a decentralized authority structure in which the person most qualified to address a subject would assume an authoritative stance, only to stand back when the topic switched. Runcorn admitted that it was all rather confusing. He was not sure who to look at when making an offer. "It's the most elasticated hierarchy I've ever encountered ... like trying to figure which side of an octopus is up." The KE negotiators would also ask for a recess at least six times a day. Whether they were just talking to each other or contacting Takeo Kano, Runcorn could not tell. But after a recess they might suddenly all change their position together, "like a shoal of fish changing course in unison".

There was another puzzling characteristic. The KE negotiators were, Runcorn felt, oddly dismissive of detail. When he or his colleagues asked for specifics, or tried to work out terms, they shrugged these off as unimportant, saying, "You can send those over later." He concluded they were more interested in general principles of cooperation and expected these to be interpreted in a spirit of mutuality. However, he found it difficult to evaluate this technique: "I thought they were being very smart ... then I thought them naïve for not being more specific."

A near disaster

The entire joint venture was nearly wrecked two weeks into the visit. Saratoga wanted contracts signed; Runcorn sent a memorandum of the agreements with KE, and the lawyers drafted the contracts. The legal office rebuked Runcorn for the vagueness of the terms. When the contracts arrived they were 50 pages long and unreadable: Runcorn was worried about what KE would make of them. Natsume, his opposite number and second in command, asked Runcorn to explain them, but when he could not, was going to take them on trust. Runcorn advised him to consult a US lawyer before doing so.

Runcorn heard nothing for a week and then started to worry. The smiling had stopped and the formality had increased. The adviser, Yuki, talked with the delegation and explained:

"They've had the contract translated and explained by an American lawyer, and they're deeply shocked. They think you're trying to cheat them. They feel they had a good relationship with you and you betrayed it. Their lawyers told them, and I quote: 'This is the smartest goddamn contract I've read in a while. If Saratoga products sell well in Japan you both win, but if they sell badly, Saratoga still wins and you lose, because you have to pay a $100,000 base royalty for handling their products in the first place. They expect to carry your products in the USA without any such stipulation. Boy, those fellows are smart!' "

In Runcorn's view they had been far too smart. He complained to the legal department which told him, "that agreement was so airy-fairy, they could have run rings around you." Yuki explained to Runcorn that the Japanese put relationships before contract terms.

"If there's an agreement to benefit each other, each side is left free to interpret this in changing situations. It's like a loose arrangement for mutuality, which is the most important aspect. Detailed contracts tie you down. The 'spirit of partnership' is what matters. You've smiled at them for weeks, and now you've offered them a contract that imposes the costs of failure unilaterally on your partners. In Japan close relationships bind, not the small print. You'll lose the partnership if you don't back down."

Then Runcorn made all senior Saratoga staff call their opposite number and apologize, and he even persuaded his CEO to call Takeo Kano. They said their legal department had not understood the "spirit of partnership" because they had not shared it and had tried to impose the wrong terms. Runcorn personally guided the new contract through the legal department.

The scouting party returns

A few days after Runcorn rescued the partnership the twelve members of the KE delegation who had been touring the USA returned. They brought back ICs, bits of silicon, brochures and specifications, and were immensely excited by their haul. "Why they should get high on advances made by our competitors I could not see. I first thought they were incredibly impressionable tourists, but most of them were well travelled so it couldn't be that." Runcorn concluded that they were simply more interested than his own staff in what was "out there". They had collected more in a month than his own marketing department had sent him in a year. Instead of being envious or belittling competitors – as Saratoga people often did – it became clear from the way KE people talked that they intended to take what they had found and reconfigure several elements into new combinations. To them competitors were less a threat than a resource.

LESSONS SARATOGA LEARNED FROM KE

The culture of Saratoga Systems gave the highest status to those who designed the integrated circuits. They were seen as creators or originators, while the rest of the organization merely implemented and then distributed what they had designed. General managers were second in the pecking order on account of their seniority, followed by marketers, test engineers, product engineers and process engineers. "We rate most highly what evolves from inside, with the environment as distinctly secondary." There was a "not invented here" syndrome, or, worse, "if we didn't think of it first it's not important".

In contrast to Saratoga, KE seemed to put process first. They were excited at the prospect of making the same products with half the manufacturing steps and at lower cost, what Saratoga called "reverse engineering", not a prestigious activity. While Runcorn believed that KE staff were not as inventive as his own, he conceded that their definition of creativity was much broader. Everyone could become creative, from the tester showing the designer how a design could test more easily to a manufacturer helping to increase the manufacturability of a design. "KE 'creates' across departments in a way we rarely do. And they prune a product of excessive elements and steps with an extraordinary zest. Yuki explained to me that a Japanese picture or a garden is incomplete until every unnecessary element has been removed. It's aesthetic for them – part of creativity."

Lines and circles

KE staff were also more "circular" in their reasoning. While Saratoga designers drew up the circuit and others "down the line" laid it out, manufactured, tested, packaged and marketed it, the designers seemed to learn little from the later steps. KE was much more insistent on the "closing the loop", that is having the marketing staff and their customers influence the designers. "We need our designers to design for everyone else in the circle, not just for a vision in their own heads; at the moment our designers feel it's someone else's problem once their design is complete. If there is trouble 'down the line', it's not their fault." In fact, a designer has considerable influence on whether a customer gets a product in time. He or she can make it easier or harder for everyone else.

Time-to-market and faster learning

The issue of how long it takes to get a new product to market, to break-even and beyond where Saratoga could start to earn profits, was now the major challenge facing the industry. Runcorn believed that KE could show Saratoga how to move products faster, and this judgement was being borne out. There were electronic fairs twice yearly in Japan, so that many companies operated on a one-year, or even six-months, cycle, discovering what customers wanted at one conference and having it ready at the next.

"You can't go for a narrow niche market unless the feedback is fast. Honda now produces a motor scooter for 19–25 year old female office workers in several colour schemes. They beat the competition by proliferating wide varieties aimed at small segments. That's an almost unbeatable strategy but can only work if you get to market fast and get the results back to the company even faster, before improving the fit. I was talking to KE about market testing one of our products and I was asked why we did not just market it. I realized that if your product cycle can speed up, then marketing *is* your test, with improved versions hot on the heels of the original product. You profit on the second or third go, even where the first fails."

The cult of creativity

What most concerned Runcorn was that Saratoga made a cult out of its creative designers. It assumes that creativity is rare and precious, that every "queen" needs hundreds of "drones" and "workers". But was creativity not something more widely shared? Could departments not be creative in their own ways and in helping each other? It had been taking Saratoga anything from one to four years to get from design to market, because its designers refused to be hurried. "You cannot schedule genius", was the argument. But why could time not be one of the variables with which creative people were asked to work? KE got to market in half the time because it was not ashamed to borrow or appropriate from other companies and build quickly on parts of other products.

Runcorn searched for a word to describe the KE style. Improvisation was close but it understated the skill, as did montage. He finally opted for meta-creativity, that is a creative combination of existing products, sub-assemblies and part-processes in a configuration which transcended these.

"There's something in Americans that loves a contest, a game in which one side wins and the other loses. Yet KE goes beyond this. They are far more interested in inventing a new game and being the sole player. I've seen them turn aside from direct confrontation repeatedly. They prefer to change the definition of the situation so no one loses face."

The higher status of marketing

Runcorn watched how the KE delegation treated their marketing staff. He had assumed, because the latter were on tour and not negotiating, that they were junior. However, they turned out to be much more influential and senior than Saratoga's marketing staff. Moreover, KE's designers went on tour with their marketing personnel. That was a clever strategy because they were shown things by fellow designers which they would not have bothered to show salesmen, and the designers learnt first-hand what customers were planning.

Seniority and job rotation

A noticeable feature of Kano Electronics was that the status of its executives was commensurate with their age and, for the most part, their time spent with the company, since turnover was very low. Runcorn had been highly critical of this system at first. "I couldn't see what they would do with the dead-wood. When we visited their plant in Osaka I was sure I'd find all the 'time-servers' and mediocrities they were too squeamish to fire."

However, the Japanese promotion by seniority meant that everyone must be trained and educated, on the grounds that their development would increase their value to the company. If such promotion was carried out without investing heavily in human resources, then a company would be encumbered with "dead-wood". In order to prevent this happening, people were rotated from job to job, giving them multiple perspectives, and each was developed to his fullest potential.

Discovering latent needs

KE taught Saratoga a concept called "latent need analysis", carried out for customers by the marketing department. Because customers can only have needs for a technology of which they are aware, and whose functions they can clearly visualize, they must be helped to look into the future to see what the sensors being worked upon could accomplish. Customers have a latent need for a product only when they realize exactly what is possible. This requires highly imaginative and expert futurology from researchers, and Saratoga is now offering prizes for the best "1999 Road Show".

For example, XY Auto's strategy is to be the world's number one on safety, reliability and theft reduction, and it is working with insurers to get premiums down as a symbol of its continuing success. Saratoga tells the company that it is developing sensors that could monitor eight different kinds of engine wear, shut off the ignition in a crash and smother the engine in foam. The car can be sealed if it gets into water, which should prevent it sinking. A thief can be locked inside the car if he does not know the code, so he cannot start it or get out. A stolen car can be tracked by emitting a signal to which the police have access. Use of the driver's thumb print can prevent a car being driven by anyone else without that driver's permission.

By describing as vividly as possible the potential of its circuits in development, Saratoga plans to emulate KE in forming a strategic alliance with companies such as XY Auto to make its products pre-eminent in safety, performance, economy, road holding and so on. Latent need analysis promises to give marketing at Saratoga visions at least as exciting as those which designers create. Saving lives, protecting passengers and averting industrial accidents are visions that can cross departmental and corporate boundaries to unify cultures. Runcorn wanted Saratoga to operate in these currencies.

Products as units and as families

Runcorn had always taken the cost-accountants' view of the value of particular products. The cost per unit was compared with the revenue generated. However, when it came to killing off losing products, the designers would make a fuss and many products survived to lose more money. KE taught Runcorn to think differently. Whether a product was worth making depended on its place in a group or family of products. This group not only offered customers "total service", so they would not have to contact other suppliers, but it also consisted of units that "gave birth" to a "second generation" and then a third. To solve a customer's problem – say closing a window when the car hits water – does not require one product, but successive generations. The first product is likely to be 70 per cent effective: the window closes if a child spills a drink. What the "generational concept" does is point a whole stream of improving products at a client's problem. If you cannot be on time with a 95 per cent solution, you supply the 90 per cent instead.

This altered the cost accounting principle that each unit must pay for itself. The "father" might conceivably be unprofitable, yet the "son" and "grandson" could prosper. It was necessary to estimate the costs and revenues from whole product families.

Organic imagery

Runcorn had been struck by the amount of organic imagery KE used. His hosts had talked as if ICs were alive.

"At school we were told this was wrong. You're not supposed to project live characteristics on to dead things. My prof called it 'animism' and the 'anthropomorphic fallacy', like saying there's a man in the moon. Yet here was Takeo Kano himself talking of chips as 'rice', 'feeding industry and each other', of 'food-chains', of product 'generations'. He even called Natsume a 'worried mother', which amused me."

Saratoga learnt to value this style.

"While ICs were technically dead, they were also extensions of human plans and purposes. You wanted your car to unlock if it crashed, to seal itself against being flooded, to stabilize itself after a sharp bend, to tell the police it was being stolen. If those who wanted these things were alive, so were these extensions of the human nervous system. ICs were modelled consciously or otherwise on the human brain."

Teams and individuals

Runcorn was convinced that KE's teams worked better than the ones he had managed at Saratoga. One reason KE products got faster to market was that the whole team identified with the project and with the customers' need for the product "family". A designer was never allowed to work on two successive generations, lest he abandon the first before it was viable. The designers spanned generations, first and third, second and fourth. They were expected to see their products through to the finish and then improve the process of making and marketing them. Saratoga's designers enjoyed starting, but avoided finishing.

Keeping promises to customers and providing them with the best quality products on time was a function of group cohesion. "You have to make commitments and keep them," Runcorn explained, "and without a cohesive group there is no audience for the promises you make." When Saratoga teams fell behind their schedule, it was regarded as a mere formality, not a promise. The only person let down was some remote planner. KE teams had a "roving fixer", a person who knew if they were falling behind and showed them how they could make up the time. He would get them more people and resources if necessary.

While Saratoga designers were usually senior, well respected and had visualized the completed product, they were often too introverted, intellectual, critical, sceptical and a-social to be team leaders. They were uninterested in holding the team together and gave short shrift to the marketing end. In contrast, KE's team leaders were either from marketing or general management. They acted as the "customer representative".

Japanese conformists

Runcorn had been prejudiced against the Japanese before the project began. He was puzzled about how they could be so successful, yet such abject conformers. He had heard the Japanese axiom, "the nail that stands up gets hammered down", and was offended by it, although he had never heard it around KE. But his views had been modified; they conformed in one sense, but not in another. He noticed that staff never questioned that they owed allegiance to their teams and to KE. In that sense they were not individualist at all. But when it came to original ideas that might help KE, their contributions could be outspoken, innovative and full of risks for each of them personally. "It's as if they know when to comply and when to originate, and they switch easily between these modes."

Working in sequence and in parallel

One way Saratoga had been trying to get faster to market was to work more in parallel and less in sequence. It takes longer if each stage in the production of an IC – design, layout, prototype, test, manufacture, retest, packaging and marketing – must proceed in strict sequence, with each stage ending before the next starts. In fact, it is possible to start the layout before the design is finished. Testing can start on completed parts of the prototype. Preparations are possible if those at later stages can know in outline what is expected of them. High degrees of overlap are possible, provided team members keep each other informed so that any one stage can start before the other finishes. Errors tend to "knock on", so a design error may be copied in layout, making two sets of corrections necessary. Hence parallel operations can waste time as well as save it. The quality of work and the closeness of communications were crucial, and here KE had the edge on Saratoga. Its teams were cohesive and stayed together over time, so it managed the hand-over between phases better than Saratoga.

Pushing free spirits or pulling them

There was a major difference in the way KE thought about schedules and times. Runcorn discovered that Japanese factories operate on a "pull" principle, and most Western factories operate on a "push" system. KE managers calculated backwards from a rendezvous they had agreed with their customers, "pulling" all the needed resources and processes towards that meeting place at the appointed time. They made the customer choose between degrees of perfection and intervals of time if the two need trading off, and they threw extra resources in if necessary. Nothing was fixed in advance, except the time and the quality required; everything else was deployed and redeployed so that the "guided missile" met its "target", making corrections along the way.

In contrast, Saratoga fixed its resources in advance through its budgeting process, and let its sales staff show off to customers by pledging perfect performance. Then they were surprised that time, the only remaining flexible factor, gave way and gave way. "As time lengthens we learn more slowly, miss more market niches and start to lose out. We end up trying to 'push' our designers, our most prestigious group, while they complain about the erosion of their freedom." It could be more than a year since Saratoga had checked with the customer. This emphasis on Saratoga's own schedule, often decided months earlier, might be the problem rather than the solution. "In at least half the cases the customer had changed his mind, even if he didn't expect us to respond to that change. He wanted the product sooner, or he wanted it later; if sooner, then some existing product in our 'library' might have sufficed, if later, he often wanted even better performance."

Competing while cooperating

Saratoga had never had a more cooperative relationship with any partner, supplier or customer. Yet the closeness was strangely empty of effect. Runcorn said, "For us cooperation bars competition. It's incompatible. But there are times when I'm reminded, chillingly, that all KE's closeness to us could make them fiercer competitors in the future, and that's precisely what they have in mind long term." KE had been negotiating with other Saratoga divisions to do its manufacturing and fast development. Runcorn regarded this manoeuvre as a strategic trap. It was the "meat" in Saratoga's "sandwich". Once KE controlled these vital skills, they would be indispensable and would take over.

MAPPING THE CULTURAL DIFFERENCES BETWEEN SARATOGA AND KE

Because of Saratoga's fears of KE's ultimate strategy, they were keen to see if the author's dilemma methodology could offer them an insight into how to use their experience to their own advantage. First it was necessary to state the dilemmas facing Saratoga.

1. The dilemma of specificity versus diffuseness

Saratoga and KE differ on a specificity–diffuseness dimension. This is shown in four ways:

- KE's unwillingness to get down to specific business until at least three days of getting to know each other have passed;
- its long ritualized preliminaries in the restaurant;
- the diffuse nature of its authority system, such as "the elastic hierarchy"; and
- its belief that broad relationships of goodwill are more binding than the specific terms of the contract.

The point is not that KE is uninterested in specifics, nor that Saratoga ignores relationships. The difference is in the starting point. KE, and the Japanese in general, start with a diffuse orientation and then close in on details. Saratoga, and Americans in general, usually start with the specifics and then expand to fill out the context (see Figure 5.1).

"I don't see us as behind or ahead of KE on these dimensions [Runcorn said]. We get to good relationships by way of fair contracts, they get to fair contracts by way of good relationships. What's important is not how we get there, but that we get there. We nearly messed up a good relationship with a 'smart' contract, but it's possible to write contracts in ways that nurture good relationships, and that's what we're learning to do. We can't change the way we think. We can accommodate their pattern."

Figure 5.1 **Saratoga–KE: dilemma 1**

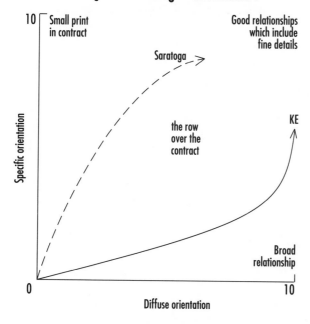

2. The dilemma of inner-directed, creative design versus outer-directed response to markets

Staff at Saratoga Systems were much prouder of design and basic invent-iveness than staff at KE, and they gave their highest prestige to designers, who had led KE in inventiveness, if not in innovation. Yet Saratoga took this much farther, indeed so far that it tended to reinvent the wheel, distrust work "not invented here" or "first thought about by others". The technological sophistication of the product was more esteemed than the value to the customer of something much cheaper and simpler. Competitors "out there" were typically underestimated in comparison with home-grown developments "in here". KE, on the other hand, delighted in what it found in the environment, borrowed without shame, reverse-engineered its competitors' products and excelled in 'meta-creativity', the synthesis of extant products into new configurations.

This was consistent with the behaviour of Japanese corporations worldwide. They had challenged the West in large part on licences obtained from Western corporations, which they had elaborated into great varieties of competitively priced products, each an incremental improvement on its predecessor. Research by Fons Trompenaars (see Chapter 2) had discovered much higher inner-directedness in US managers generally, as opposed to higher outer-directedness in Japanese and Asian managers. The Americans saw their environment as a staircase, climbed by dint of individual effort, steered from within. The Japanese saw their environment as a roller-coaster on which to hitch a rather frantic ride. Indeed, Japanese cultural tradition sees a maelstrom of environmental forces on which the skilful ride. American cultural tradition sees supermen and super-heroes, who are more powerful than the natural forces that oppose them. This dilemma is shown visually in Figure 5.2.

Figure 5.2 **Saratoga–KE: dilemma 2**

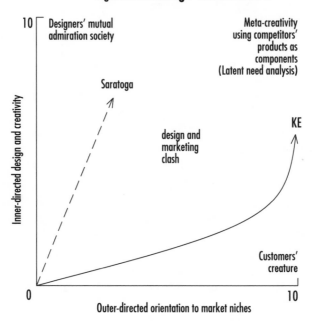

Jeff Runcorn felt that KE was much closer to reconciling inner- with outer-directed orientation. "It begins with what customers want and configures from there. We are too concerned with our own mind-stuff." Runcorn also observed that latent need analysis was important enough to be considered a reconciliation of inner-directed technological progress with outer-directed customer needs. This concept was included in parentheses in Figure 5.2.

3. The dilemma of status by achievement versus status by ascription

Saratoga in general promotes employees and bestows status according to performance and achievement. The idea is that it is up to the individual to excel and then the corporation should value him or her commensurately. It is the old Puritan notion of justification through works, presided over by a divine task master.

KE thinks in exactly the opposite way. It believes that if increasingly higher status is ascribed to older people with more experience, then they will enjoy enhanced status and achieve accordingly. For Americans, status is the consequence of achievement. For the Japanese, achievement is the consequence of having ascribed status to that person. This status is a self-fulfilling prophecy. "We give you respect, and so you achieve." The Japanese approach, typified by KE, invests heavily in human resource development and offers lifetime employment, so that employees will "grow with the company". They see their development as organized by their corporation to which they consequently owe gratitude and allegiance (see Figure 5.3).

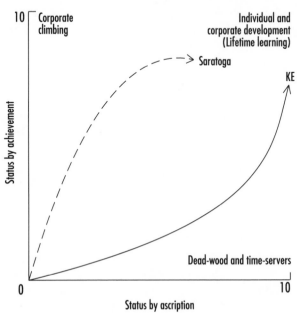

Figure 5.3 **Saratoga–KE: dilemma 3**

Runcorn said, "I think KE's just ahead of us on that one, too. Their turnover is almost zero. Ours is 9.0 per cent per annum and the more we pay young people, the more they ask from our competitors. We bid up scarce talent, and we blame unenterprising employees for their own deficiencies. Perhaps we should blame ourselves." Runcorn insisted that "lifetime learning" be added to the reconciliation in Figure 5.3. He was about to launch this programme and Saratoga was going to pay not for the job performed, but for the skills mastered. That would make employees more versatile and flexible. The products could only become more complex and variable if the people creating them were developed.

4. and 5. The dilemmas of individuals dealing with units of product versus teams dealing with product "families" and "generations"

The Japanese tend to be more "right hemisphere dominant" than Americans (see Chapter 2). That is, they think more synthetically and create wholes from parts. Americans are more comfortable with analysis and create parts from wholes by reducing phenomena to their components.

This underlying pattern is responsible for some of the differences between Saratoga and KE. While Saratoga looked at costs per unit and tried to make each individual and each product pay for itself as a separate unit, the KE approach was to deploy whole teams and "families" of products with each generation incrementally superior to the previous one. By supplying everything a customer needed, even unprofitable items, it hoped to become the sole, trusted supplier. A product was not dropped, even if unprofitable as a unit, if it contributed to "seamless service" or if it could lead to later developments. There was also the issue of whether outstanding individuals were enough to create strong teams, or if improving team spirit would help individuals to keep their commitments. Initially a chart was drawn which put individuals and units of product on the vertical axis and teams and product families on the horizontal axis, but Saratoga felt that the products should be kept separate from the people. There are individuals versus teams, and units of product versus product families. They may both have to do with the dominance of different cerebral hemispheres, but, in the view of Saratoga, as a practical matter they are separate issues (see Figures 5.4 and 5.5).

The emphasis on teams and "Group Think" could easily be taken too far in Runcorn's view. Folly was often shared for want of any dissent and the designers in Saratoga would excuse every pet project on the grounds of its imputed fertility. "We'd have 'families' so weighted down with

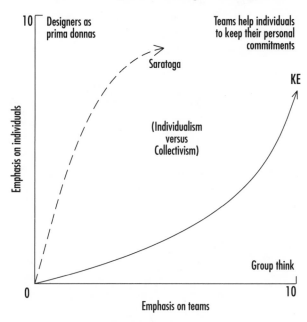

Figure 5.4 **Saratoga–KE: dilemma 4**

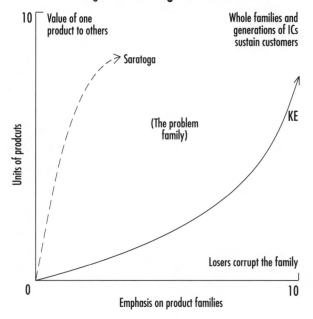

Figure 5.5 **Saratoga–KE: dilemma 5**

losers that whole projects run at a loss. I fear giving them so strong an argument." At mid-point "the problem family" was added in parentheses to highlight this dilemma. "It is important to know the gain or loss made by individual products. That way you can tell when problem families start to develop. But you should not assume that the only value that product has is its revenue minus its cost." KE had solved many of these dilemmas and Saratoga planned to copy their methods, putting general managers in charge of teams in the place of designers, and train them extensively in group process skills.

6. The dilemma of scheduling and pushing to speed up output versus the freedom and slack needed to solve problems

It is also part of the Japanese macro-culture that KE employees would arrange to be "pulled" towards an agreed rendezvous with a customer's future strategy, while the Americans in Saratoga would send one individual (a manager) to "push" another (a designer), with the result that the latter would push back. The peril of the cultural belief that everyone should steer from a point of inner moral rectitude is that collisions among the self-righteous are common. Cultures which conceive of major forces in the universe being outside individuals may agree to be drawn by those forces towards new destinies. A central Japanese axiom is "man alone is weak, but harnessed to nature can become strong". Shinto religion teaches harmony with the forces of the universe.

KE employees' encounters with the market place are, therefore, as culturally conditioned as the Anglo–US belief in striking out alone and seeking a personal path through hostile terrain.

In this case it is difficult to draw trajectories because KE has transcended the push versus freedom problem and Saratoga is still fighting between its designers and planners. The problem with pushing hard and scheduling was that only trivial products responded to those methods.

"The pulling of products towards a rendezvous with the strategies of customers means that you can reschedule every time the customer has a change of plan and every time staff hit snags. A steady stream of products means that there will usually be something that does the job and performance can be traded off against time. If the rendezvous is vital, and the highest quality essential, additional people and resources can be used to do it superlatively well and on time. In the pull system designers recreate their own schedules and are not pushed."

Figure 5.6 **Saratoga–KE: dilemma 6**

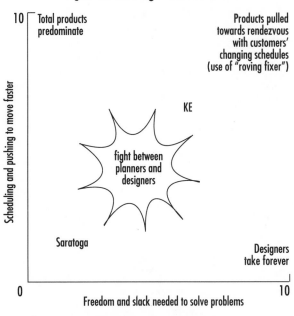

WHERE TO BEGIN: USING DILEMMAS IN PRACTICE

Runcorn agreed that Saratoga had to steer more successfully for the right-hand corner of each chart and that, since all six dilemmas tended to compound each other, these reconciliations should be simultaneous. He needed to know how to combine the dilemma resolutions and where to start.

From vicious to virtuous circles

The starting point should be with Saratoga's present dilemmas which, in their severer forms, constitute a vicious circle and could be created from what has already been charted. For example, there is reason to believe that Saratoga's culture is too specific and insufficiently diffuse, too inner-directed (ignoring what is happening in the environment) and too attached to discovering "winners" and giving them status, so that the potential of others is wasted. This vicious circle (from dilemmas 1–3) is shown in Figure 5.7 (see p. 124).

Here the elements from 12 o'clock to 4 o'clock have been emphasized so strongly they have broken off from their complementarities, the elements from 6 o'clock to 10 o'clock. The problem is self-perpetuating.

Figure 5.7 **Saratoga: a vicious circle**

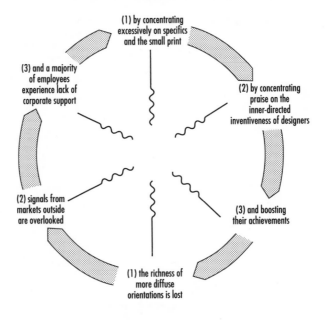

(1) by concentrating excessively on specifics and the small print

(2) by concentrating praise on the inner-directed inventiveness of designers

(3) and a majority of employees experience lack of corporate support

(3) and boosting their achievements

(2) signals from markets outside are overlooked

(1) the richness of more diffuse orientations is lost

Figure 5.8 **Saratoga: a second vicious circle**

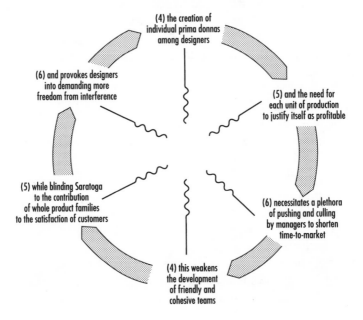

(4) the creation of individual prima donnas among designers

(5) and the need for each unit of production to justify itself as profitable

(6) and provokes designers into demanding more freedom from interference

(6) necessitates a plethora of pushing and culling by managers to shorten time-to-market

(5) while blinding Saratoga to the contribution of whole product families to the satisfaction of customers

(4) this weakens the development of friendly and cohesive teams

The very lack of support employees feel makes them cling more excessively to specifics.

It is also possible to create a second vicious circle from dilemmas 4, 5 and 6 (see Figure 5.8).

Once again, the dominant elements from 12 to 4 o'clock have provoked a breakaway by the subordinate elements of the three dilemmas, extending from 6 to 10 o'clock. The top right of the circle is at odds with the bottom left, and the problem is self-perpetuating as the designers, smarting from being pushed, reassert their positions as prima donnas.

Creating a virtuous circle from dilemmas 1–3

The viciousness is made virtuous by balancing both sides of the dilemma, with new support for the sides previously subordinated, and by creating new concepts, symbols, images and metaphors, which reattach the severed ropes and reconnect the "opposed" values to one another. The reconciliatory concepts usable by those who would heal cultures are all in the top right-hand corners of the first three dual-axis charts. In Figure 5.9 they have been written so as to reattach the values on opposite sides of the circle of dilemmas 1–3. But note that it starts with the values previously subordinated and that the specific is attached to the

Figure 5.9 **Saratoga: a virtuous circle**

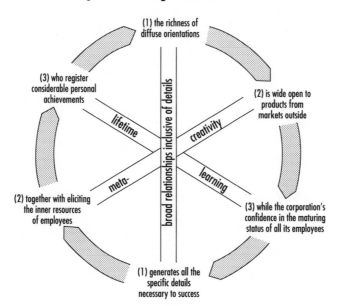

(1) the richness of diffuse orientations

(3) who register considerable personal achievements

(2) is wide open to products from markets outside

lifetime

broad relationships inclusive of details

creativity

learning

meta-

(2) together with eliciting the inner resources of employees

(3) while the corporation's confidence in the maturing status of all its employees

(1) generates all the specific details necessary to success

diffuse (dilemma 1) by relationships of broad mutuality, which KE regarded as the foundations for its joint venture. The outer-directed attention to markets is joined to the inner ingenuity of employees (dilemma 2) by a meta-creativity that uses rival products as resources for a wider synthesis. The corporation's ascription of status to all who stay with it long term is joined to personal achievement (dilemma 3) by heavy investment in human resources and the establishment of lifetime learning.

Creating a virtuous circle from dilemmas 4–6

Viciousness is similarly turned to virtue by rebalancing dilemmas 4–6 and healing their snapped sinews. Once again, the concepts of reconciliation come from the top right corners of the dual-axis charts, but in this illustration from the second set of dilemmas. As before, the order has been reversed so as to give renewed emphasis to the three "horns" that were previously subordinated at Saratoga but not at KE (see Figure 5.10).

Note that:

- the individual's commitment is joined to a coherent team by making promises to that team (dilemma 4);
- every unit in a family counts by being profitable or by generating new products (dilemma 5);

Figure 5.10 **Saratoga: a second virtuous circle**

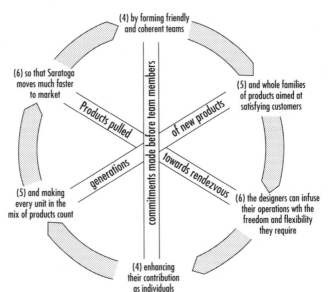

- by "pulling" products towards a rendezvous with customer's strategy, the designers can put freedom and flexibility back into their schedules and get to market on time, with additional resources where necessary (dilemma 6).

The virtuous circle takes the form of a developmental helix creating more of each of those cultural values which were previously in conflict (see Figure 5.11).

Figure 5.11 **Saratoga: a developmental helix**

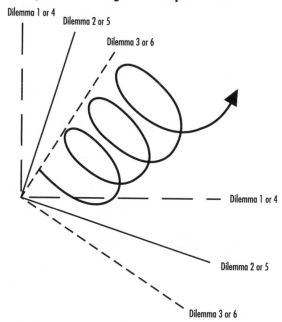

CONCLUSION

This chapter has traced the somewhat bumpy progress of one US-Japanese joint venture in integrated circuit development, manufacturing and marketing. Within the corporate culture of each partner strong reflections of the macro-culture of their nation of origin were found. While Americans and Japanese typically try to resolve their dilemmas by opposite sequences, regarding different "horns" as fundamental, both share the need and desire for reconciliation. Both have much to learn about how the other partner goes about this. On the limited evidence of this research, the Japanese may have a greater grasp of the need to create *wa* or synergy within corporate cultures.

Chapter 6

THE YEAR OF IDEAS:
HOW BAHCO TURNED ROUND

SUMMARY

BAHCO, a diversified and overstretched Swedish-based tools and equipment manufacturer, turned round from the abyss to extraordinary profits in two years. A new corporate culture was cleverly infused by the managing director: trust and respect came to dominate working patterns at every level. Using rituals and incentive schemes, the company created a climate of total devotion to sales performance and new product areas. The study shows how good communications, openness and clear focus create a culture that strives to outperform itself.

THE STUDY

Lindström takes charge

In May 1983 Anders Lindström became managing director of BAHCO. When he took over the company was accelerating into a loss-making spiral. Yet by the end of 1983, seven months after his arrival, losses were down to £7 million, and by the end of 1985, BAHCO was £20 million in profit. Lindström brought this about not by financial wizardry, but by easing the company culture into an upward spiral of productivity. The 42 year old Swede, from a farming family near the Arctic Circle, had nine years' experience of entering problem-ridden businesses, taking charge, turning them round and then handing them back. BAHCO was his fifth such corporate challenge and the one which he found the most interesting and personally satisfying. Let Lindström tell his own story.

"When I enter a company, I always look at it in its historical context, to see how its past has led to its present problems. I can then reorganize those experiences in the shape of ideas to make a better future.

"BAHCO was over 90 years old, and traditionally a maker of steel hand tools and ventilation equipment. The company invented the adjustable wrench, sometimes called a monkey-wrench. I believe that was in 1893. By the 1960s it was pretty boring, but steady, living off its early prowess. In the 1970s the management decided that Sweden was too small for the company. They would internationalize and diversify.

"The first decision was good: internationalization. The second was bad, but it was very fashionable at the time. They got a new managing director in 1978, who launched them on this policy, buying Record Ridgeway in Sheffield in the UK, a hydraulic company in West Germany, and the world's largest maker of hydraulic cranes for trucks, Hiab-Folo, which was Swedish. BAHCO went from 4,500 employees in 1981 to 9,000. It was badly over-extended and into businesses which no one at headquarters really knew about."

The BAHCO trademark was imposed on the British tool company with disastrous results. There was a slump in demand for cranes on trucks and by 1981 most economies were in recession. From a £4 million profit before it was extended, BAHCO went into accelerating losses. It was then that the shareholders approached Lindström and asked whether he would be prepared to take charge.

Post-merger depression

"I had enough reputation at that time to insist on my own terms. They must double the capitalization to show their confidence in my ability and give me a free hand. They agreed. The existing managing director was forced out in February 1983, still protesting that profitability was around the corner. In fact, 1982 showed a loss of Skr200 million, about £20 million. I took over in May 1983. The company was severely depressed and inward-looking. Job losses were imminent and everyone knew it. Moreover, they all blamed each other. Companies in France, Argentina and Sweden had been required to work together and went to great lengths to avoid doing so. They hated each other. Their styles, perspectives and behaviours were all different, and I couldn't see it was necessary."

The first thing Lindström did was to streamline the organization, getting rid of financial directorates and regional marketing coordination centres in Copenhagen, the UK and the USA and substituting seven groups based largely on product, but also separating the ill-assorted national cultures. He had them all reporting to him. The old system had given the managing director of BAHCO Record Tools in Sheffield three bosses;

now he had one. The new system cut HQ staff from 70 to 15. This took one month. "My feeling is that if you can't understand an organization chart when you look at it, then you sure as hell can't work it."

The communications strategy ...

Lindström's next step was to lighten the despair into which BAHCO had plunged. He turned his arrival at the company into a reception for the local and financial press. It was a gamble, but he needed the shareholders' confidence in him publicly proclaimed, where employees and customers would see it. So he announced the doubling of BAHCO's capitalization. The shareholders welcomed him and the press, while calling him an "optimist", decided what he had done at Ericsson he could do again. "We needed a reflection of the optimism we felt in the world outside and we got it." Lindström then prepared a "heart-to-heart talk around the coffee table" (see box) for the whole company, which was printed in a blue pamphlet and featured a photo of him holding a coffee cup. It was also videoed, so that the entire organization could see and hear him.

... and the response

There was nothing in the transcript of that talk which said "write back" or "call me". Lindström sent out 5,000 copies and 500 people wrote back to him with their suggestions and ideas. It was an important signal; they wanted to get involved.

He next turned his attention to the small town of 20,000 people in which the original BAHCO Tools was located.

"We directly employed 2,000 people in that town, so 5,000 people were probably dependent on the wages we paid and, of course, thousands more were indirectly dependent. A few months after I took over, the editor-in-chief of the local paper came to see me. He said, 'We'd like to know what's happening at BAHCO. Our readers are very concerned. But we've always been barred from the factory. As you know, rumours are flying everywhere. I'd like to do two articles about the factory, so that the town will know where we all stand. Could I please get in some time?' I told him he could get in tomorrow and talk to anyone. Well, he didn't do two articles. He did 28, none of them less than two pages.

"It was a gamble, because if things do go wrong publicity confirms this, but if things go right the publicity builds confidence and

The main points of Lindström's "coffee table" talk

1. Very hard work is needed, but this could and should be pleasurable.

2. Like riding a bicycle, BAHCO needs momentum, has to move forward, must be energized or it will wobble and fall.

3. BAHCO needs ideas. Ideas are the stuff business is made of. They release energy, advance knowledge, generate initiative and stimulate all of us. Never mind whether they are good, get them on the table where we can all assess them.

4. Ideas are a currency. If we share money between us each can only have a small part. But ideas generate ideas and they belong to anyone who can use them. You still retain your own ideas even after giving them to others.

5. BAHCO is short of money – very short – so we must generate as much as we can in the shortest time. Choose the best alternative to ease this shortage and the morale of everyone will rise.

6. We must be sincere and honest with each other, even if it hurts. The situation is too serious for evasion. You can start with me: I am largely dependent on your experience in industries I do not know technologically. Let's create a balance between your experience and your ideas.

7. Let's go one small step at a time. The road to success is paved with small mistakes from which we learn. We can't afford big mistakes in our position.

8. Only one thing makes me really angry: the failure to act and to decide. I can forgive mistakes, but I can't forgive inaction.

9. Be positive about our future, about your own and other people's ideas, about honest efforts to turn BAHCO round.

10. Keep everything as simple as you can. That means depending on people rather than controls, keeping memos short, objectives straightforward, solutions elegant.

11. Many of you have been disappointed and frustrated in the last few years. My plea is this: try once again. This time it will work.

pride. Besides, these people were working not just for themselves and their families, but for BAHCO and the whole community. I wanted them to remember this. If the paper wrote up our problems they would also acclaim any solutions, and I wanted everyone to know just how much was at stake."

Managing redundancy ...

"We needed to communicate the sheer extent of the crisis if we were to justify laying off 26 per cent of the workforce, which is what we had to do. But no one, I repeat, no one, left us without another job to go to. We had some of our older employees, who knew a lot of people, set up a relocation office, and we placed 2,000 people in new jobs by assiduous use of the telephone and strong letters of recommendation. In the end, only eight people could not be placed in jobs outside BAHCO, and those we kept with us.

"This wasn't charity, it was common sense. We had to have people pull together, trust each other, trust management and come through the crisis by helping each other. If I had simply dumped those people, no one would have believed me."

... and promotion

"You could say that I 'manage by travelling about' and by asking questions. What do I know about cranes, or ventilation, or pneumatics? Very little. But I noticed which people responded quickly to my questions and told me simply and straightforwardly what I wanted to know. Those were the people I promoted and put in charge. Those who were passive and evasive I passed by."

Choosing leaders

"For example, when I visited the ventilation group I kept asking them what they would do. I said to one manager I particularly liked, 'Suppose you were in charge of the whole ventilation group, what would be your strategy?' He couldn't have anticipated that question – those were early days, but still he had some very complete answers. He'd obviously been aspiring. He'd been there 20 years and he knew the business inside out. So I said, 'Okay. As of tomorrow, you're in charge of the whole group.' He was astounded. 'Doesn't that have to go to the board?' he asked. 'It does and it will ... but the board will support me. I'll write a letter now, putting you in charge. Please start tomorrow.' I gave him 100 per cent of my support over the next three years, and he performed admirably.

"People ask me, 'How do you dare?' Well, I'd rather judge the ability of a man or woman than second guess that person on ventilating systems. He was convincing, persuasive and experienced. We talked the same language. That's enough. I did much the same in the rest of the group."

Beer and cold sandwiches

"It's important to model the behaviour you want from others. Early on I visited one of our West German plants, an especially poor performer. The managing director didn't meet me at the airport. He sent a young controller, and that was all right because I understood just how bad the figures were by the time I got to the plant. They'd laid on a reception for me and a big lunch.

"People were dressed up and there was the German managing director, standing – rather grandly, I thought – at the top of the staircase, making his entry. I walked up the steps to greet him. 'Is that your factory?' I asked, pointing out a building some 100 yards away. 'Yes,' he said. 'Right, let's go there,' and I led the way. It was obvious he did not know the factory and couldn't make his way around and we spent some time stumbling about. 'Let's go to your office,' I said, 'and since there won't be time to eat or for any ceremony, I suggest we have some beer and sandwiches sent in.' I tell that story against myself, because there's a sad sequel. Everywhere I went for at least the next year we had beer and cold sandwiches and I love good food at a decent restaurant, so I may have rather overdone it. But at least they knew we'd be working from the moment I landed to the moment I took off again, and at least there were no further attempts to mollify me with expensive frills.

"I travelled almost continuously in those days, and when I wasn't meeting face-to-face I made a series of videos to report on the situation and lay down challenges. We also had *BAHCO News*, which laid it on the line. I told those I visited that we must be in profit by 1984, so cuts must be made now, as well as costs incurred which were necessary to make us profitable in the year following."

Creating a culture for innovation

"With all the cutting I was afraid we'd mutilate our spirit, so I also demanded at least one new product from every product depart-ment, and I wanted it by 1984. There could be no excuses; if it cost money they must spend what was necessary, despite cuts. But I made clear my belief that every department has new products buried within it, and that these must be dug up. We were going to invent ourselves out of trouble, not just cut and cut, and I wanted those inventive people given a chance to be heard.

"It had an electrifying effect on the morale of the whole group, and it saved us from what would otherwise have been a pretty depressing year. Everywhere I went there were whispers and excitement. They had something to show me, and they were so proud. Now they all wanted to talk to me. What did I think of this? Was this on the right lines? 'I like it,' I'd say, 'but it's your cre-ation and your decision and you must do it if you think it's right. I could like it and it wouldn't sell, and I could hate it and it could make a fortune. What I really like is the spirit in this room.'

"Well, we invented a new truck-crane whose distinction was that it was black instead of red – as far as I could tell – and a new, adjustable wrench which won an award and was the talk of a tool exhibition, although I couldn't tell you why, but the atmosphere was one of exhilaration. By the end of 1983, seven months after my arrival, our losses were down from £20 million to £7 million, but I knew we were well set to make profits in 1984."

The year of sales

"I declared 1984 'the year of sales'. I got commitments from all the managing directors of our companies to spend 10 per cent more of their time either in the field or talking to customers. Once again, you have to model any change in orientation. BAHCO was too inward-looking, too absorbed by its own pains and disappoint-ments, too dependent on inventions made early in its history. I needed to get people out into the environment where we would 'sell like hell'. I knew that our products were basically sound, based as they were on a strong craft tradition. What we had to do was convince others of that fact.

"I began a series of internal competitions to see which compan-ies could do more to raise sales and open markets. This is not easy with so many different groups operating in different markets with different technologies, but we got many plants buzzing. When the first small plant in Northern Sweden won, we sent our TV cameras down, with bands playing and families picnicking, and presented every employee with hand-made pieces of Swedish blown glass.

"After that we ran a competition every two months and soon I was being deluged with claims and invitations to consider this or that sales record. One of the guarantees we made to winners was total job security, but, in fact, business was already turning up in many places and I was being criticized for having laid off as many people as we had originally. Now we began to rehire.

"When the next prize awarded for sales was won by the ventilation group, there was a big party to which the employees of BAHCO Tool Co, just down the road, were also invited. They were furious, and the company won the prize three months later. I insisted that all records be open to inspection by all other companies in the group. Who wins is not so important as the fact that we can all learn from each other's successes. I encouraged travel between plants to gain information. By the end of 1984 we were £10 million in profit."

The year of ideas

"1985 was declared 'the year of ideas'. These were not just ideas about new products, but about anything that would save costs, improve quality and increase effectiveness. We all know how tired a suggestion box system can become. Some ancient engineer, who can too easily be spared from other duties, grunts his way through the box saying, 'No good', 'Tried that', 'Are you serious?'

"We start with the supposition that there are no stupid ideas and that, even if there were, no one could be certain of their stupidity. We tell stories about the telephone being rejected by the US Patent Office and the announcement in 1915 that automobiles had reached the stage where no further innovations were possible.

"We also promoted the collection of ideas. All companies are in competition for both the quality of their ideas and the quantity. Ideas are a competitive edge. So we put out the message that, for the first time ever, someone really wants to hear your ideas.

"Corporations soon learn that if they hold competitions between their groups and departments, they will get more ideas to put into the larger competition. But the more important part is getting the ideas implemented. So we prescribe the following sequence.

1. All ideas must be responded to within one week.
2. At that time the originator will get an answer plus a lottery ticket, regardless of the quality of the idea.
3. Within three weeks the company must say what it will do with the idea. If the idea is used, the originator will receive an amount commensurate with its value, sometimes a month's salary or even a whole year's or more.
4. From then on the competitor is in competition with originators of all other rewarded ideas.
5. There will be a semi-final prize giving.
6. Semi-final winners will go on to a final."

A culture tailored to favour innovation

"I remember attending one semi-final. We took the winners to the Royal Academy of Science in Stockholm for lunch. Every winner receives a crystal glass figure engraved with their name and a cheque for Skr10,000 (£1,000). We televise the proceedings and make it available to the whole company, with videotapes for each semi-finalist.

"On this occasion there were two young girls among the semi-finalists. One, I recall, had been working in the ordering department of the pneumatics company. If pumps fail then clients want replacement parts urgently, and we ship them out for overnight delivery. But because the warehouse closed at 4.00 p.m., this young girl could not ship any parts requested after that time, although she knew where to find them.

"She wanted to know – and had asked in vain for years – why she wasn't allowed into the warehouse to fetch the parts. 'They don't listen to a girl,' she said plaintively. Well, we'd taken notice now, and the warehouse was open as long as the ordering department was. The girl got her £1,000 and put her crystal ball on her desk so that no one would underestimate her ever again.

"We also honour the people who collect the ideas and first confirm them. They are mostly older people, but they are just as proud of 'their' winners as if they had thought of it themselves. For the finalists one year there was a three-day holiday in Paris. They were all workers from different factories and had never been to France before."

The results of the year of ideas

By May 1985 BAHCO had clocked up over 320 implementable ideas, which had significantly increased performance. That was several times the number for the whole of 1984. The "year of ideas" had been a triumph, and at year-end the profit was £20 million, double the year before, and as much in the black as 1982 had been in the red. The share price had trebled in value, sales had reached their highest ever. The number of employees was again increasing. That same year *Ledarskap*, the Swedish journal of business leadership, elected Lindström "manager of the year". There were still a few frustrations. BAHCO Record Tools had not recovered as strongly as the rest, suffering from the BAHCO brand name which it had never wanted, and which sounds in English rather like a coughing sheep. Its fortunes still languished. Lindström was delighted when a US company offered him £10 million for a loss-making division, but he believed strongly that everyone should have a chance to run their own life. So he told the British company about the bid and, within weeks, it had organized a management buy-out.

The (sad) sequel

BAHCO continues in profit and in the high regard of its customers and employees. But Lindström was not treated as well as he treated Record Ridgeway, the British subsidiary. The majority shareholder of BAHCO made a bid for all outstanding shares which the other shareholders could not refuse. A single financial consortium now owned BAHCO and Lindström found himself once more an employee.

"I could have been head of their industrial division, but I didn't want that ... I'd be maximizing short-term profits for the owners and that's not how I operate. I believe in the long-term interests of industry and all its stakeholders. I was really mad at the time. They'd stolen my company. I even said something rude to the press, but then I thought, what the hell, it's their right, and it's the system. Anyway, I could hardly complain. I'd put every penny I could spare into the company and now that was worth three times as much, so I quit but not without many wonderful goodbyes. I put in place people who could carry on without me and that is a lasting satisfaction."

Lindström left BAHCO at the end of 1986, after carefully grooming his successor. Two and a half years later, history repeated itself. Lindström had taken over the Carnegie Group, the tenth largest company on the Swedish exchange, which owned food stores and wholesalers. Once again the share price had tripled and, once again, promises not to sell from under him were broken. But this time he had arranged to be bought out quite dearly. When enticed to express reservations about short-termism and the profit motive for publication in this book, Lindström shrugged and smiled. "I really can't complain," he said.

CONCLUSION

What, then, can be said about the key dilemma of the macro-culture in which hierarchy encounters the equality necessary to effective communication and the eliciting of ideas? Is all hierarchy doomed? Is this the twilight of authority? Not at all. Responsibility hierarchies are unavoidable. The CEO or managing director and the top management team are responsible to the shareholders for the effectiveness with which business is conducted by their own subordinates. What is obsolete is the notion of a top-down issuance of orders along a chain of command, a uni-directional stream of instructions turning from words to acts.

Instead, the more senior a person the larger is the whole or the integration for which he or she is responsible, and the higher is the level of abstraction at which he or she must operate. The leader is thus largely responsible for the character and the performance of the corporate culture in its entirety. It is up to subordinates to excel, but up to the leader to say how excellence shall be defined.

The leader is the coach, mentor and scorekeeper for the whole team. The importance of communication among equals is that leaders like Anders Lindström and Colin Marshall cannot always tell their subordinates what they should do or even how to do it. Innovative and skilled performance depends on the judgement of the person on the job, whether cabin crew or in the pneumatic warehouse. Lindström knew that there had to be more ideas, but he was not even qualified to recognize a winning idea when he saw it. His expert subordinates had to tell him about these ideas and judge them. The equality of such relationships stems from the fact that each depends upon the expertise of the other. Subordinates give Lindström good ideas and evaluate those ideas, while their leader listens and learns. But the leader is the author and expert on the need for an idea-generating system in the first place. The authority of each has different areas of expertise, with the leader by turns humble and assertive, leading and being led.

A DIAGRAMMATIC SUMMARY

Anders Lindström faced a company so traumatized by continued failure, so paralysed by the prospect of imminent cutbacks, that he foresaw "the crash of a slow moving bicycle" without sufficient momentum to survive. His predicament could have been expressed by the three major dilemmas shown in Figure 6.1.

It is axiomatic that any company must have confidence in the future based on its past results, but BAHCO's past results showed chronic losses and its confidence was very low. Similarly any company must go out to

Figure 6.1 **BAHCO's three major dilemmas**

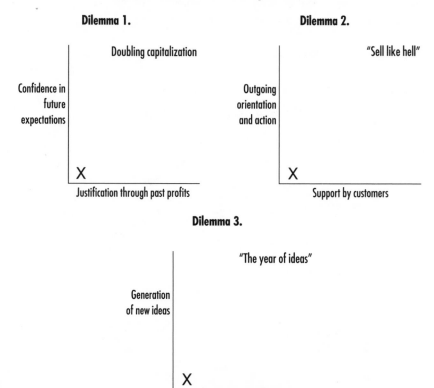

customers and win some measure of support, but BAHCO'S customers had been leaving as the recession deepened and each company shrank back into itself despairingly. Any company lives off the ideas it once generated, however long ago, and such generating risks failure and rejection. BAHCO was both fearful and sterile. It is for this reason that an X has been placed in each of the bottom left corners of the three dual axes. Unlike companies in earlier chapters, BAHCO's cultural values were not so much uneven as utterly demoralized. It lacked commitment to anyone or anything, but rather waited for the end to come.

Lindström radiated confidence in the future, substituted his own past profit performance for BAHCO's and demanded and got a doubling of the company's capitalization. He then won endorsement from the press and his employees through his "coffee table" talk. His "sell like hell" campaign and orders to the heads of businesses to meet customers also turned BAHCO outwards and won back customer support. His "year of ideas" campaign taught everyone to take the risk of generating ideas. His reconciliations are at the top right corners of the three dilemmas.

From vicious to virtuous circles

Using the six "horns" in their more negative conditions, Lindström faced the following vicious circle (see Figure 6.2).

Figure 6.2 **BAHCO: a vicious circle**

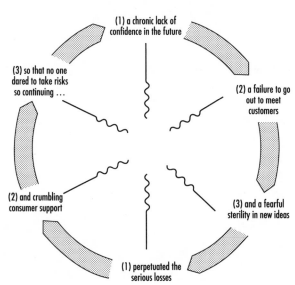

(1) a chronic lack of confidence in the future

(3) so that no one dared to take risks so continuing ...

(2) a failure to go out to meet customers

(2) and crumbling consumer support

(3) and a fearful sterility in new ideas

(1) perpetuated the serious losses

What his reconciliations accomplished was a reconnection of the company's snapped sinews (see Figure 6.3).

Figure 6.3 **BAHCO: a virtuous circle**

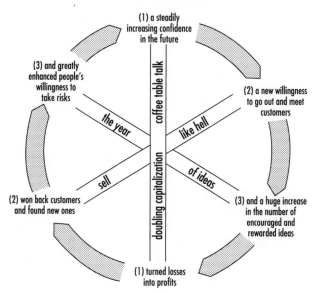

Chapter 7

THE ADVENTURES OF A TROJAN HORSE: BOXES, BUBBLES AND RUSSELSTEEL

SUMMARY

David Hurst is the vice-president and "strategist extraordinary" of Russelsteel Inc., a Canadian steel distributor with 1989 pre-tax profits in the $30 million range. He has seen his company much bought and sold since 1979. But like the wooden horse pulled through the gates of Troy, the company has proved itself in many ways more alive and resourceful than those who acquired it.

When companies are bought and sold by remote conglomerates only their hard surface characteristics are treated as meaningful. "We judge them," says Hurst, "by the boxes in which we have placed them and by arbitrary labels stuck on them. Inside the 'box' we often find the 'bubble', which gives the acquisition its life and culture, if indeed it is alive at all." There follows the story of Russelsteel, the purchased box that came alive, with a lesson for all the barterers of boxes.

THE STUDY

Simple task, subtle culture: the growth of Russelsteel

The company Hugh Russell Inc. was founded in 1962 to supply Canada's widely dispersed steel users. It grew largely by acquisitions until, in 1979, it was the 50th largest company in Canada, with a net income of $14 million on $535 million in sales – not impressive, but solvent. It was an organization in "industrial distribution", a term chosen to cover the highly diverse series of acquisitions, including the Building Supplies Group. The year 1979 turned out to be something of a watershed, and the three years which followed were years of unprecedented turbulence, disillusion and reorganization, and a complete revolution in the management culture.

Enter David Hurst

In the recession of 1981–83, the deepest in the Canadian steel industry since the Great Depression, the company's old order died and a new order was born. The unchallenged conceptualizer-in-chief of Russelsteel is South African born David K. Hurst, a Stanford MBA, whose descriptions of the company's rebirth have appeared in the *Harvard Business Review* and *Organizational Dynamics*. Hurst has been involved in company turnrounds before, notably in his native South Africa. He has transformed his experiences into an astonishingly original, astringent and far-reaching critique of conventional business strategy, dominated as it is by finance and acquisition, and he has made a powerful plea for alternative models based on the nurture of corporate cultures. The story that follows is compiled from several private interviews with David K. Hurst, from his many public presentations, and from his published works.

"My conclusions are somewhat drastic, but justified, I believe, by what we have achieved here. I'd like to explain, in the words of an article I wrote, 'Why strategic management is bankrupt'.*

"I began my management career in the 1960s, working for managers who had been taught that the principles of strategic management could be transferred successfully from one business to another. The more I saw of the results of attempts to do this, the less persuaded I was that it was really possible. By cutting themselves off from the realities of customers and operations, corporate managers often seemed to end up in a world of abstractions which provided poor maps of reality."

The conglomerate: a fictional world ...

"The logic of this world was dominated by the interests and concerns of the local financial community. It took me some time to realize that stockbrokers and investment advisers need a continuous supply of stories about companies in order to induce their customers to trade stocks. They look to corporate management to supply these. What had started out as a modest statement of corporate intentions for internal consumption would grow prodigiously to become a 'grand strategy'.

"In the benign economic conditions of the 1960s, financial results often 'confirmed' these strategies. And so the stories, once told, grew in the telling, encouraged by an adulatory business press which sang the praises of corporate management.

---

* *Organizational Dynamics*, November 1986.

"Successful conglomerates often seemed to me to become sophisticated chain letters, whose continued survival depended upon their ability to tell eloquent tales and deliver results in the short term. Gradually, their corporate managers became obsessed with quarterly earnings, accounting 'optics' and the management of the stock price. They would spend huge amounts of time searching for ecological niches in the tax system and very little on the distinctive competencies which had made them successful in the first place – competencies in businesses which they no longer understood.

"The management theory of the time was characterized by the search for, and the purported discovery of, the fundamental principles of management. Management theorists believed they had isolated the elements of administration that were common to all management situations. Because they thought these principles were universal, they believed that management skills were a-cultural and could be transferred from one business to another. Our own case was typical. Hugh Russell Inc. was a textbook case of federal decentralization, to use the term that was coined by Peter Drucker. This produces a split between the operating managers who run the profit centres and the 'investors', the corporate office heads who run the holding company on behalf of the shareholders.

"The latter were practitioners of what might be called 'the empty box approach to strategy'. Divisions and their units were moved across an abstract chessboard like so many interchangeable units taking opposing pieces from the board.

"The strategist scanned the environment, set objectives, usually financial ones, developed options, made strategic decisions, adapted the organization, so that it could effectively implement the strategy, and then had periodic strategic reviews, in case it had missed something. All this is supposed to be done by corporate office heads, far removed geographically, technologically or culturally from the units they are playing with, whose designation as 'industrial distributors' is so abstract as to be virtually meaningless. What, in fact, these corporate heads did to prevent themselves getting bored out of their skulls, was to sort out 'dogs' from 'cash cows', 'question marks' from 'stars', as pieces on a board game and go on the trail of acquisition and divestiture, buying companies that fitted within some notional concept of what the conglomerate was all about, and selling others."

... with fictional profits and cultural traumas

"In our case it was largely acquisitions, 27 of them, involving more than 40 distinct businesses. This hugely increased our size, but in the process the investment function and its needs totally overpowered the management function and its concerns.

"We did not grasp the cultural turmoil you can create by taking a company over. In some cases the companies had been built up by single entrepreneurs and, without them, were leaderless and hollow. When one of our vice-presidents was put in charge, to introduce 'the necessary organization and control', all that company's managers resigned or had to be replaced. Two other companies were supposed to be in the same business. Their merger would, on paper, create big improvements in margin and a radical reduction in overheads. Yet, no sooner were they merged than they started to fight. Their management styles were different as were their cultures and, while their markets overlapped, they were not the same. In another case, a whole group of employees resigned, started up their own business and eclipsed their original company within three years.

"There followed a disastrous diversification into Building Supplies, a family company with a rich culture, in which the original founders agreed to stay. But their money was no longer where their mouths were. After two years of profitability, the group began to sink. During those years, group headquarters received a lot of 'hockey stick' forecasts. Yes, profits could dip in the short term, but then they would shoot upwards without pause.

"The conglomerate HQ knows a great deal about historic costs, but very little about how the companies it owns are actually engaging themselves here and now, what ideas, ambitions and competencies shape their cultures, or whether the creature inside the box has long since died and only its trappings remain."

The predator strikes

"If HQ believed in these trappings, the markets did not. The pendulum had started to swing back against the fashion of diversification and the large, unwieldy conglomerates this created. Hugh Russell's poor financial returns, less than 3 per cent ROI, made it a target for takeover. In 1980 a predator struck. In the same year, the steel cycle faltered, recovered briefly in 1981 and then, a year later, plunged.

"The crunch came as the economy turned down, wiping out those of our businesses which had not provided real value to their customers. Many of our operating subsidiaries, neglected for years, fell into large losses. I'd seen this happen before. I came to realize that very few of these would-be acquisitors were villains, cynically manipulating the system. Rather they were victims of their own abstractions, tragic heroes of the stories they had told to themselves and their shareholders."

The whole concept of "management by remote control", a surviving theme of scientific management, had foundered. The financier-as-scientist at the apex of an experiment, which doles out carrots to managers and brings down sticks upon their backs on the basis of a rational model, had been exposed as a giant illusion.

Hurst believes that an organization's strategic concepts are like the hard shells built by organisms, or suits of armour worn by knights. The structures give protection and security, but at the cost of restricting shape and mobility. In North America, the corporate structures, built layer by layer during the warm climate of the 1960s, have proved highly unadaptable in the brisker temperatures of the 1980s. It had been so long since anyone looked inside the shells being bought and sold for their alleged market value, that no one had realized how many of them were already half dead and in no shape to compete for survival.

"We had seized the shell and lost the substance. I can't, off-hand, think of a more important issue facing the finance-dominated industry of Canada, the UK and USA. Are we dealing with realities of creating and growing businesses, or are we manipulating mere counters at one stage removed from reality?"

The takeover

The takeover of Hugh Russell Inc. in 1980, in a 100 per cent leveraged buy-out, was not the end of its troubles. It then merged with the large and hugely unprofitable steel fabricator, York Steel Construction, to become York Russell. Hurst recalls:

"As members of the acquired company's corporate office, we waited nervously for the axe to fall. Nothing happened. Finally, after about six weeks, Wayne Mang, now our president, asked the new owner if we could do anything to help the deal along. The new chairman was delighted and gave us complete access to information about the acquirer."

However, the information was hardly reassuring. The business had little management strength, no plan and, worse, no money. The deal had been desperately conceived to keep Hugh Russell's meagre profits and cash flow from the taxman, and to finance the large debt burden of York Steel's fabrication business. The acquirer, it turned out, needed Russell far more than Russell needed the acquirer and, more important, the acquirer had not the slightest idea of what might be done to improve its operations. For once, corporate HQ was admitting its ignorance. It desperately needed the Russell operation to survive and prosper. How it was done was entirely up to Russell.

The turnround plan – from within

"It was really a 'Trojan horse' situation," Hurst explains. "They had found us attractive, if only because we were marginally less broke, had pulled us within their walls, and now it was our spirit which took over, along with a veritable change of paradigm." Hurst joined a task force which put together a $300 million bank loan application and a credible turnround plan. York Russell survived, but only just. Interest rates of 25 per cent took their toll. Seven divisions of the 25 were closed; 16 were sold. Five of the latter, together with the steel distribution and metals businesses, were bought by Federal Industries in 1983, and with these moved the "nerve centre" of the survival plan – Wayne Mang, David Hurst and their colleagues. The Trojan horse had been towed into another city, but the group was still together, still meeting and still had the confidence of its bankers. More important, it had "a logic of recovery" encoded within it.

On "boxes and bubbles"

Writing in the *Harvard Business Review,*[*] Hurst contrasts the living processes which grow their outer shells with the shells themselves devoid of their living contents, often spectacularly beautiful, but in fact deposits from the past. He calls these living processes "bubbles" and their final structures "boxes". Boxes and bubbles complement one another, like the creature which lives within its shell. However, they are frequently misconceived being as opposed to one another.

[*] "Of boxes, bubbles and effective management", *Harvard Business Review,* May–June, 1984.

Table 7.1 **Boxes and bubbles**

Boxes	Bubbles
Strategy	Mission
Planned	Spontaneous
Analysis	Synthesis
Things as they really are	Phenomena as perceived
(the earth is turning)	(the sun is setting)
External	Internal
Strength/weaknesses	Competencies/preferences
Reductionism	Emergence
Fundamentals	Purpose
Predesigned	Evolving
Objectives	Values
Precise	Ambiguous
Targets	Directions
Focus (narrow)	Awareness (broad)
Search	Recognition
Means	Ends
Today's business	Tomorrow's business
Make it happen	Let it happen

For example, tasks are the boxes, while the roles people play are the bubbles, that is, the life-giving origins of those tasks. The structure of an organization is the box or shell formed by the dynamics of its teams which are its bubble. The compensation systems are a box created from the living history of rewards that people have exchanged. Boxes are rational, left brain, precise. Bubbles are social, right brain, ambiguous (see Table 7.1). Strategies are typically made of boxed thoughts and products, while missions are what fill those strategies with bubbles of imagination and creativity. The corporate HQ which becomes obsessed with outward appearances has lost sight of the missions of its companies, the vital complement to any strategy that adds value in the longer run.

Reading vertically down the left column of the box, the following policy statement could be made:

"The strategy consists of planning and carefully analysing things external to the organization, together with its key strengths and weaknesses. These are reduced to fundamentals from which are designed objectives, each with precise targets set for it, which focus upon and search for the means to make today's business happen." Reading vertically down the right column is like entering a wholly different realm:

"The mission involves spontaneous synthesis of phenomena internal to people and to the organization, from which its competencies and preferences emerge, and its purposes evolve from its values, initially ambiguous but finding their own direction. Employees become aware and recognize the ends which will make tomorrow's business happen."

All too often the two policy statements above exclude one another and subscribe to "hard" and "soft" approaches respectively. It is the peculiar capacity of an effective corporate culture to reconcile the hard with the soft, the box with the bubble. A company needs both to succeed.

From mission to strategy

Hurst not only believes, but has demonstrated through his successful turnrounds, that mission creates strategy, and is the soft origin of hard realities. The answer, therefore, is to read across the columns in the box.

"The spontaneous synthesis of novel phenomena is what creates the plan of analysable things and elements. The internal competencies and preferences which emerge are what constitute the externally visible organization, capable of reduction into key strengths and weaknesses. The values, initially vague, which flow in particular directions, are what make the precisely targeted objectives possible. And awareness and recognition of common ends towards which tomorrow's business can be dedicated are what energize the search focusing on the means by which today's business can be transacted."

The right column, facing forwards to the future, is the living element within the left-hand column that faces towards the past. The result is a Janus-faced organization, looking backwards and forwards at the same time, both solid shell and living substance. It is important to grasp that the backward-looking "boxes" are by no means useless. They prune, cull, rationalize and shake down the excesses of creation. They schematize and turn into routines and rules the ideas already implemented and operationalized.

Yet the shell by itself can only look backwards. The bankruptcy of most strategic thinking is that it can only play with its existing counters, but cannot bring new ones into existence, or keep its current acquisitions alive. Hard boxes do try to look forwards, but:

"They work for the future only so long as the pattern of the future mimics that of the past ... This framework assumes that capital is the scarce resource to be rationed among many competing investment opportunities.

"In fact, the current situation in North America is quite the opposite. Opportunities are scarce, while capital is plentiful ... the inability of the strategic model to create such opportunities lies at the heart of its problems."

Digging for opportunity and discovering latent potentials is the role of the right-hand column: the bubbles.

From strategy to action

What did Hurst and his team do specifically about the cultures of their steel distribution outlets to increase their numbers, effectiveness and profitability? They realized that missions, purposes, values, directions and awareness had to come from each business unit itself and that it was the role of divisional management to evoke, inform, encourage, coach, respond and, where there was conflict, to help reconcile. The Janus-faced objectives were used to encourage cultures of "both–and", in which employees would pull together because each of them saw the different faces of a single truth and appreciated that the dilemmas were reconcilable.

For example, a credit manager is both a conservative cash collector and a creative money lender who enhances earnings by accepting good risks. The cultures within the company were, and still are, encouraged to turn accepted ideas on their heads and consider the reverse. While everybody accepts that the company sells steel for money, does it not also lend money, with steel as a security, and as such is a lender of last resort?

Great efforts were made to help business units negotiate with their unions by the reconciled values of toughness and tenderness. Management was encouraged to be tough about the levels of productivity, performance and costs needed to survive and grow, yet tender in ensuring that this was done within a social context where everyone was treated with the fullest consideration possible and kept thoroughly informed about the company's position and performance: "tough on the problem, tender on the person".

Work with plant managers taught them to develop their powers to influence (bubble), from which their control (box) would follow; to be tender (bubble) so that, when they had to be tough (box), employees would quickly sense the difference. They were advised to commit themselves (bubble) and let discipline (box) flow from this. General effectiveness (bubble) should take care of key efficiencies (box). If they could first evoke (bubble) ideas and energies, then was the time to specify (box) what was needed.

A sophisticated on-line computer network allows the various branches to operate freely, and yet senior managers know what is happening because the results of all major operations and decisions appear immediately at the company's nerve centre. In this way, branch managers have autonomy, yet serious problems are caught before they become expensive. The idea is that central administration should be invisible, with information for the head office being generated as a byproduct of operating managers, running the branches as if these were their own businesses. The scheme is working well in the eyes of senior managers, and the workers and branches know before their superiors how next month's figures are going to come out, because they are in charge of the process.

The company has a variety of profit-sharing plans based on performance against budgets and return on investment criteria.

It is also typical of this company that all visitors from head office assume that they need help from the business unit they visit, to discover what is really happening. All HQ staff wear a lapel sticker which reads "I'm from head office so help me". Another crucial symbol is the hierarchy turned upside down as it was in Volvo France (see Chapter 8). Russelsteel uses a tree diagram which shows that the nutrients and the supplies come from Federal Industries and steel suppliers, while it is sales people, truckers, switchboard operators, loaders and warehousemen who face the environment and are in touch with customers. The flow of knowledge is from outside in, through the leaves and branches down to the trunk, which comprises the head office and the president.

A new type of acquisitions policy

A testament to the success of these ideas is that Russelsteel is now taking over US and North American steel distributors, whereas it was once a target. Yet no distributor is acquired without Hurst and Wayne Mang, Russelsteel's president, agreeing that the new company has latent visions and values (bubbles) that can be brought to life. Hurst's first step following an acquisition is to have the acquired company play a simulation game called Arctic Survival, which is used by the Canadian air force and rescue services. Employees pretend they are survivors of a crash in northern Newfoundland and must make choices about what to rescue from the wreck.

It is a good game for newly acquired companies whose morale may not be far from wreckage, and it teaches them quickly that only groups who share information and exchange help will survive. Hurst makes sure that, in the groups, union workers are well mixed in with managers. Because bush skills are needed, and many blue-collar workers are hunters, they acquit themselves well and win respect.

The proof of the pudding

The obvious comparison between Russelsteel in 1981 (when the bank that lent the money to acquire the company took a second look and asked for its money back) and Russelsteel now is not quite good enough. The economy as a whole and the industry have come out of recession, so that even a mediocre organization should be showing profits at this time. Russelsteel's answer is to compare its pre- and post-1981 performance with overall industry trends.

Figure 7.1 compares the variation in demand for Canadian steel from 1976 to 1987 with the return on net assets (RONA) for the Metals group of Federal Industries of which Russelsteel is the major part. Hurst and Mang's rescue package was put together between 1981 and 1982. By 1984 RONA was nearly 20 per cent; since then it has increased to 25 per cent and 24 per cent, trimmed slightly by the recent acquisitions of less successful distributors in Minnesota and Wisconsin.

Another important way of measuring the efficiency of a distributor is by the number of times inventory is turned over in a year. Fast turnover is not only more profitable in lowering carrying costs and accelerating sales, but is more "intelligent" in so far as a company will discover before its competitors which way the markets for various stocks are heading.

Russelsteel was considering an acquisition when it uncovered the fact that the small distributor under consideration was turning over stock at six times a year. The average for Russelsteel and the Canadian distribution business had been three times. The company found itself trying to invent the usual excuses as to why this small target was exceptional and the old ways were best. It collected the excuses on paper and then put a

Figure 7.1 **Russelsteel's return on net assets (RONA) trend**

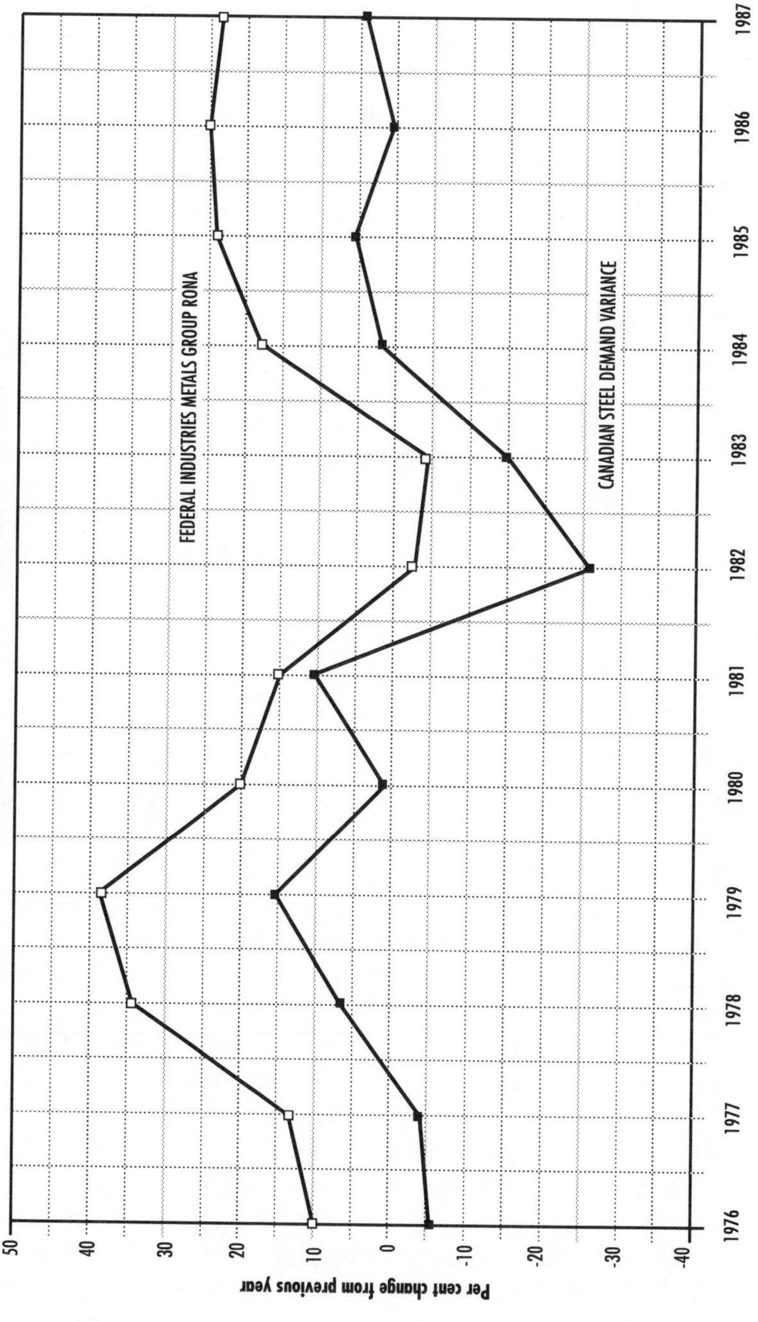

match to them, burning the lot. The company was going to monitor its inventory turnover rate, and use this as a measure of success. Figure 7.2 shows what has been achieved.

The policy of increasing inventory turn was inaugurated in July 1984, when it wavered around three turns per annum. There is obvious cyclicality, owing to the Canadian winter, but even so turns have risen some 60 per cent, with monthly rates now topping five. Hurst's US distributors have reached six.

"And we have fun"
In conclusion, Hurst said:

> "Many of my friends and colleagues seem surprised by our results. They wonder what difference creativity, ingenuity and better relationships could make in distributing bits of steel. 'Isn't it so humdrum that fancy ways of thinking simply elaborate needlessly on mundane work? Isn't this one case in which you could buy and sell boxes on the assumption that it only takes routine and control to sell batches of metal parts?' It would seem not. Our 'humble' task improves all the time. We are increasingly profitable, and we have great fun doing it."

CONCLUSION

During the late 1960s and the 1970s North America and parts of Europe went on an "agglomeration spree" that would lead, some said, to "consolidated everything". The high priests of this process argued that business strategy consisted of abstract financial formulae in which portfolios of businesses were labelled, monitored for their return on investment, rewarded or otherwise for their level of performance and acquired or divested by corporate HQs with too few other activities to sustain them. It was "scientific" management by the remotest of control. Corporate cultures were far away and shut up in labelled boxes.

With the recession of the early 1980s thousands of companies were found not to be engaging their markets effectively. Those like Russelsteel which survived and prospered did so because there was a "bubble" or strong culture inside the box. Suddenly a large conglomerate discovered that it was being sustained by one of the few of its acquisitions to retain a sense of mission competence, purpose and value. Culture counted after all.

Figure 7.2 **Russelsteel's inventory turns trend,** 1984–87

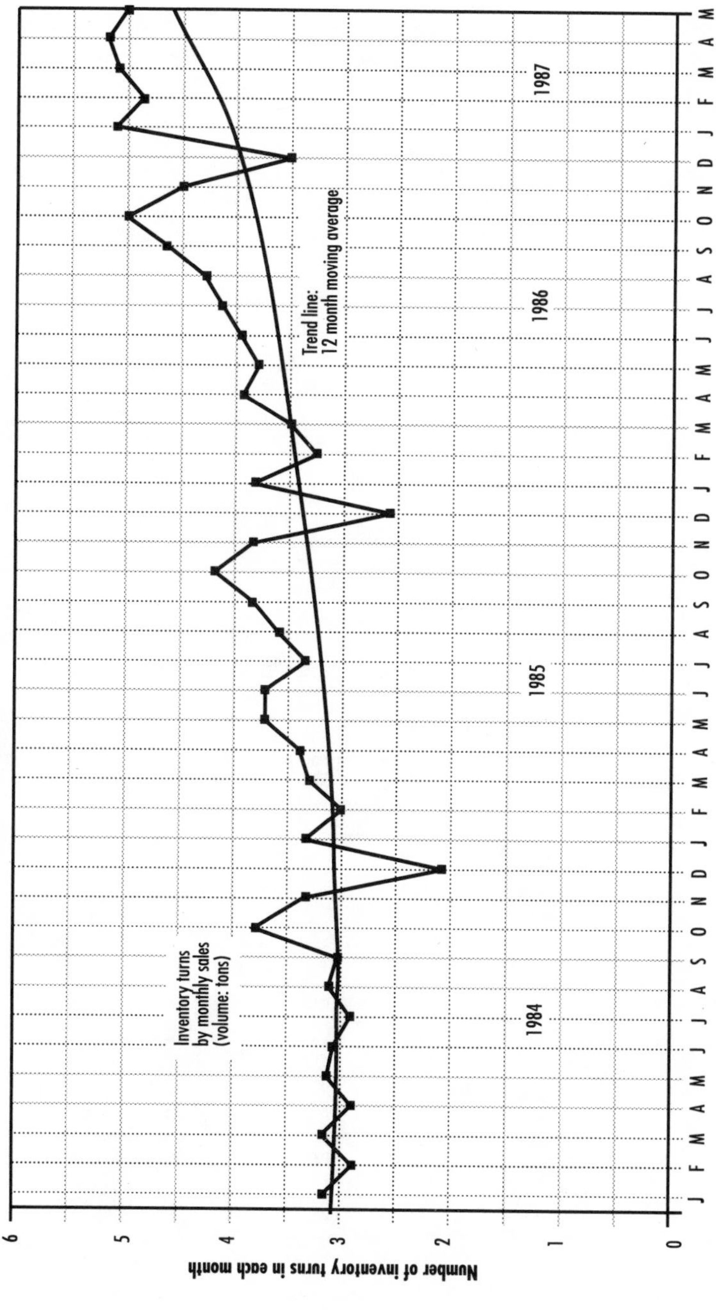

Figure 7.3 **Russelsteel: a vicious circle**

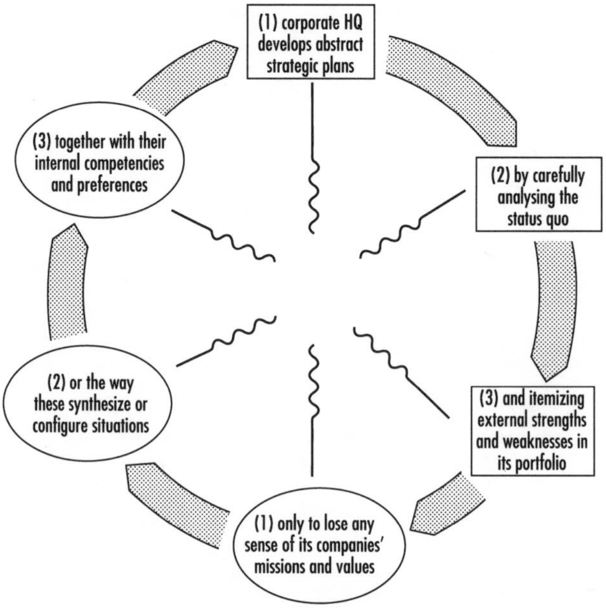

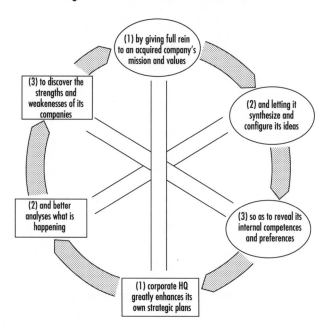

Figure 7.4 **Russelsteel: a virtuous circle**

A DIAGRAMMATIC SUMMARY

A vicious circle can be drawn in which hard "box thinking" subordinates and loses touch with "bubble thinking". This can be illustrated by borrowing three of Hurst's dichotomies: strategy versus mission; analysis versus synthesis; and external strengths versus internal competencies. Figure 7.3 shows the vicious consequences.

How did Hurst repair these severed connections when Russelsteel itself went on the acquisition trail a few years later? He emphasized that bubbles and boxes were Janus-faced including both one and the other. Every new acquisition had its mission values, syntheses and competencies thoroughly appreciated and explored.

Every acquisition had freedom to act for itself, provided the decision was entered on a joint computer system which HQ could monitor. By playing Arctic Survival where there are no easy answers and a life and death crisis, every acquisition has its initiative evoked.

Through such methods bubbles can fill the boxes with life, as shown in Figure 7.4.

Chapter 8

FRENCH WITH A SWEDISH ACCENT:
HOW VOLVO DOUBLED SALES IN FRANCE

SUMMARY

This case study looks at how a strong corporate culture can be imported into a country with different cultural values. It is a process which can produce dynamic change which may be difficult to maintain long term. Between 1982 and 1986 Volvo sales in France climbed from 10,800 cars a year to 21,000. That was achieved despite a 20 per cent fall in the size of the national market and without a large number of new product launches. Volvo France went from an average annual loss (1980–82) of Fr13 million to an average annual profit (1983–85) of Fr19 milion. The change in fortunes was almost entirely due to the way one man, Goran Carstedt, succeeded in infusing a cooperative Swedish corporate culture into the French dealers' network, and marketing the values behind Volvo to a French audience. The case study is particularly relevant to the problems of sales and marketing cultures, and demonstrates how a good corporate image and identity programme can generate strong returns.

THE STUDY

From 1986 to 1990 Goran Carstedt was president and chief executive officer of Volvo Svenska Bil AB, the distributor and importer of trucks and cars in Sweden, including the entire Volvo line as well as French Renault cars. Annual turnover is in excess of Skr10 billion (£1 billion). The son of a Swedish Ford dealer, Carstedt grew up with cars. After a doctorate in small business studies he joined the Volvo Car Corporation in 1974. Pehr Gyllenhammar, Volvo's visionary leader, had become president two years earlier at the age of 37. Gyllenhammar's view that employees needed and wanted to be involved in their work had a strong impact on Carstedt.

Soon promoted to vice-president and head of corporate planning, where Volvo produced sophisticated long-range scenarios, Carstedt found the planning process too abstract and with none of the immediate events and intense personal experiences in which he believed.

Carstedt eventually joined the French car division as roving consult-ant-cum-assistant and, after a couple of months, took over as general manager. He knew France well, having been a student in Paris at the time of the May 1968 rebellion, and now he finally had a job where the tyres met the road and he could be in the field, where Volvo's ideas were working or not working.

Dismal failure all round

Things could not have been much worse. Plans to increase sales from 10,000 cars a year to 20,000 had been laid as early as 1978. Sales prompt-ly fell to 8,000 and only struggled back to 10,000 by 1982. This was despite a growing market in which the market share taken by imports was sharply up. By 1982 Volvo's share stood at just 0.5 per cent. "It was a lousy performance," recalls Carstedt.

Failure on this scale, when Volvo worldwide was succeeding spec-tacularly and the French truck division was prospering, needed an elab-orate set of excuses; there was a formidable thicket of rationalizations.

It was said (rightly) that few French motorists even realized that Volvo was available in France. The products were said to be too old, too heavy, too stodgy, the 760 too expensive and all had stiff rear axles which were not *pointé* in France. Too much performance had been sac-rificed to safety. There was not enough support from the importer, who interfered too much and helped too little. Deliveries were slow, and promised new models were late.

Carstedt was told time and time again that "this is France". It was a Latin nation, passionate and hot-blooded, whereas Volvo was a cerebral car, something melancholy Scandinavians thought about on long winter evenings and engineered to keep the cold out. Carstedt had heard all this before and had the Italian sales figures in his briefcase to show that Latins could buy Volvos in large numbers. But he knew better than to assault their defences frontally. In his view, a "negative story" has to be reinter-preted, with the same facts but altered meanings. Piece by piece he began the reconstruction.

Reconstructing a negative culture into a positive one

Fond as he was of France, Carstedt had no intention of letting his Volvo philosophy go. If the French were not buying Volvos in sufficient num-bers it was because they had not yet understood the car and the culture that made it. He was going to convince them. It was not as if Volvo was a mass-market volume car-maker which millions of French people had to buy. Volvo was aimed at discerning drivers and there were surely enough of these in France, even if the origins of the vehicle and its value system were foreign.

Carstedt had worked in planning, the heart of the company, where its values and strategies were generated. He was going to say to French motorists, in effect, "Here is something different which is worth buying". Volvo, he felt, had a style not dissimilar to the spirit a previous, and now wealthy, generation had fought for in 1968.

"The Volvo which Pehr Gyllenhammar was realizing represented the best in Scandinavian culture. We'd pioneered the Kalmar factory which broke up the assembly line into circular work-stations, where teams worked in progressive stages of assembly of the whole vehicle. At the Uddervalla factory we had even got out of sequential stages altogether. Each car was built from A to Z by 15 'car craftsmen' who, when they had finished the car, would sign it personally."

He sees Sweden as the conjunction of two major world trends.

"We are a very individualistic nation and yet we've been social democrats almost continuously since the war. We've had to combine the initiative and commitment of the individual with the ethic of social concern for the welfare of others. From the convergence of these two streams has emerged our paramount concern with building safe cars."

The Volvo corporate culture: safety, equality

"We pioneered the windscreen that does not shatter, the crush-resistant car body and the three-point safety belt, on which we still have patents. These ideas come not from any analysis of markets but from Swedish and Volvo cultures themselves. I remember taking my kids ice-skating near our home in Paris. There must have been more than 100 children at that rink. Ours were the only ones in crash helmets. Swedes take care of each other."

Volvo's philosophy also shows up in its management culture. "If you believe in people and their latent capacities, then the more authority you 'give away' to them the more you get back in initiatives and ideas even you did not foresee. We believe in radical decentralization, in pushing authority down to the level where those dealing directly with customers have the freedom to exercise it."

Finding out what members of the corporate culture think is an essential first step. Sympathetically conducted interviews are crucial.

He began his efforts with nine regional meetings with the 150 French dealers around U-shaped tables, where he took the coordinative rather than the boss role. He said simply, "I want to know from you what you think should be done and what Volvo can do to help you sell more cars. Tell me what we are doing wrong, what you want from us, and I'll see it is done if I possibly can." That surprised them. No one had ever taken the dealers seriously enough to ask their advice. It was, "Why don't you do better? Don't think we can't drop you." Here someone was listening.

The challenge to double sales ...

"Much of what they mentioned I had anticipated and, within weeks, we had new systems on line. But I needed to issue a challenge. We knew roughly how many people repurchase a Volvo car after a certain number of years, so we could expect 4,000–5,000 repeat sales annually. Around 20 per cent of our future sales would come from this source. That meant we had to persuade 70–80 per cent of people who didn't know Volvo to try it and buy it. That was a tall order, but we had to double sales and that was our target."

Quietly, yet relentlessly, Carstedt was chopping away at the forest of excuses, clearing the ground for his positive reinterpretation of the Volvo culture. He earned two nicknames at this time, *Le Vol du Nord* (the northern wind) and *ça je n'accepte pas* (I don't believe that).

Carstedt went back to Volvo's HQ in Sweden and gave them a complete strategy analysis with all the numbers. They loved it and, of course, he had friends there who wanted to see the philosophy come alive. There were plans to speed up delivery, computerize ordering, make car financing less expensive, do better customer research, coordinate national with local advertising and fill vacancies caused by high turnover.

... and break down the hierarchy

The least effective and the most common way of implementing a strategy is for each level of the hierarchy to define what is required of the level below. Instructions quickly become meaningless.

But Carstedt had no intention of dumping his strategic plan on the heads of dealers. They would not have appreciated it, and they would have seen their salvation as being in the hands of those higher up. His message :"No one's going to save us but ourselves". "To them I was the son of a car dealer, and we were going to do this job together," he recalls.

"One of the first things I noticed was the existence of a hierarchy stretching from Volvo in Sweden, to Volvo France, down to the dealers, with customers at the bottom. If Volvo France was called by head office, they virtually saluted them, and three copies of the report, beautifully bound and describing what ought to be happening, was back in Sweden within days. If a dealer called the French head office, he was either ignored or yelled at. He wasn't one of us. If he didn't perform, we'd change him. The dealers were passing on our behaviour to their customers."

Carstedt drew a cartoon, which turned the hierarchy upside down. "The customer was king. The dealers were his courtiers and it was our job, mine, Volvo France's and HQ's, to make sure the dealers had what they needed."

Carstedt hired a conference centre on the outskirts of Paris and invited all the dealers and their wives. He began with a film he had had shot, *Où est Volvo?* (Where is Volvo?). It used humour to explain just how bad things were. Assorted citizens were asked about Volvo and Volvo dealers and gave expansive shrugs and elaborate gestures of indifference. One old man was questioned with his back against a Volvo sign. *"Je ne sais pas,"* (I don't know) he replied defiantly. Then, to show he was not senile, he reeled off a dozen names of cars. Everyone in the audience laughed, a trifle ruefully.

Carstedt then presented the new car models for 1984 to the dealers. This was done live from an outside studio and televised on a big screen in front of the audience. The room from where the products were presented was an immaculate showroom, beautifully appointed. It was obviously in France because the announcements were all in French.

Dealers in the audience could be heard asking whose showroom it was and where had it been shot. Then Carstedt lifted the curtain behind the screen on which the film had been projected. The entire showroom had been created for that film and for that day.

Investment from the bottom, not the top

It was intended as an example of what was possible, of how a dealer's showroom could look. The message was, "You have to upgrade your showrooms and invest in expanding your facilities. We'll give you all the support we can, the blue and white panels and logo, 60 days' credit, all the advice you need. We could try to double our sales by doubling the number of our dealers, but that would increase your competition. So we'd like to do this first, to see if all of you can, on average, double your sales." A comprehensive programme for upgrading a dealership was offered; 130 of the 150 dealers participated in it during the next two years.

"I knew at the time what they needed to invest, Fr150 million or more. I could have 'proved' it by showing what Mercedes, BMW and Alfa-Romeo dealers were spending, but they'd have blown up. In the programme we outlined, every dealer worked out what he needed to invest and calculated the returns. As it happened, they invested more than Fr400 million."

National advertising campaign based on research into cultural values

Volvo France still had to attract customers into its showrooms in the first place. Its French advertising agency had put a Volvo car in the grounds of a castle and called it a *carrosse* (royal carriage). The 340 had been lifted by helicopter and perched atop a red rock against an Arizonian backdrop. Carstedt saw no point and no intelligible message. No one could tell him what it was supposed to mean.

Despite warnings that the French were unconcerned with safety and with Volvo's sober values, he decided to find out. Research from RISC, a Paris company, showed that, on the contrary, safety and reliability were values very much to the fore among French people at the leading edge of emerging values. These values were of more than sufficient strength to sustain an appeal for quality cars.

Another study showed that, given a choice between luxury, sportiness, relaxing, good service, modern technology, sober reliability, multipurpose and safety, 41.2 per cent of the French sample put sober reliability in their top two choices. Another 30.6 per cent put safety first. No other descriptions scored as well as these. With 10,000 killed annually on French roads, Swedish values were relevant after all.

Advertising to sell cultural values

These advertisements were clever plays on words, which the French love. But they also reconcile dilemmas and integrate values. One advertisement reads: "Performance is measured in seconds ... and also in years", and the copy below tells you that Volvos last many years longer. Another shows a little girl strapped safely in the back seat of a car. The caption reads: "You need to protect the future, especially when the future is behind you." Carstedt believes that there is nothing in the world that is more important than keeping your children safe. He also appreciates the strategic use of time, configuring the future and the past in the present, rather than extended in a straight line. The care we take today makes the future and the past we carry with us into a resource.

At the annual advertising awards ceremony, Volvo's campaign won the top prize in the automotive division. It seemed the French could respond to safety after all.

But the biggest marketing effort is inside the corporation

In September 1984 Carstedt invited the entire French dealer network, together with their wives, to visit Sweden and see key Volvo facilities. "80 per cent of our marketing efforts are internal ... to help dealers assume the Volvo identity and take pride in the quality of the vehicles and see that their own service is an inseparable part of this."

The chartered plane landed at Gothenberg where they visited the Torslanda factory. "Later we gave out prizes to our best dealers in front of our own president and senior managers and showed off our latest models and what was on the drawing board."

An unusual corporate ritual

"The next day we booked our own train and took it through some of the most beautiful parts of the Swedish countryside passing Skövde where we took them to the engine factory. The place is immaculately clean. The workers are young and attractive – many are women – and it is high-tech, high-touch and electronics. We then took them up to Old Stockholm to see the sights, and from there to a Viking party where we drank schnapps, wore helmets, ate with our fingers and threw the debris over our shoulders.

"For lunch the next day we gathered in Stockholm City Hall, where Swedish fiddlers in traditional costume and singers of folk music fêted the guests. At that point I gave a speech. My French was never too successful, but I think they gave me points for trying. I said: 'For two years now I've been trying to explain to you that there is something special about Volvo: our philosophy and values are important to our success. And to understand Volvo, it helps to understand something about Sweden. So we've invited you on this trip to see our factories, to meet our people, to see our lakes, forests, trees and houses for yourselves. Now we're here, in the heart of Sweden, in the room where the Nobel dinners are served before the prizes are given, and you have the Nobel menus before you to remind you that this is the place that gives hospitality to the greatest achievements and the finest quality of which all of you can be a part.' "

New organizational structure and communications system

Earlier, in January 1984, Carstedt had introduced a new regional organization for Volvo France. "We had to get closer to the dealers, not just psychologically but geographically. France is a large country. If you want the importer to be responsive to dealers, rather than throw his weight about, it helps to regionalize." Four regional offices now serve the dealers closest to them.

A year later he launched an electronic dealer communications network. This allowed dealers to ask each other and the regional offices for help and advice.

"We focused on people, activities and relationships and not primarily on the product. The product was the context of our work, but its people, and the services they provide, are what add value to a distribution company.

"I love French culture but I am also critical of it ... It is still very hierarchical. The way our kids were treated in school, for example. The disparaging remarks made by teachers to parents in the presence of their children shocked us. My son, Peter, came home shaking after being publicly humiliated ... and yet they get children to learn far more than you imagine them capable of. But it's still *le patron, le chef* ... authority, it seems, is seen as a permanent attribute of personality. For Swedes it is assumed or laid aside depending on what you know and whether the situation makes that knowledge relevant."

France without the hierarchies?

"This is not just my opinion. I consulted André Laurent, the French cultural researcher at Insead, and he gave me his comparisons between Sweden and France on issues of authority (Table 8.1, p. 166). Notice that over half the French managers feel they 'have to know the answers', although this is increasingly hard as business grows more complex. Nearly three-quarters believe that

Table 8.1 **Attitudes towards management: France and Sweden compared**

	Agreement (per cent)	
	Swedish	French
It is important for a manager to have at hand precise answers to most of the questions that his subordinates may raise about their work	10	53
When subordinates are given more freedom and more possibilities to take own initiatives, it is necessary to strengthen the control of their work at the same time	38	71
Personal relationships between managers and their subordinates should normally be avoided	20	64
It is preferable that private life and work is kept clearly apart	32	68

Source: André Laurent, *The Cultural Diversity of Management Conceptions,* Insead, 1982.

you can't give subordinates local initiatives without also increasing controls, 64 per cent avoid personal relationships, while 68 per cent clearly separate their work life from their private life.

"I was determined to counter all these tendencies. I believe Swedish attitudes are more conducive to the highest levels of customer service, but I also knew from my Paris days and from my experience of human nature that people will respond to being respected by those who lead them. Information is power. Give your subordinates all the information you can and facilitate its sharing among them and they will seek responsibility and achieve it.

"The effect was marvellous to watch. The young French cadres were just incredibly bright, curious, intelligent and flexible and their energy was unbelievable. I believe you get more out of a culture if you seek to correct its weaknesses than if you simply go along with them. I had to use my influence at head office to transfer some Swedish managers who were not responding fast enough to Volvo France. I wasn't going to let that energy flag."

A new corporate ethic: "we", not "them"
Carstedt also declared war on all memos designed to record excuses and cover backs. "I want to see no memos of that kind at all … none! Damn

it, I want you to go to that person and help him solve the problem, get a grip on it and on that person, so you really work together in finding the answer, and when you've found it, let others know, too, because we're here to learn and to teach each other." Carstedt created two symbols to convey his point. One had a square of four fingers pointing out what is wrong with the other; the second had four hands grasping each others wrists in genuine support.

"What I think I did was to redefine the word 'we'. 'We' were now the importers and the dealers working together, no longer 'us' and 'them'. People kept asking me in the early days, 'How can we motivate them?' That's the wrong question. It's how can we stop demotivating them, how can we stop trying to get them to do what we only talk about? It becomes 'we' when you start removing the obstacles and start responding to their agendas. Instead of this interminable 'it's your fault, no it's your fault', I invited all concerned to focus on the relationship and asked, 'How can we build and improve our relationship?'"

Cultures are patterns
Carstedt sees corporate culture as patterns which keep repeating themselves. The relationship between Volvo Sweden and Volvo France is repeated in the relationship between Volvo France and its dealers, and is repeated again in the relationships between dealers and customers. If Volvo Sweden responds to Volvo France, then the latter can respond to dealers, dealers can respond to customers and *le client c'est le roi*.

You do not "motivate", you show
But failure at any level will ramify throughout. "You won't get your people to care about customers unless you show your people that you care about them. They'll pass on your concern. You don't 'motivate' your employees, you show them the concern you want them to express to customers."

Innovations as part of the learning process
Carstedt also introduced a steady stream of innovations, many at the request of dealers and customers. There were studies of 'ownership economy' designed to reduce repair costs and obtain lower insurance costs because of Volvo's safety record, improvements in second-hand values were plotted and distributed, and the car rental market was breached.

New technology was brought in and Minitel, the French data network, was used more effectively, deliveries speeded up, automatic payments through computers introduced, credit control improved, the administration of warranties overhauled, expert systems supplied to dealers to use in their computers and so on. The innovations were ceaseless. All were part of an ongoing dialogue of learning from each other.

Carstedt moves on

Carstedt left France in mid-1986 to become president of Volvo Svenska Bil and then has moved on to head the North American operations of AKEO, the Swedish furniture exporter. But the sequel to this story is sad. No sooner had Carstedt left Volvo France than the "spirit of Volvo" began to ebb. By the end of 1986 market share was already slightly down; thereafter it fell steadily until, by the end of 1988, it was back to the level of 1983 (see Figure 8.1).

Carstedt points out that, although market share fell, overall sales did not, since the entire market was buoyant. Hence the dealers did not lose money on their investments and Volvo's sales are still well up on 1983. Nevertheless, the tendency of a culture to revert to the form most typical of its macro-culture should not be underestimated. It needs continuous effort to go against a national trend and, when "the strange Swede" stopped intervening, business-as-usual returned to some extent.

Carstedt's successor was not of the same ilk. He preferred hierarchy and control. The dialogues dried up and the numbers turned down. The oasis of relative egalitarianism and close personal relationships had been created in a culture which did not give those values as much support and, without Carstedt there to pump the bellows, the flame died. This is a tribute to the skill of a single leader. But it also shows the fragility of a corporate culture when its architect moves on.

Management models

Carstedt is developing additional concepts which help to account for the successes Volvo and he have enjoyed.

"I picked up from the university that you have to have a theory and a hypothesis. The world simply can't be made sense of, facts can't be organized, unless you have a mental model to begin with. That theory does not have to be the right one, because you can alter it along the way as information comes in. But you can't begin to learn without some concept that gives you expectations or

Figure 8.1 New registrations 1978–88: Volvo's market share in France

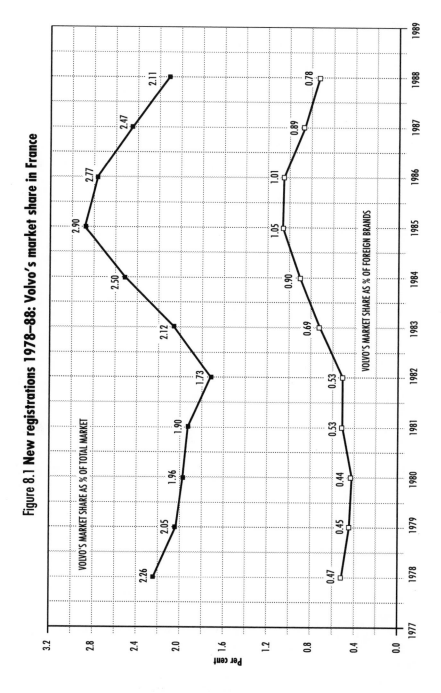

hypotheses. The very condition of expecting something alerts you to the fact that it's happening or, more important, that it's not happening. We learn in contrast to what we anticipate. Our theory becomes our strategy, our hypotheses become policies, directives and advice, facts grow from implementations as new insights, resources and structures grow from revised hypotheses. As the learning circle revolves, we conceptualize, sell, listen and interpret and then think again." (See Figure 8.2.)

He sees leadership as a bridge. It can join theories with facts, strategies with implementation, ideas with their execution, thinking with doing

Figure 8.2 **Goran Carstedt's learning system**

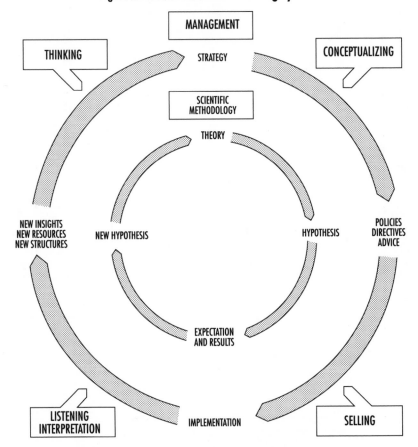

The inner circle represents the theoretical operations of a science.
The outer circle is the management equivalent.

and brain with muscle. The leader is there to make sure that people learn by contrasting one side with the other, modifying each accordingly.

CONCLUSION

Between 1982, when Carstedt arrived, and mid-1986, when he left, Volvo dealers in France increased their expenditure on upgrading their own facilities tenfold, from Fr3–4 million to Fr30–40 million. Sales doubled from 10,800 cars a year to 21,000. The number of cars on display rose by 80 per cent, salesmen doubled, mechanics increased by 80 per cent. Volvo had a 0.5 per cent market share in 1982. This more than doubled to 1.05 per cent at the end of 1985. Its share of imported cars rose from 1.7 per cent to 2.9 per cent. All this happened in a market for cars which fell 20 per cent overall. Turnover was up from Fr462 million to Fr1,034 million. From 1980 to 1982 profit after tax averaged minus Fr13 million. From 1983 to 1985 profit before tax averaged Fr19 million. In January/June 1982 Volvo was 14th in the league of car importers; by January/June 1985 it was ninth, increasing its share by 65.4 per cent and overtaking Mercedes, Datsun, Mazda, Alfa-Romeo and Toyota in the process. The only other company to do as well was GM with a completely new model.

While Carstedt's synthesis between cooperating and competing was a powerful one, he at least had the Swedish macro-culture on his side. Sweden, too, is an interesting example of social democratic capitalism, and he utilized this fact to woo the French.

A DIAGRAMMATIC SUMMARY

When Goran Carstedt came to Volvo France, he confronted a dispirited organization complete with its own "mythology of failure", with dealerships which passed on to the customers the distance and disdain with which they were treated by a foreign company which knew nothing of France and its "Latin temperament". Dealers had invested little in their dealerships because they had little confidence in the future value of their relationship with Volvo, which then blamed them for investing so little. The circle was clearly a vicious one (see Figure 8.3, p. 172).

This vicious cycle is full of mutual antagonisms.
1. "Cold" Swedes affronting "hot" Latins.
2. Importers talking down to dealers who refuse to invest.

Figure 8.3 **Volvo France: a vicious circle**

(1) a foreign importer "cold", melancholic and dull

(3) so customers purchased very few cars, perpetuating the impression of ...

(2) talked down to its dealers threatening to replace them

(2) the dealers failed to invest in their showrooms

(3) who passed on this indifference to customers

(1) who being "hot" and romantic would not buy a car anyway

Figure 8.4 **Volvo France: a virtuous circle**

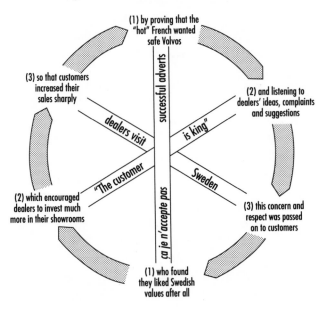

(1) by proving that the "hot" French wanted safe Volvos

(3) so that customers increased their sales sharply

(2) and listening to dealers' ideas, complaints and suggestions

successful adverts

dealers visit

is king"

"The customer

Sweden

ça je n'accepte pas

(2) which encouraged dealers to invest much more in their showrooms

(3) this concern and respect was passed on to customers

(1) who found they liked Swedish values after all

3. Customers treated badly by dealers and not buying.

Carstedt joined the severed ropes by several bold initiatives.

1. He refused to accept "hot–cold" myths, establishing by an advertising campaign that enough French people wanted Swedish values.
2. He used "the customer is king" and the model showroom to raise considerably dealer investment in showrooms.
3. He treated the dealers with social democratic respect and invited them to Sweden.

The result was a virtuous circle (Figure 8.4).

Almost at once the system began to learn and to develop with more listening, more respect passed on to customers, more money spent on showrooms and thus more cars were purchased. The process is helical (Figure 8.5).

Figure 8.5 **Volvo France: a developmental helix**

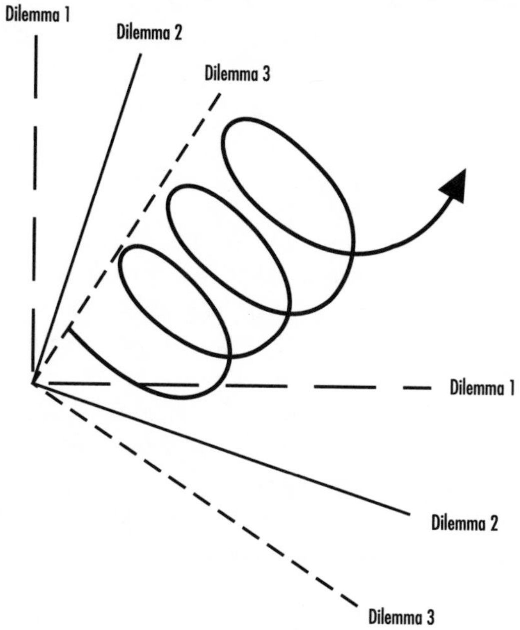

Chapter 9

THE CASTLE OF CARE:
NORTH AMERICAN TOOL AND DIE

SUMMARY

The North American Tool and Die company (NATD) is now widely considered to be the best job-shop for high-precision tool and die making in the world. This is a result of a home-grown, but internally consistent management culture, which promotes free speech and substantial rewards for quality work and innovative ideas and encourages employees to perform to the highest standards as acts of affection for each other, viewing NATD as a family resource. The culture turned a company with low morale into one where the 95 or so jobs are widely sought after, absenteeism is almost nil and quality is supremely high.

THE STUDY

The castle of care

The company is strategically located in San Leandro, south of Oakland, on the edge of California's Silicon Valley. It is housed in a rather undistinguished building in the warehouse sprawl that covers much of the South Bay. Yet, by reputation, NATD is a bright jewel in the USA's increasingly tarnished industrial crown. Ever since Tom Peters and Bob Waterman made a public television sequel to their work on excellence in corporations and pronounced the company "excellent", the managing director, Tom Melohn, has been fighting off admirers. "We don't show people around the factory any more ... the folks felt like goldfish. There isn't much to see anyway. Of course, customers are shown around, but we've stopped the tourists."

"I don't read them [says Melohn, gesturing at the books above his desk]. It's not that I don't agree with what they say ... They're very kind to me. I'm afraid that if I start to pick up all those buzzwords – 'Theory Z', 'quality circle', 'management by walking around' – I'll screw up my gut. God gave me a set of beliefs and they work. They are not for everyone, nor for everywhere, and they don't work for punk rockers, but they work here and now and for the foreseeable future – I hope. If I start using fancy ideas I could lose the respect of the folks that work here."

Melohn is perhaps the least academic but most successful person included in this book. Yet he possesses a powerful personal philosophy which is far less interested in articulating beliefs than in acting out their detailed implications. He is that rare creature, an idealist not enamoured of the ideas themselves but highly involved in the particular people they point to. "He who would do good must do it in minute particulars," wrote William Blake, and Melohn is a remarkable exemplar of that axiom.

The value of personal touch

When interviewed for this book, Melohn came into the office late with a dozen boxes of doughnuts he had personally bought for the workforce. Doughnuts with pay cheques is part of the ceremony held on the last Friday of each month. It is a small gesture of appreciation among the dozens of personal notes and appreciative words which pervade the company. Such sustained levels of mutual admiration might feel uncomfortable if the tension was not persistently relieved by a corporate sense of humour, which Melohn personifies. A mobile made of rejected parts dangles from the ceiling above his desk, "Valuable because they are so rare". There is a safety helmet with horns and a siren, so that the employees who gave it to him can hear him coming. A collection of cartoons includes a well-dressed New Yorker exclaiming, "Help, I'm trapped inside a banker!" and a boss saying to his subordinate, "Come in, Frank, I've been eager to communicate downwards to you".

Melohn explained that Plant 30 had just opened. "We call it that so some dumb buyer will think there are 29 others ... before we tell him." The small San Leandro office is called "The World Headquarters".

Background of a leader

Melohn explained how he came to buy the company with his partner, Garner Beckett.

"When I was a kid, the others collected baseball cards. I knew the names of the people running the *Fortune* 500. Don't ask me why. I dreamt of running a major consumer package goods company and did everything I could to realize that. But the closer I got to the top, the clearer it became that my idols had clay feet, round heels or no heels at all. It was an evolutionary shock. I tried to get out with the help of venture capitalists but couldn't. When I was passed over for president I said to hell with it and quit. No more quiet desperation ... that was 1977. I still can't tolerate the way major corporations treat their people. I decided to do it differently myself.

"I was fascinated by Silicon Valley, then growing at 30 per cent per year. But if you are like me and can't screw on a number plate or operate a tea-urn, you're likely to be captured by your 'French chef', that's the star employee who wants 20 per cent of your profits now, 50 per cent next year and leaves the year after to set up his own company with your money. Besides, Garner and I didn't have the capital to break into computers, so we settled for a job-shop supplying precision parts to the Valley. There was an ad for NATD in the *Wall Street Journal*. God moves mysteriously."

The strategy: growth and quality ...

While Melohn's ideas have to be inferred from the rich corporate culture he has created, he began with a clear strategy and simple philosophy whose sophistication is in its implementation, not its basics. The strategy was to grow as Silicon Valley expanded and, as competition hotted up and the Japanese made inroads, to supply the rising demands for quality, precision, service and prompt delivery at the lowest cost. NATD is now an integral part of its clients' competitive edge in world-class products.

Melohn has won enough respect to choose his clients carefully and to eliminate what economists call "opportunism" from his strategic alliances. He will only supply companies which:

1. are growing faster than their industry;
2. are "decent people" to work with and honour their agreements;
3. pay their bills promptly.

... required a culture of respect and attention to detail

To the best of his knowledge, NATD is sole supplier to its clients. He delivers "just in time" if required. But Melohn has succeeded, not so much because his ideas are better, but by showing his workers such respect and affection that he taps deep, latent reserves of skill, ingenuity, zest, creativity and a capacity for painstaking precision. In a sense his technical incompetence is his forte. He has to respect "the gang" as he calls them. He has to delegate and trust, and his gratitude to those who compensate for his own deficiencies is heartfelt.

"The person actually doing the job knows it better than anyone, and if you treat them as you would like to be treated yourself, then the whole company will learn what that person knows and has discovered. [The room starts to shake as Melohn's hand bangs monotonously down upon the surface of his desk.] That's a punch press," he explains. "It does that 40 times a minute, eight hours a day, five days a week. I lack the skill to operate it. I'd go crazy if I tried. What I can do is create a context where the person who does that for me and the rest of us knows that we really appreciate it. On the genuine quality of that appreciation depends the quality of his work. This country had better learn that, or rather remember it, because it's not just Japanese, hell it's American! Unless we recapture that part of our heritage, we'll go down the tubes commercially."

Melohn was never taught about corporate culture

No one seems to have taught Melohn how to make a corporate culture coherent, or how to organize a "learning community". Everything he does is home-grown and its internal consistency appears to be a consequence of his own integrity writ large, and the result of relationships in which his subordinates speak out. "If you don't understand, yell! If you don't agree, yell! We'll work it out between us."

The company has an ESOP (employee share ownership programme) in which all of the 70 or so employees over the age of 21 share the company's earnings. The younger ones get a cash equivalent. The stock is distributed free each year and acts as a powerful confirmation and appreciation of the company's growing quality. Melohn and his partner do not dilute the share pool. "I'm not really interested in money as money," he admits. "Now the profit I'll fight for, because that's my score card." Melohn is notorious for his $15 red trousers and his 1985 Olds truck in its non-reserved parking space.

But the culture also rewards quality in the short term. Every four weeks the company awards $50 and an engraved plaque to the "superperson of the month" who has made the greatest contribution. Melohn is especially on the lookout for innovative ideas, not the kind dropped into suggestion boxes, but those worked through to practical application. When one worker realized he could fit a tight part if he first cooled it in the refrigerator, his cheque and his plaque were presented to him by ceremoniously opening an ice-box door. The worker who thought of a completely new way of storing material had the building named after him.

Corporate rituals ...

The monthly ceremonies follow Melohn's axiom "have fun", but they have other purposes. Loyalty is rewarded by silver dollars, presented on each anniversary of an employee's stay with the company. The monthly statistics on quality, productivity and costs are read out, whether better or worse than was hoped. Everyone knows the company's strategy and learns of the extent to which it is being attained. Praise from customers and the press is also shared and is posted with the plaques, where employees rather than customers can see it.

But Melohn is careful that he does not reward substantial innovations with symbols alone or nominal payments. For the employee who automated a whole sequence of steps there was a genuine share of the gain the company had realized, as indeed there was for the person who developed a method of attaching twelve fasteners in a single operation. Where a group has worked on a valuable idea, everyone in the group shares the gain.

... and special events

Occasionally there is a major event. The Japanese president and vice-president of New United Motor Manufacturing, the joint venture between Toyota and GM, visited NATD with a whole retinue. Melohn consulted the Japanese cook at his wife's sushi shop and constructed a large sign reading *"Yo-Ko-So Irashai-mashita"* (welcome to our new partners). His visitors told him that the quality he had provided was better than that available in Japan or anywhere else in the USA and they shook hands with the employees who had done it.

"You should have seen us! We were 10 feet tall. Hell, we are a small company and they are giants. I've never had a visit from as much as a vice-president of one of our US customers. Yet the Japanese came down en bloc to say thank you to a job-shop.

"Do you know NUMMI? That used to be the worst plant in the whole GM system: the highest level of strikes and stoppages, the highest grievances, the worst safety, absenteeism and turnover and the worst quality and productivity. So they closed the plant and fired 5,000 workers. Then Toyota offered them a joint venture and they had to reopen. They rehired 3,000 of the same 'trouble makers' and now they're the best plant in the whole GM system on the very same criteria. Productivity is 50 per cent higher in the joint venture than in other GM plants. If they treated their workers the way they treated ours on the day they visited, I know why they turned around."

Melohn takes care to circulate throughout the whole company every letter of congratulation that is received, annotated in his own inimitable style.

Melohn has recently invented a ceremony that symbolizes everyone's reliance upon others. Along with the doughnuts, he distributes pay cheques at random, but with each person's name on the envelope. The recipient must then find the person to whom the envelope belongs and hand it to him or her. "That person made your own pay cheque possible," Melohn tells them. "In reality you are paying each other."

He wants the company to be seen as a resource by all of its employees. Accordingly, any worker can apply to borrow a company truck at the weekend for moving house or belongings. If insurers are slow to pay any employee, the company throws its weight and its telephone calls behind the case. There was a recent search for a Korean-speaking doctor for a Korean employee with complaints he found hard to describe in English.

A learning culture

No one has told Melohn that the latest fashion on the consulting circuit is to have employers pay for skills rather than for particular jobs, and that the versatile, multi-skilled employee can be used more flexibly. Once again he has got there by himself, with the help of the gang. His people never stop learning, unless they want to. There are night classes on the premises run by Chabot College for those who want to advance, and there is job rotation for everyone who wants it. Melohn celebrates those who came as sweepers and now manage.

But do you not get ripped off if you are so kind and nice? ...

Most business people will be aware of the appalling results of wilful attempts by members of institutions to be nice to each other.

"Surely NATD is going to have its generosity exploited? Nice guys finish last, and all that? All the publicity and the hoopla will flatten you as customers and admirers rush to the sunshine company. Don't employees raise their expectations of you faster than you can fulfil them? What's to stop your ego being hyped with admiration? Don't customers see your kindness as 'weakness' and promptly screw you to the wall?"

Melohn is thoughtful.

"On the subject of my ego, I will only say that I'm married, with children whom I enjoy, but who remind me that my philosophy does not work with everyone. I limit public appearances to one a month. The gang does not expect too much, partly because the publicity doesn't occur in the media they see or read, partly because the US blue-collar worker is a long way from being indulged in our society, but mostly because we select our people very carefully."

... not necessarily

"From 300 applications I interview around 20, and we take two, sometimes three. I look for neatness in the application and completion, because that is the kind of work they will have to do. I look for membership in churches, any church or synagogue, community chests, little leagues, scouts. I want people to give to their communities, not just get. If they come for an interview I have them interview me about the company. Their questions tell me a lot. Are they assertive? Are they curious? Do they care? And we have 'engagement parties' where they come in to work for a day at our expense and we see if we like them.

"But you are right about some of our customers. They think we're too decent and nice to be tough ... and they're wrong. Certain vendors believe that, because they are large and we are small, they can float on what they owe us. They can't. Our terms are payment within 30 days. After 34 days we stop the shipment of their parts. It's simple. They break their word. We stop doing business.

"Because we're sole suppliers, each party is vulnerable to the other's pressure tactics. There has to be trust. I had a $2 million vendor in this office in 1984 who tried to screw me to the wall on price, after we'd agreed. We had a discussion. I cursed him out of the room and told him not to come back for three years. He laughed, 'You can't turn down a contract this size!' 'Wrong,' I told him. 'What I can't afford is to work for a company that breaks its word. Please inflict yourself on my competitors.'

"That was three years ago, and last week they were back. It's not only wrong values, it's stupidity, because I'd stand this whole company on its ear for an honourable customer like Hewlett Packard. If they have an emergency they can count on us."

This is no Eden

"But this place is no Eden. We discovered sex last month. We have an open telephone line the employees can use. The rule is no long-distance calls and they stick to that, but a few weeks ago we got a bill from one of those 'dial-for-porn' outfits, and I wanted to know who had done it, and they knew and they wouldn't say. But the man I suspected resigned a month later, so perhaps they took care of it in their own way. I wouldn't have fired him myself."

Also, in some ways, Melohn's very kindness can become coercive by engendering in workers a very strong sense of personal responsibility, with guilt if anything goes wrong. He told the following story.

"I meet every Wednesday with the head toolmaker, and we go over each project to make sure we're coming in on budget and on time. We got to one of them recently and he said, 'Boss, we're going to be late.' I said, 'What's the matter?' He said, 'Jay is working on this one, and we can't lick it.' So I said, 'OK, let's get him and the engineers in here and figure out where we're in trouble and how to solve it. Then I'll call the customer.' Now Jay is 34 or 35, has two kids and a wife who sells Tupperware. He came in with the engineers, we had our meeting, then, after the engineers left, he stood in the doorway of my office and started to cry. And he said, 'I'm sorry I screwed up your record 100 per cent on time delivery.'

"How do you pay him for that? Here's the part. It's three-thousandths of an inch thick. That is so thin that the metal on one part of the die hits the metal on the other part of the die. It's almost impossible to make, and we did it in one die. Other people would tackle it with two or three dies. How do you pay a guy to make something like that? Jay is making $16.00 an hour here, but he could go elsewhere and easily get $17.50. Even so, he stays here. He cares."

Not that tears are unusual in NATD. Melohn cries frequently and unashamedly, most noticeably on public television when asked to describe the efforts of his people to work to microscopic tolerances.

To do Melohn justice, he does not reproach his workers individually for failure. He believes that responsibility must be shared. A foreman explained:

"I made a quotation on one part that was much lower than the time it actually took. The company lost money. I had the feeling that everyone tried to solve the problem as if he had made the mistake. They weren't all saying, 'Bruce made the mistake, and he's going to solve it.' The whole tool room tried to figure out what to do to solve the problem. I didn't feel guilty that I had made a big mistake. Their attitude was, 'You made this quotation, but I was there, and I thought the same thing. I didn't change my mind until I saw that there was something wrong with it.'"

Melohn does not believe in safety manuals and establishing official policies. He has had fluorescent orange stickers designed which read: "We care about you! Please be careful!". Because people get used to these if they are stuck in one place, he sticks them on each job order in a different place so that the reminder is constant. Accidents, turnover and absenteeism are now almost nil. The hundreds of applicants lined up for every vacancy remind employees of what they have, a most unusual culture.

The operating results ...

Tom Melohn not only mixes toughness in with his tenderness, he has the hard results which vindicate his soft orientation. The company he bought with Beckett was marginally profitable in 1978. It had low morale, poor safety and high turnover. Within four years Melohn could report in the *Harvard Business Review* that sales had gone from $1.8 million to $6 million, pre-tax earnings were up 600 per cent, the price of stock had risen by 30 per cent or more each year, the reject rate was down from 5.0 to 0.03 per cent (it stood at 0.01 per cent in 1988) and turnover had fallen from 27 to 3 per cent. In addition accidents had virtually ceased.

... and some reservations

Melohn's dislike of rubricizing what he does may have the result that what grew with his personality could die with it. Ideas about relationships certainly lack the life and immediacy of those relationships, but they are more generalizable and can teach "at a distance".

There is also a danger that the celebrations of Melohn's tenderness may miss the tough side of him. Customers play his game and honour his values or they do not play. Only cooperative people are recruited to NATD. It is not reformatory. Melohn is good enough to get his way with the environment. But his oasis of honour is tenaciously guarded and liars are cast out.

A DIAGRAMMATIC SUMMARY

In this particular chapter no vicious circle was encountered. North American Tool and Die was a stunning success by the time the research was conducted. Yet enough is known of the kind of pressures to which such small job-shops are submitted and what some companies tried to do to NATD to enable a fairly accurate picture of the vicious circle that might have been to be constructed (Figure 9.1).

It was shown that some customers try to cheat their job-shops, reducing agreed prices and often paying months late. Yet Melohn helped his workers meet exacting standards by binding them together with bonds of intense mutual respect and affection.

Figure 9.1 **North American Tool and Die: a vicious circle**

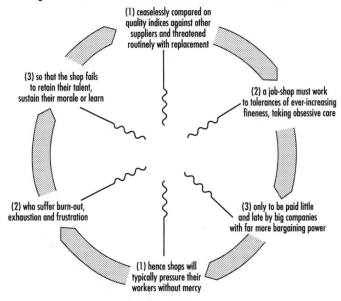

1. He publicly rejoiced in 99 per cent plus quality ratings, plastering his shop with letters of appreciation from customers.
2. A "superperson of the month" and gain sharing scheme celebrated a continuing capacity to meet and surpass challenges.
3. Banishing exploitative customers from his sight allowed Melohn to pass on to workers decent treatment by his clients'.

This is the virtuous circle (see Figure 9.2, p. 184).

Such success if self-intensifying, self-perpetuating and constitutes a helical growth dynamic (see Figure 9.3, p. 184).

Figure 9.2 **North American Tool and Die: a virtuous circle**

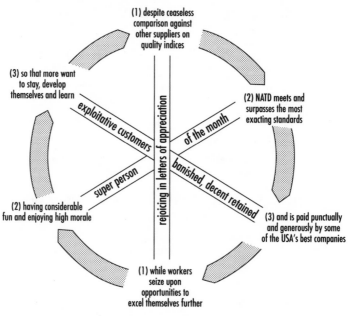

(1) despite ceaseless comparison against other suppliers on quality indices

(3) so that more want to stay, develop themselves and learn

(2) NATD meets and surpasses the most exacting standards

exploitative customers

of the month

rejoicing in letters of appreciation

banished, decent retained

super person

(2) having considerable fun and enjoying high morale

(3) and is paid punctually and generously by some of the USA's best companies

(1) while workers seize upon opportunities to excel themselves further

Figure 9.3 **North American Tool and Die: a developmental helix**

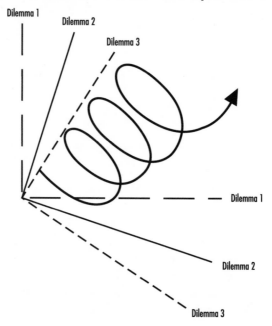

Dilemma 1

Dilemma 2

Dilemma 3

Dilemma 1

Dilemma 2

Dilemma 3

Chapter 10

WHERE ANGELS FEAR: INTERVENING TO CHANGE A CORPORATE CULTURE

It is possible to intervene to change a corporate culture. The method involves a cumulative investigation into values, myths and rituals, using interviewing and group discussion. This process provides a clear understanding of the cultural paradigms of how a corporation functions, and how it learns from its environment. At this point the parameters of business can be shifted away from unilateral manipulation of objects into multilateral sympathetic systems that allow rapid innovation and feedback. This chapter examines how to alter a corporate culture.

MODES OF INTERVENTION

Changing a culture to increase a corporation's effectiveness is a hazardous undertaking. Consultants have an advantage in seeing corporate dynamics as vivid, unanticipated and different. Long-term members of a culture may take it all for granted and be so accustomed to some limiting conditions as to regard these as necessary and normal. But if outsiders see more, they can usually do less, since they are not well known or trusted. Attempts to change culture depend on liking and trusting your colleagues.

In this chapter, cultural change will be considered as a process in which consultants help a CEO to act. It will be assumed that consultants make the discoveries and map the culture, while an influential insider, preferably but not necessarily the CEO or managing director, implements those changes. Appendix 1 shows what kind of help is available.

Table 10.1 (see p. 186) shows the fundamental process of culture intervention and management.

1. FIND THE DANGERS

> Locating the black sheep ➔ elicits cultural taboos and violations ➔ enabling you to tread more carefully.

"Fools rush in where angels fear to tread" is a well-known saying that could apply to many attempts to modify a corporate culture without

Table 10.1 **The mechanics of culture change**

Modes of intervention	Cultural phenomena elicited	Cultural change induced
1. Locate the black sheep	Taboos and violations	You can now tread more safely
2. Interview and observe	Values, conflicts and dilemmas	Substitute dilemmas for social conflicts
3. Review findings with group	Theatrical and dramatic scenes	Suggest happy endings
4. Review past and present history	Surface myths, stories, scenarios	Reinterpret myths, retell stories
5. Explore all higher logical types	Metaphors, images, symbols, ceremonies and rituals	Revision, create new images and symbols, renew rituals
6. Discover logics by which current system learns	"Old" paradigms of manipulating employees and customers unilaterally	New paradigms and epistemologies created for better innovation and quicker learning

adequate understanding of its dynamics. Cultures of even the most benign variety can turn very nasty when their patterns are violated. An important principle to remember is that the strength of a culture is best and quickest discovered by violating it. Since you cannot violate a culture and remain credible or welcome within it, you must discover what taboos have been broken and what were the settled opinions which were violated. You may need to study the corporation's "black sheep" to discover, what they did to make people so upset. This will tell you which carpets are wired, where the bodies are buried, who and what are not mentioned.

Locating black sheep was especially important for the two sets of consultants considered in Chapter 3, for the culturally "shocking" behaviour of drafting the contract in Chapter 5 and for a leader like Goran Carstedt (see Chapter 8) who came into French culture as an outsider.

There was a taboo, for example, against admitting how bad things were at Volvo France, and an even stronger taboo against accepting responsibility for the situation. Carstedt could have blasted these defences and insisted that what worked in Sweden could suit the Latin temperament fine. He could have told dealers straight out what they needed to invest. But he did neither of these things. He asked questions, used humour to show that Volvo was virtually unknown, and created his own model of what a dealership could look like. This allowed enthusiasm to develop and investment to be volunteered.

The author of this book and his consulting colleagues faced even stronger taboos in the Western Oil safety case (see Chapter 3). "Tough" drivers did not show solicitude or fear and they not only refused to "snitch" on each others' violations of safety regulations, they would have sanctioned anyone who did so. Had the consultants said straight out, "You ought to care", or simply ordered the drivers to expose violators, their reaction would have been angry and emphatic. Similarly, in the Fairmont plant of Annheuser-Busch, Royal Foote faced strong revulsion against "cosy relationships" between managers and unionized workers. Had he instructed them to increase their levels of social intimacy, he could have been run out of town on the proverbial rail.

Violations can be useful

The reason violation is so useful is that it makes the "invisible" nature of culture visible. So long as everyone complies, culture may not be articulated. Its rules remain hidden. Those intuitively obeying these rules may even be unable to articulate them, so much have they blended with the scenery. But, when a taboo is broken, the trip-wire releases a flare. The miscreant is revealed to all in a sudden illumination and shocked voices exclaim "We don't do that here!"

The cultural rules at GM

An example of considerable insight achieved by flouting rules was John Z. de Lorean's deliberate violations at General Motors. His transgressions enabled him to discover just how strong were the basic assumptions listed below, all of which were brought forcibly to his attention.

- A company the size of GM can largely have its own way with its environment.

- Power relationships with subordinates, suppliers, dealers and sub-contractors are legitimate ways of transacting business. Those with clout should use it.
- Human nature responds well to large monetary rewards or punishments tied to short-term profits.
- GM as an entity is more important than the personalities of those who serve it, who should efface themselves accordingly.
- Years of dutiful subordination give to those promoted the right to inflict on their subordinates similar humiliations.
- What cannot be easily counted and monitored by the finance department is not important, i.e. safety, quality, customer satisfaction.

De Lorean attacked all these cultural rules. He publicly proclaimed that mediocrities not achievers were being promoted so that the boss promoting could maximize his power. He denounced short-termism and derided group-think. He talked back to superiors and campaigned for better quality and safety. While, with hindsight, nearly all his criticisms were justified, the way he tried to change the culture was a total disaster and ended, predictably enough, in his own forced resignation. Shouting your opposition to your corporation's culture is the quickest road to martyrdom rather than success. You simply taunt the culture until it destroys you. De Lorean's subsequent adventures in Northern Ireland and the catastrophe of his gull-wing sports car also suggest that his chief talents were theatrical. His self-celebratory protests were no more viable and effective than the culture he attacked. Nevertheless, a black sheep like de Lorean can tell a more subtle interventionist a great deal about the culture in which he was operating.

Cultures are alive

It needs to be stressed that a corporate culture is alive. It is not a thing, not a harness or inert structure, and it is not a mechanism, although it may try hard to resemble one. It is a living system which will literally turn upon you in a friendly or unfriendly fashion when you try to handle it. It is as conscious as you are and will wonder what you are up to, even as you wonder about it.

A culture cannot be made to do anything. The most that can be done to corporate cultures is to trigger their own energies and directions. This is true even if you have the formal authority to give them orders. What should be the case according to the legal–rational definition of your "power" may not be the way the world really works.

"Black sheep" can also be used as foils by skilful change agents. Nick Georgiades (see Chapter 4) mocked British Airways's earlier military traditions. The aircraft "on parade" when they should have been flying, the pilots with "scrambled eggs" on their uniforms, were pointedly ridiculed. He engaged in building a more caring and spontaneous staff by attacking the methods by which social distance and formality had long been maintained.

Companies tend to define what they are by emphasizing what they are not. "The black sheep" has wittingly or otherwise confused these categories. Interviewers should:

- ask about any short tenures or abrupt departures;
- when embarrassment is reported seek its source;
- when someone loses a dispute try to find out why.

The main purpose of these inquiries is to avoid repeating the errors which marginalized the "black sheep". You can now tread more safely.

2. BRING CONFLICTS INTO THE OPEN

> Interview and observe ➜ to elicit value conflicts and dilemmas ➜ substitute for social conflict.

The interview is the heart of the process of investigating culture. Nothing is more important, and a successful outcome will depend on the skills of the interviewer. The interview can not only elicit the values in contention, but it is in itself a minor theatre or drama (stage 3) in which myths and stories surface (stage 4), metaphors, images and symbols arise (stage 5) and ways of learning are described (stage 6). Those who investigate culture are inevitably a part of that culture. There is no way they can avoid "interfering" with the culture being studied. Carrying a clip board and looking dispassionate and detached will elicit a dispassionate and detached response, and much of that culture's richness will be missed.

In the case of Annheuser–Busch (see Chapter 3), for example, interviewing and training others to interview in the same style was virtually the entire intervention. The consultants arranged for the first line supervisors to interview the hourly workers, the second line to interview the first line, and so on to top management. The effect was to draw information up into the organization from the lowest levels to the highest, to move what was merely inside individuals into the culture at large, and change it from "low context" (impoverished information) to "high context" (rich in information). Employees began to do their work better and communicate more effectively as they learned more about each other.

In short, the interview well conducted provides a model for improved human relations, as well as eliciting vital information which the culture needs to comprehend.

What is learned may be excluded from the culture

Interviews can reveal what the members of a culture believe as individuals. That is not necessarily the same as what they affirm as employees. Many corporate cultures greatly reduce the permissible variety of individual expression. The interviewees may be trying to use the interviewer as a messenger for what they are culturally constrained from saying. If this message is passed on it may cause offence, and its originators may deny authorship. Yet if it is not passed on those who gave it may feel betrayed. Indeed, this can constitute a serious trap for consultants (see box).

No need to mention dilemmas or conflicts

The author of this book uses interviews to elicit dilemmas and social conflicts. But there is no need to announce this. Indeed, people may be scared off or feel you are "looking for trouble", and social conflicts may be exacerbated. The dilemmas uncovered at Western Oil were volunteered while interviewees addressed their own concerns, not those of the interviewer.

What interviewers looking for dilemmas should do is naturally and without artifice be especially interested when a respondent hesitates, equivocates, expresses ambivalence or perplexity, experiences ambiguity or divided loyalties and/or admits to inner conflict. At the first sign of such experiences, these should be sympathetically explored and the dilemma will take shape. Here, for example, is a statement from a driver with Western Oil:

"Management keeps yelling that we won't only kill ourselves but the whole depot could go up in an explosion. The only way to stop that, they say, is turn each other in for any offence against the safety rules we see. Hell, I'm not a stool pigeon! And I don't snitch on friends. Still it's true that we could all go up in flames, thanks to one clotsy character."

The consultants' nightmare

Two consultants were hired by an independent college of a US state university to recommend ways of removing friction within the faculty and in the faculty's relationship with the administration. They were to report to the dean who was their contractual client. They interviewed the parties concerned, who seemed to be holding something back. The fifth person to be interviewed, a senior professor, suddenly said, "the dean has to go". From then on virtually all the interviewees used the same phrase with various degrees of finality and vehemence.

It became clear not only that the dean was very unpopular but that the consultants were caught in an orchestrated strategy to get rid of him. Their plight was worsened when the dean gave a family party at his own house for the delivery of the consultants' report.

One of the consultants gave a heavily censored version of their findings, only to be interrupted half way through by the senior professor who had first demanded the dean's dismissal. He had taken the precaution, he said, of monitoring what many of those interviewed had told the consultants. A wise precaution, since this was a travesty of the true opinions of the faculty. Could anyone doubt that after this pretence was over the dean would be given the real report, a secret one? There was pandemonium.

Two weeks later the dean resigned. "I must take responsibility," he wrote to the faculty, "for the shockingly unprofessional conduct of the consultants." There was probably nothing the consultants could have done in such a tinder box. But the story well illustrates why dilemmas must be dealt with before they become social conflicts, which in their last extremities will poison an entire culture. Dilemmas will become social conflicts if they are not reconciled in time. In their advanced stages they are extremely dangerous for the mediator.

Or take another statement:

"We're all on incentives ... see? If I don't make my quota of gas stations I don't get paid as much, never mind traffic. It's hurry, hurry and get moving. But if there's an accident, then the tune changes. You were going too fast! You never read the pamphlet! They want us to drive like maniacs - only safely."

But an explicit dilemmas methodology is not required to understand the major issues in a culture. Most of the leaders in Chapters 3–9 had an intuitive grasp of what they were up against and used personal judgement. Some leaders are far wiser than they know or can explain.

Leaders must be masters of paradox

For example, at British Airways, Nick Georgiades and his successors grasped very quickly the key issue that, while the demeanour of cabin and ground staff – their "emotional labouring" towards customers – could make or break the airline, such staff were largely without the power to initiate improvements or control events. He also saw that staff could not be expected to care for passengers if they were not themselves cared for by supervisors, and that what a manager achieved was only half the issue. Equally vital was how he or she achieved it. Georgiades, then, had a sound grasp of the interdependence of emotional labour and empowerment, of showing care and being cared for, and for achieving goals in a way that sustains subordinates rather than grinding them down.

At BAHCO (see Chapter 6), Anders Lindström saw at once that he had to cut the staff by 26 per cent yet somehow maintain its morale and sense of forward movement. Insisting on the generation of new products and on getting his dismissed employees new jobs was an inspired way out of this dilemma. He knew that you cannot call on people to contribute ideas without simultaneously organizing the reception and reward of these ideas. Outstanding leaders have a sense for these vital balances, in whatever way they are expressed. David Hurst of Russelsteel refers to that balance in terms of "bubbles" and "boxes" (see Chapter 7). The Meridian consultants at Annheuser-Busch speak in terms of steering between the "rock" and the "whirlpool".

Making sense of "opposites"

But why do values take this curious form? Most people assume that values are like objects and ask, "Is this a good thing?". But values, as John Sculley (CEO of Apple) has pointed out, are contrasts or, as the social anthropologist, Gregory Bateson, used to say, they are "differences that make a difference".

Drivers at Western Oil who refuse to report their colleagues for safety infractions will typically describe themselves as "loyal" but those who might report a colleague as "snitches". They could drive safely, given a chance, if "kick-ass management" were not so "production crazy".

Values are contrasts

The contrasts between loyalty and informing, or safety and "production crazy" cannot simply be accepted at face value. The leader's task is to reconstruct the culture so that these conflicts are first defused and eventually become complementary forces, mutually reinforcing the best aspects of culture rather than continually attacking them. What he or she needs to avoid are patterns of social conflict. These are invariably indicated by a contrast between a positive and a negative view of the same issue. From the point of view of Western Oil drivers it was a positive/negative conflict between loyalty to colleagues on the one hand and informing on the other. The management at Western Oil also had a conflictual view, this time a negative/positive one. They experienced the fact of collusion among workers as being in conflict with management's wish to have violations reported.

Western Oil emerged from the conflict mode into a dilemma between two equal choices. There are important gains in this move from social conflicts to dilemmas. If the members of a culture are to own the new culture offered to them, then their own positive efforts and the justifications of their views must be part of the final picture. If the conflict can be presented as a choice between equally unacceptable alternatives (that is, as a dilemma) then neither side will be quite so prone to attack the other. A balanced view would admit neither collusion nor informing. Leaders or consultants are not going to promote the *bête noire* of managers or workers. Rather, they will seek to eliminate both threats. Some corporate cultures may be too far gone into factionalism, but if a manager or worker so much as hints that the other side has a point, it is more effective to pick up on these inner doubts than to solidify the battle lines.

Having reduced its social conflicts to a dilemma, Western Oil had to work at bringing the opposing sides into a positive complementary relationship. It began systematically courting errors in the form of "unsafe acts" witnessed, and groups worked with those who perpetrated these acts to reduce them. Reporting a violation was turned into an act of loyalty since this protected the employee from management sanction. However, the employee had to appear before a representative group of those fellow employees whom his act had endangered. Work schedules were redesigned to reflect safe productivity.

3. PLAY OUT CORPORATE DRAMAS BASED ON THE FINDINGS

Review findings with group ➔ to elicit theatrical and dramatic scenes ➔ to enable you to suggest a "happy endings".

Once you are in a position to share with a representative group from the company some of the cultural elements discovered in the course of the interviews, you will learn how open this culture is to its members. How much of what they have said privately will the group admit as its cultural domain? A repressive culture may simply deny that remarks qualifying or criticising it were ever made. A narrow or low-context culture may agree that such remarks were made but treat them as the utterances of private persons, irrelevant to the common task. Many corporate cultures believe that only operational issues matter, that people, their feelings and idiosyncracies should be kept out of the affairs of a business.

Introduce as much as possible to the culture ...

The more elements that can be admitted to the corporate culture you are trying to change the better. The effect of employees' morale on the corporation is crucial to its culture. Volvo (see Chapter 8) held seminars in which its employees were invited to discuss dilemmas of work and home, conflicting duties to family and to the company. Major Japanese corporations take wide responsibilities for their employees' total welfare. North American Tool and Die (see Chapter 9) lends its facilities to employees to improve their non-work lives. British Airways (see Chapter 4) acted to end the separation between work and home. The point is not to intrude into private lives but to make sure that public and private obligations do not become unnecessary sources of tension. Let the employees bring the greatest parts of themselves to their work.

... but do not overburden the table with issues

But remember that if you succeed in getting much of the interview material admitted to the culture, it will have to be dealt with. The task should not seem insoluble. More issues than can be managed would threaten the culture's capacity to cope. So when presenting the tensions found within the culture to the group, it is important to communicate the solubility of these dilemmas, along with the conviction that great gains in performance are achievable by such resolutions.

Several of the leaders described in the case studies "reviewed their findings with the group" and "elicited dramatic scenes". In BA the devastating research findings, describing the company as "cold, aloof, uncaring and bureaucratic" were presented to cabin crew and ground staff in "Putting People First" seminars. The staff were then invited to devise solutions to this crisis, with Colin Marshall appealing personally for their help and listening to what they told him. Through "Customer First" quality circles reviewing and designing solutions were institutionalized, with staff newly empowered to improvise and create on-the-spot solutions.

Here an intuitive grasp of dilemmas is evident. The very problems caused by congestion at airports and unavoidable delays gave the cabin crews opportunities to improvise. BA actually increased its popularity with customers when crew were seen to be striving to redress problems that were clearly not of their own making. Anders Lindström also fed back to his employees the full extent of BAHCO's difficulties during his "coffee table talk", setting scenes far more conducive to the rescue of an ailing company.

Tom Melohn of NATD not only reviewed customers' congratulations and compliments monthly with all employees, he almost begged for dramatic scenes that could enable him to forestall genuine mistakes. "If you don't understand, yell! If you don't agree, yell! We'll work it out between us." David Hurst of Russelsteel puts all his new acquisitions through the simulated dilemmas and dramatic game "Arctic Survival", chosen because it gives workers with practical skills a lot to say and do.

Do not let "organizational theatre" get out of hand

The likely response from the group to which the issues in tension are fed back is a minor re-creation of the dramatic conflicts around these dilemmas. Professor Iain Mangham of Bath University has written of "the theatre of organizations". The acting out of some of the values in dispute will give you a chance to observe directly how conflicts are conducted in the organization.

At Western Oil, for example, the consultants were careful, when reviewing union and management tensions, not to start the quarrel up again, but there is usually a skirmish or two around the familiar issues. For example, the accusation that the drivers were "a bunch of neurotics" for complaining about exhaust fumes leaking into the cab was partly replayed in front of the consultants. The union for its part had counter-accusations. "Jim was in intensive care when his supervisor leaves a safety manual at his bedside with key passages highlighted. The man's half dead and they are chiefly concerned with getting the company off the hook."

The clash between noble ideals and base motives, or even between two noble ideals, makes for good theatre. The protagonists stand on the stage and try to personify some eternal verity. The Dauntless Driver, deserted by an ungrateful company as he struggles for life. The Dedicated Manager, keeping vigil by the bedside of one of his "boys". None of it has much to do with business as actually conducted, and what makes for dramatic contrast also makes for perpetual conflict. The theatre of organization tends to over-generalize, finding in particular circumstances some universal lesson about the oppression of workers or "the right to manage", which tempts each side to declaim "they shall not pass".

Avoiding dangerous dramatic conflict

Humour and questioning can be used to debunk conflicting stereotypes. While consultants would be quite unwise to laugh at their clients, they can usually laugh with them, and investigation will often show that the corporate culture keeps its members from excess by teasing them. For example, the drivers of Western Oil were not, as it happened, exponents of dangerous driving. They had invented a character called Calamity Wayne, supposedly once employed there. This epithet was designed to challenge the credentials of macho styles of driving.

4. REINTERPRET THE CORPORATE MYTHS

Review past and present history ➔ to surface myths and stories ➔ so that you can reinterpret the myths and retell the stories

Corporate cultures are historical. They pass through crises, suffer defeats and achieve victories and their current values are very much a consequence of these past experiences. The value dilemmas you have already collected from interviews and the dramas you have seen enacted by the group to which you reported are only going to make sense if placed in the context of the company's history.

A potted corporate mythology: Apple Inc.

Apple Inc., which John Sculley joined in 1984, had a much repeated history which included all six levels of cultural phenomena (Table 10.1, p. 186).

Level 1: IBM as taboo. Once upon a time there were only corporate computers, which gave vast powers to US institutions but which left individuals feeling powerless.

Level 2: discovery of hackers' dilemma. But two youths in their early 20s, Steve Jobs and Bill Wozniak, struck a telling blow for the counter-culture. In a garage they created the first personal computer, designed to give power to the person and liberate the individual.

Level 3: dramatic and theatrical enactment. Just as Prometheus stole fire from the gods, Steve Jobs "stole computing from the corporation" and brought it back for the use of ordinary persons. So fast is technology developing that the corporate super-computer of 3-4 years ago can today arm each individual.

Level 4: historical myths and scenarios. Steve Jobs taught his employees that "the journey is the reward". By this he meant that the accumulation of skills and knowledge in a continuous process of accelerated learning was the key to personal satisfaction and corporate success. Even great products would soon be obsolescent, every great discovery would soon be bypassed. All these were "ports of call" in an endless journey of discovery to expand the mind of man.

Level 5: new metaphors, images and symbols. The logo, or symbol, chosen by the company depicted a multicoloured apple from which a bite had been taken. We are in an "Electronic Eden" rediscovering fateful knowledge.

Level 6: old paradigm yields to new. Knowledge is inherently different from selling objects in exchange for money, because those who give knowledge can never lose it. It stays with them in a paradigm beyond scarcity, which is why Steve Jobs gave Apple computers to every Californian high school. Computer literacy is in the mutual interest of all. The computer is coextensive with mind itself. The network is a global village. Apple is in the business of learning and discovery by a world community of scholars.

Deciphering and "reading" corporate stories

The history of the contending values within an organization can often be "read" by uncovering corporate stories. A story repeatedly told within a corporation, especially to recruits, may be regarded as an important message about how protagonists have tried to mediate dilemmas and succeeded or failed in these attempts. Nearly all stories have recurring clashes between people and/or values in which one side wins, the issues are resolved or both defeat each other. Twists and turns of fortune or joke collisions between values improve the story.

Stories may be positive or negative towards the prospects of solving problems. North American Tool and Die was full of positive stories, "The client who tried to cheat Tom and was banished for three years"; "The day the vice-president of Toyota thanked each one of us personally". Volvo France, in contrast, was the victim of a highly negative story with which Carstedt had to contend on his arrival. It went something like this.

"The Swedish people who make Volvo don't understand the French. We are hot-blooded Latins, with dash, romance and style. We like cars that perform and are in fashion. Volvos are too sober, too safe, too pedestrian, too cerebral and too practical, consisting of largely old models, which have not changed noticeably in years. Scandinavians have a temperament that dwells on accidents and upon keeping warm. The French have more *joie de vivre*. Despite heroic efforts to move these melancholy motors, we have not been very successful."

Reinterpreting a story to change a culture

A crucial aspect of changing a culture is to retell, reinterpret or transform a story which otherwise spells defeat. Goran Carstedt did that in Volvo France. By taking the dealers and their wives to Sweden and giving them the grand tour, the story of moody Scandinavians and dull cars was totally recast to read as follows.

"Volvos are made in Sweden by small, dedicated groups of craftsmen who make and sign each entire car and who manage themselves. Volvo symbolizes for the world an individualism married to social concern, to which the virtues of safety and reliability are the key. There are enough French people of discernment and good sense to think of their families and future responsibilities. With the new support we are getting, the Volvo message is one we can deliver with pride and with success."

Colin Marshall transformed an organization of titles, ranks and committees with his resonant reproach. "My name is Colin Marshall. I'd like you all to remember that." The story, told and retold around the organization, signified personal responsibility not roles, names not titles and insignia, one-to-one communication not committees. Without formal instruction the titles disappeared from doors and were replaced by names.

New stories give meaning to new incentive and pay schemes

Stories provide context and interpretation. Unless the basic story line changes, attitudes will persist. Harrison Owen, the US culture consultant, tells of the CEO with a reputation for deviousness, who gave all employees a $1,000 Christmas bonus in a bid to change their attitudes to him. It was a costly mistake. When Owen reinterviewed the employees they only mused, "What is that bastard up to now? What does he want from us?". Contrast this with David Hurst's reinterpretation of strategy as a creative bubble arising from the grass roots which shows clearly what new stories can accomplish.

5. LOOK AT THE SYMBOLS, IMAGES AND RITUALS

> Explore all higher logical types ➔ to elicit metaphors, images, symbols, rituals ➔ revise these. Create new metaphors, images, rituals.

Corporate cultures are full of metaphors, images, symbols and rituals. These are words or visions which stand for the values, dilemmas and myths of a culture.

Rituals describe the culture and reinforce its values

Take the ritual which John Sculley describes from his days at Pepsi Co. Every month Nielsen presented Pepsi's sales against Coca-Cola's for the previous month, including gains or losses of market share of less than 1 per cent, but still worth million of dollars. For this monthly ritual juniors entered first, sitting near the walls, then more senior executives, then the Nielsen team and then the president, to whom a waiter brought a Pepsi poured into a Tiffany glass. The monthly figures were presented, the president growled or beamed and signalled the end of the proceedings by leaving.

The ritual symbolized the hierarchy, the order of deference, the sacred liquid it was all about, the centrality of marketing, the toe-to-toe combat with Coca-Cola, the reward of success and the punishment of failure. Symbol comes from the Greek word *sym-bol* and means "to throw together". When values are symbolized or enacted ritually, they are thrown together and held fast. The organization's value system was partly present in the ritual described. The Japanese *ringi* ritual, in which an agreement is passed around and initialled, is a ritual of consensus, celebrating *wa* or harmony, a major Japanese ideal.

Use them to celebrate achievements ...

Rituals can be used to celebrate achievements, for example, the "super-person of the month" awards at North American Tool and Die, which acclaim the highest contributor. The "cheque ceremony", in which employees are given their salary cheques at random and must find the person to whom the cheque belongs and present it, is a celebration of interdependence – "We all work for each other" (see Chapter 9).

IBM has an annual extravaganza for the 80 per cent of general service engineers who exceed their quota for the year. They are invited to an expensive resort on Coronado Island in San Diego. The opening picnic lunch is Mexican with *tostadas* a foot high. The results for the year are flashed up on multiple screens to thunderous applause. Specially invited singing stars croon amid ice clouds. Hired actors mix with senior managers to lampoon recent corporate events, and in a grand finale the words "You are Special" are picked out in the darkness by pinpoints of light.

... and give balance at crucial moments

Ritual can be used to redress an imbalance of values which arises for any reason. It can be crucial to say goodbye and to mourn if the company is merging, relocating or changing its form. Death is typically accompanied by a gathering that affirms the living memory of the deceased, comforts those who grieve and declares faith in an afterlife. Likewise, any serious change within the corporation needs to be accompanied by a ritual affirmation of the bonds about to be severed, and the relationships soon to be lost, and the meaning of the work accomplished. Harrison Owen, the US consultant and episcopal priest, is a major convenor of corporate rituals designed to assuage loss. Companies which separate their employees brusquely from one another in the endless reshuffling of assets should not be surprised if these people find it hard to commit themselves anew.

Reconciliation through symbols and metaphors

How can you take a painful dilemma and resolve it using metaphors or images? How can contending viewpoints be tamed by symbols? In Chapter 6, for example, Anders Lindström uses the image of a bicycle to reconcile change with continuity and action with discovery. A company so deep in trouble may slow until it wobbles and crashes, so he tells his employees that they have to "pedal". Only movement can allow them to create.

New metaphors and images, such as that of the cyclist, are good ways of communicating to a culture the need to reconcile its values. A metaphor has been defined as "the likeness of unlike categories". It is accordingly of use in conveying the potential synergy among contrasting values and heralds the chance to reconcile dilemmas. It is an invitation to all to try to combine their values.

One important symbol used by Goran Carstedt was a "clenched wrists" motif, which symbolized people working together to help each other. He wanted this image to replace the previous one of four hands each "pointing the finger" in a loop, casting blame at their neighbours. Carstedt also used his "Customer is King" diagram which significantly placed the dealer who serves the customer on step two, with the importer and the manufacturer on steps three and four respectively. This symbolized the need to serve the dealer if the customer is to be properly served.

How images describe the culture of an organization

A most important contribution to understanding the "organizing image" or metaphor which patterns corporate cultures has been made by Gareth Morgan of York University in Canada. Morgan interviews and observes corporate executives at work to discover the dominant image among them of the corporation they serve. In his book *Images of Organizations** he shows how organizations are experienced by their members in the images of:

- a mechanism;
- an organism;
- a brain;
- an aesthetic culture;
- a political system;
- flux and transformation.

The machine is the classical image and still probably the dominant one. Activities are preprogrammed, routinized, repetitive, powerful, reliable, efficient and precise. Employees should behave in a way that maximizes machine potentials since this is the key advantage. Economies come from speed, volume and scale. The ideal is rationality. Examples are the factory and the bureaucracy. The organism is the image that arose to contend with mechanism. Here growth and development are stressed,

* Beverley Hills, Sage Publications, 1986.

with employees having an intrinsic need for the care, nurture, facilitation and interdependence of living systems in a benign environment. In the political image, the corporation is seen as a power and bargaining structure between contending groups. Increasingly corporations see themselves as brains which learn from experience and process complex information internally from professional disciplines and externally from signals coming from the operating environment. Others see themselves as coded knowledge in a state of flux and transformation into different products. Finally, some model themselves on aesthetic cultures creating beauty, comfort and satisfaction for customers.

6. CREATING NEW LEARNING SYSTEMS

Discovering logics by which current system learns ➔ elicits "old" paradigms of manipulting objects ➔ enabling "new" paradigms and epistemologies to be created for better innovation and faster learning.

To discover the logic by which an existing culture learns, it needs to be asked: "What would have to happen for you to change your mind?". The answer lies in that culture's paradigms. A paradigm may be defined as a criterion of judgement. It is what tells you the kind of phenomenon you are expecting and looking for. It presumes that the field of study consists of certain entities, and therefore shapes the entire learning system of the corporation.

The corporation intending to use its culture as its source of strength must ensure that after an intervention to adjust the culture, systems are available for continuing to adapt and transform the company in the future. That means looking at the organization's criteria for judgement – its paradigms – and adjusting them if necessary.

What do cultures learn?

There is overwhelming evidence that we "know" before we look, that corporate cultures have categories and concepts which affect the realities they experience and the lessons they learn. It is part of the paradigm. Thus Howard T. Geneen's "unshakeable facts" are not usually tested either, nor is the Asian idea of a rhythmic universe of complementarities. These are all "givens".

Epistemology is a subject very close to all this. It asks: "How do we set about the task of learning and discovery?"; "What are the best paths to knowledge?"; and "What kinds of knowing should we pursue?". The paradigms and epistemologies of a corporation are crucial parts of its culture and the final point of any investigation into culture.

Perhaps the best way for companies to proceed in this complex area is to examine their current paradigms and see whether these exclude the sort of information and processes that are increasingly seen as factors of business success.

In most traditional corporations – those based on a paradigm of mechanization and the mechanical sciences that most dominate production - such a culture learns in the manner idealized by Newton and by nineteenth century experimental physics. It produces and supplies things, manufactured in parts and then assembled. The more it can produce at progressively lower costs and higher profits the better. Its ideal is to predict and to control what its employees will do and what its customers will buy. The corporation acts with demonstrable efficiency to achieve these goals. This machine learns after a fashion. If its predictions do not come true or if its controls do not produce the behaviour it seeks, these will be re-engineered until they work better. The machine culture learns only about deviations from its own operating manuals.

New paradigms for business

The paradigms of information age business are, however, very different from this; and consequently involve alternative learning systems. Whereas the machine culture assumes that reality and business consist of things, units, atoms and objects with precise definitions, the alternative view sees business as a matter of processes, waves, dynamisms and patterns with imprecise boundaries. In the old, nineteenth century paradigm, business performance could be explained analytically, by reducing complex problems into parts and isolating difficult areas. But in the fluid, alternative paradigm proposed here, explanation – and hence learning – involves synthesis, combining smaller parts into complex wholes.

The new paradigms adopted by the businesses considered in the case studies in this book suggest other observations too. The phenomena of the business world are no longer cumulative and linear with inbuilt fixed onwards and upwards trends. Now, businesses deal with systems, whose properties are circular, cybernetic and self-correcting, in short the defining features of a corporate culture listed in Chapter 1. Likewise, the corporation's relationship to its environment is less and less one of control, prediction and manipulation. Replacing that cause-and-effect paradigm is one that stresses instead the achievement of finest fit with the operating context, harmony within the organization, and a synergistic relationship with the environment.

New learning

Under this more subtle paradigm, a new epistemology, or type of learning, becomes possible. Instead of learning merely about its deviations from the rule book, a corporate culture can learn actively from the patterns and processes it experiences. By synthesizing such information and using the self-correcting properties of a culture, organizations can ensure that they achieve a constructive learning relationship with their operating universe. This enables a company to develop synergy with, and generate profit from, the patterns of change in the economy.

By shifting their cultures away from the mechanical model and towards the fluid one, corporations modify their logic of learning so that they can adapt to a changing world. The mechanical model still has its uses, and should not be supressed simply because its relevance has decreased. However, in the information age, organizations need a paradigm that can deal with complex relationships, with employees and with customers, and around subtle questions of value. British Airways is an example of an organization that needs machine-like principles to operate its craft safely and efficiently. But the social infrastructure that learns to do these things better needs a logic of development and enquiry, so that the culture can persistently improve itself. Within that fluid paradigm of learning, personal service and care, there has to be space for the old and still valid paradigm of mechanical accuracy, precision and analysis.

CONCLUSION

The essential point to remember about a culture is that you cannot study it without already starting to change it. You must decide, therefore, what you personally believe in and, as you engage the culture, make those convictions available to anyone who challenges you or enquires about your intentions. This applies equally to consultants and leaders.

The eliciting of taboos by locating black sheep is a sensible precaution. A culture partly defines itself by what it is not.

When you interview to elicit value conflicts and dilemmas you are modelling how authorities might better listen, understand and respond so that information is drawn up into the organization. Even if you get no further, the culture may be richer for your efforts.

When you review findings with the group you are helping them to admit many important elements into their culture and thus to themselves. By arranging these values as complementary patterns, you render them more acceptable and more soluble.

By helping the group reinterpret its history, myths and stories, you can give these new force, new meaning and new direction. These stories have dilemmas encoded within them and ways of managing dilemmas are idealized.

A corporation's metaphors, symbols, images and rituals are similarly models of dilemma resolution. These are all ways of handling "opposing" injunctions. You can surface them, appraise them and, if needed, qualify their meanings.

Finally you must ask how this culture learns. Is its thinking still based on the ideal of the efficient mechanism, or is it a self-augmenting culture that learns from its experience of engaging the environment?

The truth is that the modern knowledge-intensive world economy is a "learning race" in which only corporate cultures with a thirst for discovery can survive.

A DIAGRAMMATIC SUMMARY

There are dilemmas for the consultants or managers who are attempting to change culture, quite apart from the dilemmas the organization may face. Anyone seen by an organization to be trying to change it faces potentially dangerous issues that could explode. Three hazards are especially perilous.

  1. What individuals reveal the group will deny.
  2. Dilemmas unearthed may trigger simmering conflicts.
  3. The old paradigm will attack any prospect of a new one.
These dilemmas can constitute a vicious circle that all too often hinders an attempt to change culture (see Figure 10.1, p. 206).

Three major attempts have been made in this book to reintegrate and strengthen these ropes.

  1. The high-context, enriched culture can do more sophisticated and information-intensive work. If this is emphasized strongly enough senior managers may agree to admit the contents of the interviews to the corporate culture.

Figure 10.1 **A vicious circle**

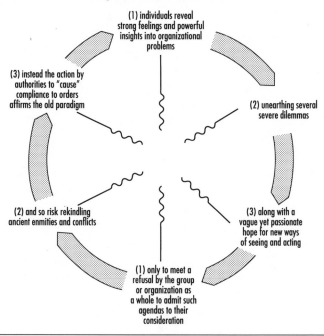

(1) individuals reveal strong feelings and powerful insights into organizational problems

(2) unearthing several severe dilemmas

(3) instead the action by authorities to "cause" compliance to orders affirms the old paradigm

(3) along with a vague yet passionate hope for new ways of seeing and acting

(2) and so risk rekindling ancient enmities and conflicts

(1) only to meet a refusal by the group or organization as a whole to admit such agendas to their consideration

Figure 10.2 **A virtuous circle**

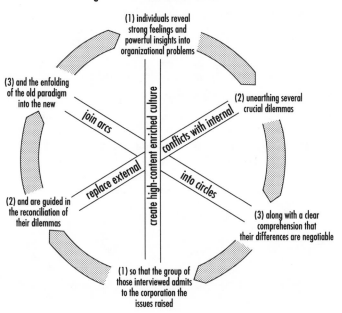

(1) individuals reveal strong feelings and powerful insights into organizational problems

(3) and the enfolding of the old paradigm into the new

(2) unearthing several crucial dilemmas

join arcs

create high-content enriched culture

conflicts with internal

replace external

into circles

(2) and are guided in the reconciliation of their dilemmas

(3) along with a clear comprehension that their differences are negotiable

(1) so that the group of those interviewed admits to the corporation the issues raised

2. Dilemmas which are internal conflicts wrestled with privately are far less dangerous than external or factional conflicts. People do not have to agree with one another to discover congruence among their value preferences.

3. The old paradigm of mechanical cause and effect is part of the new paradigm. An arc is abstracted from a circle when we think in causal terms. The broader truth is that "the effect" feeds back. Hence a "new paradigm" can be created from a conflict between two parties, each trying to "cause" the other to behave.

With practice a "virtuous intervention" is possible (Figure 10.2).

Despite everything written here, the fear of angels is well founded. Luck and much goodwill will be needed on all sides. Headlong assaults on the ineffable are not guaranteed to succeed.

Who does what, where and how

Worldwide there are probably in excess of 20,000 consulting groups or individual practitioners who invoke the idea of corporate culture. It is by now axiomatic that strategies will not work effectively without some prior understanding of the organization's "character", "climate", "history", "environment" or culture. Hence, few who would guide a company through the change process can afford to ignore the question of culture.

Despite this swelling chorus of "culture vultures" the field is massively derivative. Never in the field of corporate consulting has so much repackaging been done by so many from the ideas of so few. The following consultants, each with distinctive competencies in diagnosing and assisting change, may be judged to have "started something". Their ideas may soon be seen in many places, branded with the logos of the other consultants. But for full understanding of an approach the original work should be examined. It can then be tailored to your own unique circumstances and the context of your company.

The following account is a tentative and partial description of some consultants whom consultants consult – meta-consultants, perhaps, or pattern-makers. This list: is by no means an inclusive or comprehensive its purpose is to give readers insight into some of the most challenging thinking on corporate culture. Any attempt to arbitrate among the qualities of various practitioners is inappropriate. Culture is a many sided phenomenon. Those participating in its making and understanding are equally diverse. Those described here are simply a selection known to the author, who have influenced the approach taken to corporate culture in this book.

THE McKINSEY MODEL

Tony Athos is a former from the Harvard Business School and co-author (with Richard Pascale) of *The Art of Japanese Management* – the book which just beat to publication *In Search of Excellence** by Tom Peters and Bob Waterman.

Warm squares, cool triangles

The close similarity of the two books was no coincidence. All four authors had been members of a team hired by McKinsey to create a model which the consultants could nail to the masthead, one that could do what the "Cows, Dogs, Stars" model had done for the Boston Consulting Group. Their joint product was the seven "S" diagram (a version was used by British Airways, see Chapter 4, p. 93). The original diagram (see Figure A1.1, p. 209) has superordinate goals in the centre. These are what integrate strategy, structure and systems with style, staff and skills.

Obviously, this diagram has undergone various forms of interpretation, and Tony Athos has encountered interesting issues in the application of the mode.

"We are at the beginning of a 'strategic era'," Athos claims. "The silicon chip is to our time what the steam engine was to the industrial revolution. This means that

---

* New York, Harper and Row, 1982.

Figure A1.1 **The McKinsey seven "S" diagram**

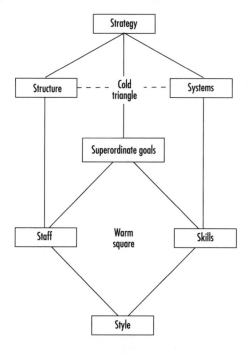

we are awash with information; uncertain, ambiguous, imperfect information from which we have to make and assert our own meaning which we then offer to customers. But meanings can only be generated if we create harmony and coherence, the Japanese call it *wa,* among all seven Ss. The strategy has to be one for which the systems are in place and which the organization's structure is capable of delivering. Staff must be capable of working the strategy through and must have the skills to learn through it and from it. This, in turn, will require the appropriate management style. The whole is orchestrated by superordinate goals to which all employees commit themselves, often using spontaneously improvised means of realizing these. This totality constitutes the organization's culture, a pattern which is more or less harmonious."

But corporate cultures are not usually harmonious. A very common condition is tension or conflict between what Athos calls the "cold triangle" and "the warm square". The cold triangle consists of strategy, structure and systems, while the "warm square" consists of staff, skills, style and superordinate goals. "There is nothing so dispiriting as creating a composite model only to find that nearly everyone you talk to wants to deconstruct it into polarized elements. It usually turns out that they are obsessed on a subset of the model depending on whether they are 'hard' or 'soft' in their approach to organizational culture."

Strategy, structure and systems are the favourite elements of the hard crowd, who believe that all the rest will fall into place if their cold triangle is constructed right.

Personnel people, human resource types and the vast majority of organizational behaviour types are "warm squares". They tend to believe that a vaguely humane style and lashings of human skills development for the staff will automatically create a benign culture from which "strategy" and "structure" will spontaneously emerge, with "systems" generating all the right numbers.

An organization works by the levers with which top people are comfortable and would prefer to pull

They "pull" strategy, structure and systems far more often than they "pull" the others. These are typically given lip-service and assigned to low-voltage departments like personnel. They are attended to only when things are going well, and are often seen as frills, veneer, gloss or froth. Style is usually expected to adapt itself, while the staff are expected to grab for themselves the necessary skills and find superordinate goals and meanings in what the strategy tells them must be done in any case.

Obviously, the coherence needed to generate meaning in an information era is less likely if there are only three levers to pull rather than seven, and if the human side of the enterprise is largely neglected. Table A1.1 illustrates the tensions which Athos reports finding most frequently, as the cold triangle polarizes with the warm square. Analysis tends to clash with and subordinate interpretation; quantification lords it over verbalization; measurement excludes other forms of evaluation; design becomes all important, with implementation expected to follow; skills in abstraction eclipse experience and personal knowledge. The Japanese and other Asian cultures would regard the two columns in Table A1.1 as a sort of *yang* and *yin,* natural aspects of each other.

Table A1.1 The dichotomies between cold triangles and warm squares

△	□
Analysis	Interpretation
Quantification	Verbalization
Measurement	Evaluation
Control	Guidance
Science	Arts
Top–down imposed	Bottom–up participation
Big brain	Little people
Design	Implement
Bold	Deliberate
Win/lose	Win/win
Competition	Cooperation

Two consequences arise from the polarizing habit of the US individualistic macroculture. The first is that, given a choice of modelling himself on masculine or feminine stereotypes, the American male employee invariably prefers the left-hand column. The dismal second consequence is that, in any struggle or conflict between the hard and soft approach, the former is bound to win. Hence those favouring adversarial and win–lose relationships will inevitably force people who work cooperatively and search for win–win relationships to lose any contest. This is not because the right-hand values are not crucial to organizational effectiveness – they are – but because, once polarized against the left-hand values, they become non-viable on their own. Isolated "soft values" cannot survive attack.

This problem goes to the roots of US culture. Individualism and masculinity combine to form a seriously top-heavy corporate culture in which the Ss of the cold triangle attempt to drive all the rest. Executives who try to develop their subordinates are described as "hand or handkerchief holders" and "breast-feeders". Japanese men have no problem playing support roles. "I am the wife of the plant manager," one Japanese accountant told Athos. He meant that he had to use tact in offering support. Yet, to most Americans, the warm square is "wifey stuff". If anyone teaches well or is supportive of others, they are immediately suspected of not being top-flight.

A central finding of both books, *The Art of Japanese Management* and *In Search of Excellence,* was that excellent companies combined tightness with looseness, competition with cooperation, top–down direction with bottom–up participation and productivity achieved through people. Hence the main thrust of Athos's current work is with CEOs, getting them to reconcile and synthesize squares with triangles. This involves riding out the frequent protest by subordinates that the leaders are "inconsistent in their values". Athos believes that if this combination can be achieved, the whole discourse of organization behaviour could disappear. It is a "creature of the divide", a largely impotent protest on behalf of the human factor.

Anthony G. Athos, 11 Pleasant Street, Gloucester, Mass. 01930, USA.
Tel: (617) 283 4645.

MEREDITH BELBIN

Dr R. Meredith Belbin is the managing director of the Employment Development Unit Ltd, a consultancy based in Cambridge, UK. After many years of working with experimentally formed teams at the Management College at Henley, he appears to have developed a powerful system for building top executive teams and improving their performances.

Balancing the roles to build top executive teams

The method consists of administering a simple questionnaire whose purpose is to discover what roles managers prefer and customarily play in groups. They may, of course, enjoy several roles and be versatile enough to contribute whatever any situation requires. However, most have definite preferences and a very marked tendency to play preferred roles in every situation, if necessary by displacing other team members.

Belbin found at Henley that he could construct experimental groups from these declared preferences and predict with fair accuracy the results of the performance of that group in computer-simulated management situations. Using "Teamopoly", a modification of the well-known property board game, in which winning and losing are telescoped into short time intervals, Belbin gets team members to revert to their most basic, occasionally their most primitive, role-playing. All of this is carefully recorded by observers. A crucial discovery from this research was that teams chosen for unusually high levels of intelligence failed more often than they succeeded, with average placement of fifth or sixth out of eight. This posed the question of why so much potential comes to so little fruition.

Main concepts and ideas

As a result of research lasting twelve years, Meredith Belbin identified eight roles necessary to the functioning of effective teams. They were as follows.

1. The plant. So called because these imaginative, creative and idea-generating persons were originally "planted" in experimental groups to see what effect they would have. At their best, plants originate the best strategies and the most ingenious solutions. At worst, they are impractical, up in the clouds and obsessed with their own "genius".

2. The chairperson. The person who can evoke from other team members their fullest potential and best contributions. He or she keeps before the team their major objectives and confirms or denies the relevance of various contributions towards these objectives. A good chairperson is open, respectful, calm, controlled, self-confident and fair-minded. At worst, they will be overwhelmed by the sheer variety of opinions and pressures.

3. The shaper. The person who takes the idea and runs with it, pushing it through committee, getting it operational, and turns it from an idea into a reality. Good shapers are dynamic, outgoing, forceful, energetic, the "doers and shakers" of the corporate world. Bad ones are tense, impatient, irritable and ruthless.

4. The resource investigator. Less creative than enthusiastic about the new. This person enjoys exploring, discovering and collecting novel resources to be deployed in gaining the team's objectives. A good one will be extrovert, enthusiastic, sociable and curious with extraordinary powers of initiative and improvisation; a bad one will be easily bored and distracted.

5. The company worker. Succeeds by putting the company's objectives before his or her own and ensuring that no necessary job, however personally unfulfilling, is left undone. The best ones are conscientious, conservative, disciplined and practical. The worst succumb to "group think" and confine themselves to received ideas.

6. The monitor evaluator. The team's critic, appraiser and surveyor, who challenges half-baked ideas, makes hard-headed judgements about feasibility and tempers idealism with realism. Ideally a sober, detached and prudent person, but risks being a nay-sayer, wet blanket and obstacle.

7. Team workers. The group's social specialists: sensitive, kindly, responsive, warm and healing. They repair and maintain the bonds of the group, relieve tension and increase conviviality. Should promote *esprit de corps*. A useless one will dither in crises when not everyone can be assuaged.

8. Completer–finishers. The people who work the project through to its completion, taking pains to ensure that no details are missed. They are crucial to the quality control of complex products. The perfect completer–finisher is orderly, conscientious, responsible and perfectionist. The worst are compulsive, anxious and nit-picking.

Balancing the roles in a culture

The theory now explains why a team of super-intelligent individuals fails. High IQ individuals have such an investment in their own cleverness that they are more critical than supportive, more analytical than synthetic, more assertive than responsive, more competitive than cooperative. Put them all together and they shoot each other down. Similar disasters occur when a team is composed entirely of "plants". They create an effusion of ideas which no one can shape into a reality. It is the same with any team composed of one type only.

What are the crucial predictors of a successful team? They are as follows.

- Chairmen with high integrative capacities who can both extract the potential from their teams and organize these resources into attainable objectives.
- The existence of one strong plant to supply creative ideas and strategies a second plant makes success less probable).
- A wide spread of complementary roles and attributes, that is a plant matched by a shaper, a monitor evaluator and a completer–finisher to assure quality.
- Versatility and adjustment to imbalance. This means that individuals can switch roles to whatever is missing and, therefore, needed in the particular situation. Predicting a team's success is even surer when the criteria above are combined. For example, a single good plant with a close relationship to a competent chairman in the team experiments finished in the first three of eight competing companies 90 per cent of the time.

Belbin's work is confirmation of a major premise of this book: a culture is not simply a collection of human and physical resources but the pattern by which these are joined, balanced and synthesized.

Dr R. Meredith Belbin, Employment Development Unit Ltd, 2 Little St Mary's Lane, Cambridge, CA2 2YX, UK. Tel: (0223) 60895.

CORPORATE RENEWAL ASSOCIATES

Corporate Renewal Associates (CRA) is a London-based consultancy which works with clients on issues that are blocking their ability to achieve and sustain high-level performance. The founder and managing director is Leslie Dighton.

Renewing corporate cultures

Dighton argues that organizations which achieve high performance over time have learned how to renew themselves continuously in terms of their ideas and behaviour. Those that have not learned this fail to keep pace with their markets and technologies. They age, become insensitive to their environments, and adapt too slowly. Even high-performing organizations can become self-indulgent over time, thereby losing their competitive edge and creating the conditions for their decline.

Typically, CRA gets involved with organizations which are at significant turning points, such as merger, deregulation, poor results, new leadership. Such turning points often necessitate radical change and a new frame of reference.

The symptoms of poor functioning seldom come singly. Loss of good people, poor customer service, slow decision-making, defensive attitudes and other ills are interdependent and develop in the context of the organization as a whole. Addressed in isolation, they tend to recur. Their cumulative effect is perceived to be disabling.

The group finds that clients generally want two things: first, a total approach to the whole system – strategy, structures, top teams, key skills, support systems and processes of all kinds – to ensure that everything repositions itself in a new direction with the relevant capability and at the right pace; and, second, solutions generated internally from the client's system, and not imported from outside on the basis of someone else's best practice, which may not be relevant or achievable.

Diagnostic framework

CRA uses a diagnostic framework with four main interrelated components (see Figure A1.2). The largest diamond at the centre represents what is potentially attainable if Vision (top), Implementation (right), Energy (bottom) and Values (left) were optimally developed. The small, irregular diamond at the centre represents chronic under-performance.

Figure A1.2 **CRA's diagnostic framework**

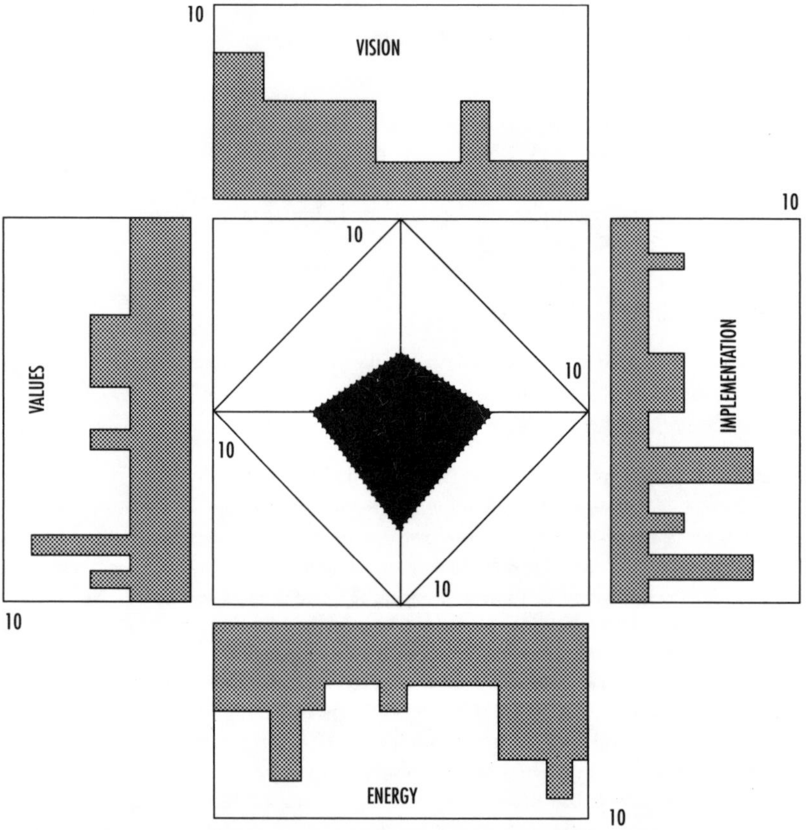

The bar chart at the edges show the client's performance in key areas. This client is higher on energy than vision (represented by the dotted diamond in the centre). Ideally, an organizaton will achieve a mapping shown by the large central diamond.

Mapping the components

Each of the four sides expresses a profile based around multiple components. For example, Vision: Is top management aware of the fundamentals of its business? How good is market and competitor knowledge? How complete is its information base? How good is functional integration and consensus building? These evaluations are done by the management team in conjunction with the consultants. External views and comparisons against best current practice are also obtained.

The Implementation profile enquires into roles, structures, accountability, management information and personnel systems. The energy profile looks at the leadership, its style, motivation, selection and power delegation. A clear indicator of problems is when high-performing businesses build walls around themselves to avoid central interference. The values profile investigates what paradigm is in use within the organization. Are clients blinkered by internal views or can they respond to market changes? Are they centralized or decentralized? Do people work together openly or are they secretive and distrustful?

The collection of these data is not a neutral process. It alters understanding and develops potential energy for change.

CRA aims to act as a catalyst to management but occasionally at the implementation phase it becomes a temporary interventionist to ensure that the necessary information reaches the appropriate parts of the organization and the force for change is maintained. The sign of success comes when the insiders on the joint teams start taking initiatives and assume ownership of the process.

CRA reckons that this approach is generic to all organizations, and it has worked in just about every sector. The high level of involvement means it manages only about six or eight clients at a time, and even these must be at different points in the cycle of change.

Leslie Dighton, Corporate Renewal Associates Ltd, 24 Fitzroy Square, London W1P 5HJ, UK. Tel: (071) 387 9226.

MIT SYSTEMS DYNAMICS GROUP

Peter M. Senge is the director of the Program in Systems Thinking and the New Management Style at the Sloan School of Management at MIT (Massachussetts Institute of Technology). The program uses a number of methods organized around the study of systems dynamics, a field made famous at MIT by the work of Jay Forrester. However, Senge's approach is to begin with the existing mental maps and current working assumptions of those running particular organizations. He takes the values and processes of an organization and shows how these generate results which that culture may not intend and which could be improved upon to create a more effective corporate strategy.

Starting with the client's own model – a computerized view of systems dynamics

The Systems Dynamics Group is a department of the Sloan School rather than a consulting organization. However, there are many corporate subscribers, including Apple Computer, Hanover Insurance, Shell, Kollmorgen, Ford, Analog Devices, Cray Research, the Royal Bank of Canada and others. These meet several times a year to exchange experiences on putting cybernetic models and learning systems to work.

Membership is confined to "metanoic" organizations. The word is from Greek, meaning "shift of mind". Hence this group shares certain key assumptions: that an organization, steered by intuition, can nonetheless monitor itself systematically, thereby improving its judgement; that, when all employees are aligned around a shared vision and purpose, the culture can learn from its experience how to engage its environment more effectively.

Key concepts

Senge begins by asking how it is that people learn skills of extraordinary complexity. For example, a person learns to play a piano key by key and bar by bar until they can play simple tunes, then complex tunes and, finally, "hear" the music as they read a full orchestral score. They have an intuitive grasp of these wholes which are stored within their minds in patterns and configurations which, once learned, sink into automatic assemblies of skills.

There is also a bridge between the intuitive feel that the music is better or worse and the operation of the rational mind. Intuition itself has patterns, and the systems approach can make these patterns explicit and subject to rational critique.

This is not the rationality of the traditional hierarchical organization where authorities try to control their subordinates' behaviour in mechanical-type sequences of cause and effect, or plan and implementation. In highly innovative organizations like Cray Research or the Kollmorgen Corporation it takes 100 innovative contributors to create one super-computer or piece of electro-optical equipment. There is no one at the apex of these corporations who could cause innovation to happen.

Employees are aligned in the sense that personal goals are co-extensive with the organization's purpose and hence with one another, so the fulfilment of individual and corporate aspirations are mutually supportive. This implies neither conformity nor continuing consensus. On the contrary, there will be strong tensions and conflicts among the organization's values. But because its purpose is superordinate, differences will be resolved and dissent or opposition will not be allowed to block resolution. Aligned organizations, then, empower their members who trust each other not to be perfect or without error but to keep trying to create an integrity among their tasks.

Using software to map organizational dynamics

The MIT Systems Dynamics Group develops computerized case studies to map the organization's dynamics on software. This gives the managers in that corporation a simulation of their own operations, a "game" whose rules they can modify since it is their own. It also provides for college students a simulation of real corporate problems and decisions, less abstract and more participative than reading written case studies.

For example, Senge and his team developed a "claims game" from a study of how property and liability insurance claims were settled at the Hanover Insurance Co. in Worcester, Massachusetts.

The first attempt by Hanover to map its working processes showed limited systems awareness, with arrows moving in only one "causal" direction, few feedback loops, and a separation of the main elements from one another. The personnel function, crucial to how new adjusters are hired, trained, leave or grow in experience, could not be fitted into this early map of the process, except by a vague and imprecise sense of general connectedness. There was only a vague notion that the number and quality of experienced adjusters relate to how well claims are settled.

After 22 sessions in which systems dynamics were used to organize the executives' own categories, a much more sophisticated map emerged, which enabled executives to study the linkage between an increase in new claims, productivity, staffing needs and adjuster quality. Mapping the dynamics of the system in this way showed that Hanover Insurance was receiving "a sting in the tail". Claimants are either overpaid, in which case the company suffers, or they are underpaid, in which case costly litigation and adverse court settlements will sharply increase costs. The fact that one set of standards in the system is hard edged and unambiguous (pending ratios, settlement times, production ratios) while another set is ambiguous, soft and fuzzy (the "quality" of the settlement) eventually damages the "hard" performance of the company. Poor quality settlements cost by far the most in the end.

These relations can be charted on a software map, enabling management to see the problem, described by themselves, on the computer screen before them. They can experience the effects of a culture that avoids ambiguity and clings to key ratios upon their organization's overall performance. Making these perceptions does not guarantee a solution to the problem. Despite months of lip-service to the quality of settlements, old habits reassert themselves. Cultural patterns are hard to break, but the best way may be to observe the errors in simulation, and then deliberately change the rules and practise a new game.

This "new game" could experiment with hiring better and more experienced adjusters, paying them well above the industry average and investing heavily in "fast, fair and friendly" negotiating skills. Although this would increase costs in the short term, it could be seen whether this would greatly decrease the costs of litigation and adverse judgements. It could give Hanover a reputation for fair dealing which might also be cheaper for all those concerned. In the long term it could pay handsomely.

Peter Senge, Program in Systems Thinking and Organizational Learning, System Dynamics Group, Sloan School, MIT, 300 Memorial Drive, Cambridge, Mass 02130, USA. Tel: (617) 253 1575.

ARGYRIS AND SCHON

Chris Argyris and Donald A. Schon are co-creators of the theory and practice of "Action Science". Chris Argyris, trained as a psychologist, is a professor at the Harvard Business School. The author of some 25 books, he has acted as consultant to the governments of the UK, France, West Germany, Greece, the Netherlands, Italy, Norway and Sweden, as well as hundreds of corporations. His current preference is to act as consultant to firms of consultants.

Donald Schon was trained in philosophy at Harvard, worked at Arthur D. Little for many years and is a professor in the Department of Urban Studies and Planning at MIT. He gave the BBC Reith Lectures in 1971 and is best known for his book *The Reflective Practitioner.*[*]

---

[*] New York, Basic Books, 1983.

Action Science: from single-loop learning to double-loop learning

The point of departure for their approach is the perception of two kinds of error: un-designed error, which it is the purpose of all education to reduce; and designed error, which is the particular focus of their attention. The big question is how rational creatures can knowingly design a mismatch between what they intend and what eventuates. Argyris and Schon find the procedures of "Normal Science" (rigorous laboratory experiments) inadequate "because they have nothing to say about these designed errors which we have repeatedly discovered".

Designed errors can soon become defensive routines practised by a whole organization. What does it mean to say that an organization learns, or blocks its own learning, by designing errors? Organizations may be said to learn, or mislearn, when their members jointly share a task system and evaluate their own performance. Members will typically share some theory of action, establish roles and share an image or map of how the organization functions. This is its culture. Any modifications made to these theories, maps and images through studying the experience of their use is organizational learning. Designed errors are shared ways of evading threat and embarrassment. Among the lessons an organization can learn are ways of bypassing certain threats to its stability and comfort.

Argyris and Schon distinguish the kind of learning which arises from the Action Science which they advocate and the learning arising from Normal Science based on the methodology of physics.

Pay by performance

In order to understand how these two "sciences" compare, consider a case typical of those addressed by Argyris and Schon.

A CEO is determined that his corporation should "pay for performance", that is that the abler and harder-working employees should receive payments commensurate with their higher performance. Unfortunately, the system of evaluation has proved highly fallible, as many discovered before this. The total wages bill has soared. There is an inflation of evaluations deemed "excellent" and "good", while poor and mediocre performers are not being confronted with their shortcomings. If it is assumed that "fear of upsetting the workers" has led supervisors to "smoothing behaviour" in which the problem of evaluating poor and mediocre performance was evaded, how might Action Science resolve the issue?

Whereas Normal Science would seek to show that values of x (fear of upsetting the workers) are connected to values of y (behaviours which smooth over negative evaluations), Action Science would begin with self-questioning by a supervisor. "If fear of upsetting workers is part of my design or intention, will this lead me to smooth over vital differences in my evaluation of their performances?" The focus is on what practising people seek and intend.

Action Science would also look at the specific context in which the manager operates. It might conclude, for example, "that no evaluation crammed into three minutes can hope to distinguish better from poorer performance while maintaining the employee's confidence in that evaluation."

Normal Science is also in search of unilateral or one-way determinations in which x determines y. But influences are often mutual and multilateral. For example, the fact that the feelings of poor performers have been soothed and smoothed (y) for several years may perpetuate and exacerbate the fear (x) of suddenly having to tell the truth, so y also determines x. It needs Action Science to capture such self-perpetuating cycles.

According to Argyris and Schon, only Action Science permits a corporation to criticize and modify the culture through which it learns. Most learning is single loop, which compares performance to fixed standards which are not themselves questioned.

What becomes possible if people are willing to change cultures and the standards embedded in them is double-loop learning. Here the corporation designs its own learning rules. Instead of performances being judged against fixed and unchanging standards, the culture considers whether:

1. its standards are worthy of the potentials and aspirations of its employees; and
2. its standards are appropriate to changing competitive environments.

Loop 1 compares performance to standards. Loop 2 compares standards to actual, potential or required performances. The employees learn from the standards before the standards are re-examined critically by employees.

Defensive routines based on evading the unpleasant truth of an employee's alleged "inferior" performance tend to wither away in the face of double-loop learning. This happens for several reasons:

- the appraisal interview is now itself assessed for what can be learned from it;
- the employee is not necessarily "inferior" at all;
- the standard is possibly outdated;
- genuine innovation may be going unmeasured and unappreciated.

Thus the meeting of supervisor and employee becomes a shared search to understand a discrepancy in which either standard or performance or both may need to be modified.

Double-loop learning consultants

Consultants using the double loop learning approach include the following.

Chris Argyris, Humphrey Hall, Room 13, Harvard Business School, Boston, Mass. 02163, USA.

Donald A. Schon, Department of Urban Studies & Planning, Room 9-517, MIT, 77 Massachusetts Avenue, Cambridge, Mass. 02139, USA.

Robert Putman, 184 Mill Street, Natick, Mass. 01760, USA.

Diana M. Smith, Action Design Associates, 21 Janison Street, Newton, Mass. 02160.

Bill Isaacs, 69 Fayerweather Street, Cambridge, Mass. 02138, USA.

The Systems Dynamics Group, E40-294 Sloan School, MIT, 50 Memorial Drive, Cambridge, Mass. 02139, USA.

Michael Sales and William Joiner, Action Management Associates, 883 Barrett's Mill Road, Concord, Mass. 01742, USA.

JUANITA BROWN

Juanita Brown builds corporate cultures by organizing not simply the top management team, but all employees. She prefers not to stop there, but to include the community as well. She did just that between 1985 and 1986 with a large paper mill in the southern USA, the vertically integrated subsidiary of a national consumer products company. The surrounding town was economically dependent on its mill; even the houses and shops would be worthless if the mill closed.

A vision for the whole community

Juanita Brown had originally been called in by the senior management group for whom she facilitated the process of constructing a vision. She took them through her customary sequence (see Figure A1.3).

Figure A1.3 **Juanita Brown's circular sequence**

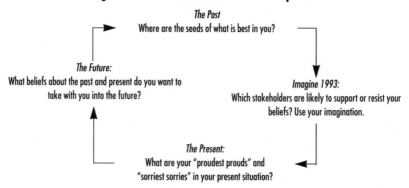

The Past
Where are the seeds of what is best in you?

The Future:
What beliefs about the past and present do you want to take with you into the future?

Imagine 1993:
Which stakeholders are likely to support or resist your beliefs? Use your imagination.

The Present:
What are your "proudest prouds" and "sorriest sorries" in your present situation?

She went round and round the circle with her group until all elements had been included and all members felt commitment to, and ownership of, the vision which had emerged.

When all goes well – as it did on this occasion – she invites management to let everyone participate: the employees, spouses, sub-contractors, banks, schools, the community. What kind of environment do we want? What kind of town? What is to be the relationship of the business leaders to their community?

"We dedicate ourselves to 'three qualities': quality of life, quality of product and quality of process.

'"The power of these meetings is that a lot of people in the same room contribute their interpretation to a chosen theme or image. We can get everyone's version affirmed, and pledges by management made in this public fashion are not lightly broken. We are building 'a high commitment work system'. To set a positive tone, the three days of discussion are kicked off with celebrations and entertainment."

The plant in question showed major increases in productivity. Accidents were also down. Cost per ton dropped from a 1983/84 index of 481 to 421 in 1985 then 361, 337 and finally 315 in 1988. Net profit rose every year since her work began. She does not attribute these gains entirely or even largely to her visioning exercises. Changing technologies also played a major role. But she believes the creation of a genuinely shared vision did make a significant difference.

Not all Ms Brown's interventions are on so vast a scale. She likes to act as consultant to in-house consultants and does extensive seminar work in Scandinavia. She has done an "Airports of the Future" project for SAS, a "Station 90" project on the ground support that air travel will need in the future, and the NAVIA project on envisioning the future of SAS and its stakeholders, customers, partners and sub-contractors.

She is also consultant to The Institute, a Scandinavian top management group. Her other speciality is merger negotiations, and her clients include Proctor & Gamble, the San Francisco Foundation and others who desire anonymity.

Terror in cultural change

But Juanita Brown is included here for her grasp of the fact that all wilful efforts to improve culture and "do good" have their dark side, which you ignore at your peril. She fell seriously ill after strenuous work in Latin America. That brought to a halt what she calls her "Little Miss Muffet days". She was trying too hard to be cheerful, positive, helpful, responsive and dynamic. "My nervous system packed up on me."

"There is underlying fear, even terror in much of cultural change. Because its aims are so good, people feel morally coerced into going along, but that can be fatal. You can't have people 'participate' unless you have the time and the skills to orchestrate that, and to admit your own limits and feel panic at the sheer weight of public responsibility is a totally natural reaction. I've had people blow up in my face. 'We don't want to evaluate each other! We'll lose our friends.' I don't agree with that ... but I agree that the feeling is strong and legitimate and must be expressed so that we can deal with it. There's so much energy in those fears. We can't afford to lose those energies. There's an equivalent terror in me. We have to talk about it. Trying too hard can turn you into an utterly superficial and inwardly desperate person."

Juanita Brown, 497 Loring Avenue, Mill Valley, Ca 94941, USA.

JAMES WILK ASSOCIATES

James Wilk Associates Ltd, based in London, is a most unusual international consultancy in strategic management.

A principal consultant takes the client's problem back to a "management think-tank" of fellow consultants, who take turns in backstopping each other. The think-tank not only asks naïve questions about the relative nakedness of emperors, but comments upon and criticizes the principal consultant's relationship with the client, noting points missed and coaching him or her in greater awareness, on the basis of taped recordings of the meetings or open telephone lines. The claims for this approach are bold. "We specialize in the rapid solution of intractable problems and in bringing about major transformations in large corporations by means of the smallest intervention possible. The principal analyst, D. J. Stewart, calls this "the science of justified intervention".

The approach has three lynch-pins:

- an unusual insistence upon the rigours of the natural sciences;
- the use of the client's existing corporate culture; and
- "minimalist intervention" in that culture.

More than other consultants discussed here, James Wilk Associates identifies itself with scientific methodology. This is not the Action Science of Argyris and Schon, nor F. W. Taylor's misnamed "scientific management". It aims to apply the cybernetic principles discovered in information science, physics and biology to human enterprises. "Managemement cybernetics" would be the technical term. It is a feature of the general systems approach that systems in all disciplines are deemed to have principles in common.

The client's existing culture is conceived of in system terms, with feedback loops that are either not working satisfactorily and/or are creating unintended effects. JWA works with the managers to co-design a range of interventions which, taken together, will bring about the desired transformation. "Each manager that we need to involve," Wilk explains, "and this would usually be only a handful in each division, just goes on doing his or her ordinary job. When they're satisfied and we're satisfied that our hands are on the right levers, we pull them in a concerted manner."

A light touch should suffice

"Minimalist intervention" means making an intervention that is small in the expenditure of time and effort yet has maximum impact and transformative power. It derives from the principle that if anyone truly understands a living organizational system, a mere nudge at the right point will send it off in a new direction, like touching a spinning gyroscope. Organizations are in an analogous state of dynamic equilibrium: they are circular systems packed with the energy of their own momentum. Minimalism is thus more than a philosophy. It should prove that the diagnosis of the client's problem was accurate. You have demonstrated good analysis when your nudge alters the system in the way you intended.

JWA's methods reflect the approach of the Japanese and Asians, whose martial arts and business practices involve joining themselves to the momentum of the opponent. JWA relies on the managers within the existing corporate culture to help discover where the best points of intervention can be found. This method involves the climbing and descending of a daunting abstraction ladder, from the general cross-disciplinary principles of cybernetics at the top, to the specific issues faced by the organization in its day-to-day reality at the bottom. Does JWA not lose the comprehension of the client in the process? Not, it claims, if caution is exercised. In any event, models based in cybernetic sciences have, it believes, far greater validity than the *ad hoc* models encountered in most consulting. "We use universal laws defining inviolable constraints on how things actually work."

James Wilk himself contends that there are no "soft" problems in corporate culture. There are only hard problems to which inappropriate thinking was applied to precipitate a host of "soft" exceptions. "We find the whole dichotomy between soft and hard to be spurious both in concept and in practice." Values, ideas, opinions and so on, all conventionally seen as "soft", can be treated rigorously by cybernetics.

JWA is particularly adamant about what it does not and will not do. It does not get involved in training or organizational development. It does not carry out research or studies and it never writes reports. It does not design or run programmes, give advice, make recommendations, or confine itself to working on processes. It thinks with and not for clients, and makes only joint, not solo, interventions.

Strategy grows from culture

Strategy must be a natural expression of the potential latent in a culture. Because corporate cultures are unique, the products inspired by a culture can be original and incomparable to the offerings of competitors. Hence, a competitive strategy should begin with the culture of the organization.

In an age where hierarchy is coming close to being regarded as an anomaly and rationality itself is questioned, JWA gives managers the role of intelligently redesigning systems already in motion, removing constraints on already active patterns. This should ensure for the system greater discretion, quicker feedback, and the capacity among subordinates to learn how to be more effective. The leaders neither need some extraordinary vision, Wilk argues, nor do they need to resort to push and shove. They need only nudge the spinning wheels of corporate culture, developing patterns of greater harmony, elegance and value. The "nudge" is a way of transforming organizations that respects their continuity.

James Wilk Associates Ltd, 4 Norman Avenue, St Margaret's, Twickenham, London TW1 2LY, UK. Tel: (081) 744 2030.

PIPER TRUST

Piper Trust provides creative management consultancy and venture capital to the retail sector and leisure industries. It specializes in managing development and innovation. The consultancy is based on a particular understanding of systems dynamics. An organization develops a culture in which various decision-rules are formally or informally embedded. That culture must systematically learn from the feedback generated from its operations.

Systems principles in the retail sector

A large retailer cannot make sense of the overwhelming mass of information it generates (thousands of breakdowns by product, type and size, turnover per square foot) unless it knows what it wants, has a vision of where it wants to go and approaches its data with a set of working hypotheses. Retailers tend to drown in their own statistics. Anyone who thinks that "getting close to customers" will automatically bring success should study large retailers. Because they are able to supply such huge varieties of product lines, they typically lose both interest and preference, about what is in demand and why.

Automated reordering procedures develop a suck-in-and-discharge mentality. The process of moving boxes and filling shelves expands until it totally dominates consciousness. Customers choose and retailers move merchandise in the direction of that demand. That is the pattern which will emerge unless a conscious effort is made to create an alternative culture. Only if you have a vision can you begin to see events and demands in the market place as either confirming or negating that vision. Without initial questions to put to customers, there can be no answers, only a sporadic flow of products which would boggle the mind, were it not for the bureaucratic categories that do your thinking for you and will continue indefinitely unless checked.

Piper uses the "Whole Brain Model" (see Figure A1.4, p. 224) from the work of Ned Hermann to understand and then to influence corporate cultures. Research showed that most retail stores on the high street or in shopping centres are overwhelmingly lower left, or quadrant B. They are planned, organized, detailed and sequential "stock-movers". In contrast, the HQs of these large retailers are finance and statistics oriented (in the upper left quadrant A). These people are logical, analytical, quantitative and fact based. The retail business as a whole, then, is overwhelmingly left hemisphere dominant and male oriented, but there is usually an enormous tension between centre and outlets.

Figure A1.4 **Whole brain model**

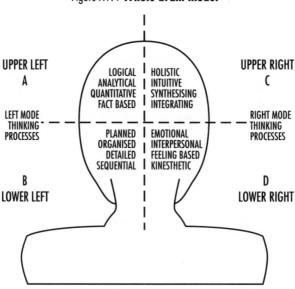

Source: Ned Hermann, *The Creative Brain,* Lake Lure, NC, Brain Books, 1988

Drowning in statistics

The irony is that women customers do most of the buying, and they fall largely into the bottom right quadrant, that is emotional, interpersonal, kinesthetic. What is missing is the "intellectual holism" of the top right quadrant, a vision that synthesizes and integrates all employees into a coherent culture dedicated to serve the customer. Without that top right mode the retail conglomerate drowns in its own statistics. It cannot make sense of what the customers, whom it barely understands as people, are really seeking. Only a whole vision can speak to a whole person. The world of numbers and boxes is blind to patterns and people.

Figure A1.5 **The Piper vision**

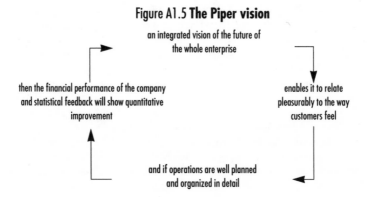

As an example of how this theory works, Piper recently produced a model vision for a chain of kitchen shops called "The Kitchen as the Heart of the House". These would build on the symbolism of a place around which the family revolved, was fed and whose style and cheer helped to hold the family together. Piper discovered that those in quadrants A and B had the greatest difficulty in understanding the concept.

Piper proposes a cultural model to enable the whole retail organization to learn. The cycle must be guided from point D and come full circle through the other three brain quadrants.

The Piper Trust, Eardley House, 182–184 Campden Hill Road, London W8 7AS.

OTHER CONSULTING ORGANIZATIONS

Many of the larger general management consultants also carry out distinctive and original work in the area of corporate culture. It is not possible to list even a selection of them here. When assessing a consultant's approach to corporate culture work, look for awareness of the complexity of the issue and the need to tackle it at several levels.

Boston: culture in five dimensions

The Boston Consulting Group, for example, while equating culture with leadership, defines five simultaneous dimensions in which culture must be approached: vision, overriding goals, strategy, beliefs and, finally, actions. It uses group sessions to establish consensus on the decisions made in each dimension, and oversees the introduction of appropriate corporate rituals and communications programmes to maintain momentum between the different planes of activity. Like most, Boston emphasizes that change must be gradual and coordinated, never sudden or total. Understanding what beliefs and values already exist leads to decisions as to which to emphasize and which to de-emphasize.

Some consultants have an avowed preference for installing a particular management culture, and the Milan-based Ambrosetti Consulting Group has enjoyed success with Italian methods based on developing management networking and coordination systems in companies that choose to be (or have to be) diffuse and dispersed. Ambrosetti specializes in integrating cultural programmes into complex organizational structures.

Strategy first, then culture

Many consultants see culture as the key to reinforcing a strategy. The market development oriented "hard" approach of the US-based Doctus group is a good example. Doctus aims to tailor culture to provide whatever the client needs to support strategic goals. This approach is most appropriate for technology-based companies (which are the biggest client group), particularly since they make a point of including organizational behaviourists in every consulting team.

Culture first, then strategy

The contrasting approach is typified by the Scandinavian group Indevo, which bases its work on the principle that culture should lead business strategy: the organization's attitude should encourage repeated adjustment of strategic direction in response to continuously changing environments. Indevo sets up participative structures in client companies and concentrates on improving communications in order to create foci for regular strategic adjustment.

Accountancy-based consultants focus on productivity

In the larger accountancy-based consulting firms, corporate culture consultancy does not always fall into a particular department and is sometimes offered as a collaboration between divisions. In such cases, the emphasis is usually directed at productivity improvements.

Coopers & Lybrand "manages" clients' cultures by providing a hands-off umbrella service covering communications, training, quality and productivity using a team of specialists from different departments coordinated from the Human Resources consulting division. It focuses on the values and norms that govern workplace behaviour. Deloittes, another consultancy-based group, also has a hands-off philosophy, but it focuses on modifying management systems to release the blocked potential of operating personnel.

Training-based approach

Another question is the degree of implementation consultants can (or should) give in a field where the issue of ownership is so crucial. One consultancy that considers implementation through training an integral part of any corporate culture assignment is the UK-based Coverdale Organization. This group specializes in the theory and practice of team development, and runs training services at all levels for clients. The aim is to build up cultures where people work together effectively. Sheppard Moscow is also known for culture work followed up by training and implementation.

USING CORPORATE IDENTITY CONSULTANTS

Before leaving the subject of consultants, a note should be added about a special type of service which is often encountered in this field.

Identity and culture

"The work of the corporate identity consultants, to quote the catechism, is about the outward manifestation of an inward and spiritual grace," said Wally Olins, speaking in the early 1960s. Since then Wolff Olins, today operating in London, San Francisco, Barcelona and Copenhagen, has become the world's leading consultant on corporate identity and the designer of its clients' logos, shopfronts, billboards, signs, stationery and facades. Wolff Olins's clients include Repsol, Renault, Prudential, Audi, Unilever, AKSO, ICI, the Department of Industry (DTI), Bovis, British Telecom and Volkswagen.

The word symbol comes from the Greek *sym-bol*, "to throw together". The power of symbols is that they can throw together several crucial aspects of the corporate culture encountered by customers and personify these in the public's mind. Symbols can be very powerful and they can come to stand for deeply held convictions and experiences.

This book has been much concerned with dilemmas. It is no coincidence that the cross symbol has inspired Christians for 2,000 years and has come to stand for an inward spiritual struggle intuitively grasped by millions. You "bear your cross" when faith and doubt, hope and despair and many other forces pull you in opposite directions.

It has been claimed that design comprises less than 15 per cent of the cost of most products, yet accounts for up to half the perceived difference in value. The design of a corporation's identity should be such that each part includes the pattern which unites the whole. Seeing that part, whether it be a livery or billboard, a can, a letterhead or a TV commercial, it should be possible to visualise the whole.

Clients come to identity consultants, says Wolff Olins, because they sense a mismatch between how they are perceived and how they would like to be perceived. With both the world and the customer constantly changing, there is a vital need for continuity in the meaning of that company to others.

Ideally a company would create an identity from its authentic culture, so that there was congruence not simply among the visible manifestations of the company in the proliferation of its symbolic forms, but also between those symbols and the behaviour of its employees. This is asking a lot of the consultant who should have both design expertise and staff able to facilitate the development of culture, so that signs and symbols stand for genuine service, rather than being contrived to disguise weaknesses.

Identity consulting is important, because it is one of the few principles of cohesion as opposed to division which is well performed in Western economies. It is a vital "right hemisphere" function (see Chapter 2) in the sense that it connects, harmonises and makes whole that which is perpetually threatening to come apart. It also represents an important aesthetic element in the conduct of an enterprise in its attempts to make solutions to customers' problems elegant, fitting, proportionate, customised and stylish, and to cultivate customer loyalty.

Increasingly organisations teach their customers, beginning with instructions on how to use a product or service, but growing far beyond this to embrace computer literacy, nutritional intelligence, effective communicating and so on. It follows that a corporation's design needs to elicit the individual's potential to learn.

How corporate identity consultants operate

Identity consultants need to start at the top, with those initiating changes in strategy. What meanings will be confirmed, retained and strengthened by these changes? What are the consistent themes, the skeins of continuity within the changes? Consultants must be involved in the process of change. Any problems found will need solutions, which must be communicated to employees and customers and implemented. The designs comprising the new identity must be able to accomplish all this. They must personify answers to problems, ways of communicating and forms of implementation.

Who are the major identity consultants?

The largest corporate identity groupings are controlled by the media giant WPP. These include Sampson Tyrel, Coley Porter Bell and the Business Design Group. Groups originating in the USA include Wolff Olins, Anspach Grossman and Portugal, and Siegal and Gale. In the UK some newer aspirants are the Michael Peters Group, Loyd Northover, Landor Associates and the Conran Design Group.

Corporate culture and corporate identity are clearly convergent and before long both groups of experts will colonise each other's territory to create a seamless whole.

Resource index

WHERE TO GET HELP WITH DIFFERENT ELEMENTS OF CORPORATE CULTURE

Below is an index of the features of corporate culture mentioned in this book. Academics and consultants tend to specialize by feature. It is not a comprehensive list.

Anxiety, Stress. An inevitable accompaniment of cultural change, it is measurable and manageable.
Contact: Dennis T. Jaffe or Cynthia D. Scott, ESSI Systems, 764A Ashbury Street, San Francisco, Ca 94117. Tel. (415) 759 9366.

Attunement. A word coined by Roger T. Harrison for the capacity of all instruments in a cultural "orchestra" to achieve harmony.
Contact: Roger T. Harrison, 1909 Grant Street, Berkeley, Ca 94703. Tel. (415) 849 3103.

Ceremonies. See *Rituals.*

Coherence. (See also *Attunement* and *Synergy.*) Coherence is the name of a Soho consultancy which aims to make design, advertising, literature, video, internal training and other aspects of communications consistent with each other.
Contact: David Bernstein or Sarah Maynard, 37 Dean Street, London W1V 5AP. Tel. (071) 434 2631

Creativity. (See also *Intrapreneuring.*) Achieved by techniques designed to minimize destructive criticism and blockages in the culture.
Contact: Tudor Richards, Creativity and Innovation Unit, Manchester University, School of Business.

Creative Leadership. The Center for Creative Leadership is deservedly well known. Leans rather heavily on personality testing individuals.

Contact: CCL, 5000 Laurinda Drive, Greensboro, North Carolina, 27402.

Crisis Management. (See also *Theatrics.*) Here the notion is that a crisis obliges you to affirm your ultimate values since your very survival is threatened. Anticipating potential crises has an effect which can be salutary.
Contact: Ian I. Mitroff, Center for Crisis Management, University of Southern California, School of Business, Los Angeles, Ca 90089. Tel. (213) 743 8318.

Cross-cultural Management. Consists of studying the national characteristics of various groups of managers and attempting to make the best multinational use of their predispositions. Such understandings are important in mergers, joint ventures and negotiations.
Contacts: Fons Trompenaars, Centre for International Business Studies, De Lairessestraat 90, 1071 PJ Amsterdam, Netherlands. Tel. 20 664 0743. Professor André Laurent, Insead, 77305 Fontainebleau France. Tel. 60 72 40 00. David Wheatley, Employment Conditions Abroad, Anchor House, 15 Britten Street, London SW3. Tel. (071) 351 7151.

Cybernetics. For the special attributes of "self-organising" cybernetics systems.
Contact: Fernando Flores, Action Technologies, 2200 Powell Street, Emeryville, Ca 94608. Tel. (415) 654 4444.

Viable Technologies Inc., 34 Palmerston Square, Toronto, Ontario, Canada M6G 2S7. Tel. (416) 535 0396. Plus many of the practitioners covered in Appendix 1.

Design of Systems. (See also *Cybernetics*.) For the redesign of organizational systems see Appendix 1. Also of interest is the matching of organizational structures to the task required, or "requisite organization".

Contact: Elliott Jaques, SST Ltd, PO Box 2364, Arlington, VA 22202, (703) 521 3873 or 19 Bolton Street, London W1.

An interesting structural typology of organizational systems which "mandate" corresponding cultures has been created by Professor Henry Mintzberg.

Contact: Professor Henry Mintzberg, Faculty of Management, McGill University, 1001 Sherbrooke West, Montreal, Canada H3A IGS. Tel. (514) 398 4017.

For purpose-built information networks, whether temporary (for conferences or projects) or permanent.

Contact: Frank Burns or Lisa Carlson, Metasystems Design Group Inc., 2000 North 15th Street 103, Arlington, VA 22201. Tel. (703) 342 6622.

For "architecturally designed" solutions to any impasse in an organizational system, the world-renowned expert is Russ Ackoff.

Contact: Russ Ackoff, INTERACT, 3440 Market Street, Philadelphia, PA 19104. Tel. (215) 386 2500.

Dilemma and Paradox. This is the speciality of the author of this report. Peter Vaill takes a softer but persuasive view of paradox.

Contact: Peter B. Vaill, School of Business Administration, George Washington University, Washington DC. Tel. (202) 994 7597.

A more measurable and structured approach is taken by Robert Quinn who looks at management styles.

Contacts: Robert E. Quinn, School of Business and Public Administration, State University of New York, Albany, NY. Kenwyn K. Smith, Department of Management, The Wharton School, Philadelphia, Pa 19104. Tel. (703) 521 3873.

A dilemma board game has been invented by Strategic People, who claim that it raises the consciousness about key issues.

Contact: Pam Pocock, Pepys House, 48 Station Road, Chertsey, Surrey KT16 8BE. Tel. (0932) 563213.

Environment. This was a useful term for studying corporate culture before it became fashionable. It has been argued for some time that the corporation's internal culture must match the features of the external culture and possess the same "requisite variety". This approach has been pursued for many years by Igor Ansoff, the "father" of strategic thinking.

Contact: Igor Ansoff, US International University, 10455 Pomerado Road, San Diego, Ca 92131.

Flow States. Cultures are increasingly being seen as "states of flow and mutually strengthening processes". The following take such an approach.

Contacts: Professor Jerry I. Porras, Graduate School of Business, Stanford University, Stanford, Ca 94305-5015. Tel. (415) 723 2850. Linda Ackerman, 1925 Rhode Island Ave, Mehean, Virginia 22101. Tel. (703) 241 8110.

Futures. (See *Scenarios of the Future*.) Elliott Jaques has also developed a way of measuring orientations to the future to see which managers have the potential to manage longer "timespans of discretion". See *Design of Systems*.

History as Culture. Many consultants routinely look at the organization's history as a clue to its culture. A prime advocate of this position is Andrew Pettigrew, who researched ICI longitudinally.

Contact: Professor Andrew Pettigrew, University of Warwick, Coventry, CV4 7AL. Tel. (0203) 523918.

In continental Europe:

Contact: Alden Lank, IMD, Chemin de Bellerive, PO Box 915, Lansanne, CH 1001 Switzerland. Tel. (21) 618 0111.

Identity, Corporate. (See also *Appendix 1*). Wolff Olins looks at overall design as a contribution to identity and as a reflection of strategic performance.

Contacts: Wendy Pritchard, 22 Dukes Road, London WC1H 9AB Tel. (01) 387 0891.Coley Porter Bell, 4 Flitcroft Street, London WC2H 8DJ.

A young company moving fast with a similar approach to Olins.

Images of Organizations. (See also *Metaphors*.) This is the speciality of Gareth Morgan and is discussed in Chapter 10.

Contact: Professor Gareth Morgan, York University, 4700 Keele Street, North York, Ontario, Canada M3J 1P3. Tel. (416) 736 5095.

Intervention Skills are specifically taught and addressed by Sheppard Moscow.

Contact: Sheppard Moscow Ltd., Beaumont House, Willow Grove, Chislehurst, Kent BR7 5DA. Tel. (081) 468 7975.

Intrapreneuring. The concept was invented by Gifford Pinchot III and refers to innovating within a large company by bringing entrepreneurial processes within the corporation. Some significant successes have been claimed.

Contact: Pinchot & Co, 40-49 Orange Street, New Haven, CT 06511. Tel. (203) 624 5355.

For a British interpretation:

Contact: Roy Williams, Developments Associates Group, Kenneth Pollard House, Castlebridge, 5-19 Cowbridge Road East, Cardiff CF1 9AB. Tel. (0222) 344 457.

Japanese Culture. It is best to stick to the experts.

Contact: Professor M.Y. Yoshimo, Graduate School of Business, Harvard University, Boston, Mass (E17). Tel. (617) 495 6305.

For the best Western interpretation:

Contact: Professor Ezra Vogel, Center for Asian Studies, Harvard University, Cambridge, Mass 02136.

For a prominent Japanese-American interpreter:

Contact: William G. Ouchi, Graduate School of Management, University of California, Los Angeles, Ca 90007. Tel. (213) 825 7935.

Leadership. Major contributors to leadership and culture include Professor Warren Bennis.

Contact: Professor Warren Bennis, Department of Management and Policy Sciences, University of Southern California, Los Angeles, Ca 90007. Tel. (213) 743 8317.

For additional emphasis on long-range planning:

Contact: Bert Nanus at the same address. Tel. (213) 743 5229.

Professor John Kotter studies the responsiveness of leaders to different cultures.

Contact: Professor John Kotter, Harvard Business School, Boston, Mass 02163.

For a highly original British approach to leadership and culture:

Contacts: Alistair Mant, New Age Network Ltd, PO Box 467, Hove, East Sussex BN3 7FZ (0273) 207381. Manfred Kets de Vries, Insead, 77305 Fontainebleau. Tel. 60 72 40 00.

Learning and Learning Styles. (See also *Paradigms*.) The topic of accelerated corporate learning is taken up by Arie de Geus, until recently with Shell.

Contact: Arie de Geus, Strategy and International Management Department, London Business School, Sussex Place, London NW1 4SA. Tel. (071) 262 5050.

That managers learn in radically different styles and require information to match those styles is taken up by Joint Development Resources.

Contact: Jerome D. Rhodes, Joint Development Resources, 24, Cecil Parks, Pinner, Middlesex, HA5 5HH. Tel. (081) 866 1262. (See also *Two Cultures.*)

For learning that makes elaborate use of interactive media, video, software etc:

Contact: Bob Garratt, Media Projects International Ltd, Cameron House, 12 Castlehaven Road, London NW1 8AW. Tel. (071) 845 5657.

That planning is best regarded as a form of learning from error is the position of Don Michael.

Contact: Don Michael,1472 Filbert Street 511, San Francisco, Ca 94109. Tel. (415) 775 1839.

Learning was also the specific focus of many of the consultants discussed in Appendix 1.

Managerial Grid. This is an instrument for monitoring progress along at least two reconcilable axes.

Contact: Robert R. Blake and Jane S. Mouton, Scientific Instruments, Austin, Texas.

Mental Mapping. See *Transitional Objects.*

Metaphors. See *Images of Organization.*

Myths. See *Story-telling.*

Paradigms. How paradigm change is affecting professional disciplines and corporate learning.

Contact: Jay Ogilvy or Peter Schwartz, Global Business Network, 37 Poplar Road, 94704 Ca. Tel. (415) 527 9408.

Participation. Schemes for workers and employees, including quality circles, gain sharing, Scanlon plans, quality of life programmes, have been collected and carefully evaluated by the Center for Effective Organization, which also designs programmes appropriate to different situations.

Contact: Professor Edward Lawler, Center for Effective Organization, University of Southern California, Los Angeles, Ca 90089-1421. Tel. (213) 743 8765.

Peak Performance. Cultures capable of generating peak performances.

Contact: Charles Garfield, 652 Bair Island Road, Redwood City, Ca 94063. Tel. (415) 960 0700.

Renewal. (See *Appendix 1; Creativity* and *Intrapreneuring.*) Corporate renewal is the speciality of Robert Waterman.

Contact: Waterman and Co, 100 Spear Street, 1505, San Francisco, Ca 94105. Tel. (415) 974 5757.

Quality Circles, Quality of Working Life. See *Participation.*

Rituals, Ceremonies and Mourning. Corporate "funerals", wakes, celebrations, rebirths are orchestrated by the episcopal minister, Harrison H. Owen.

Contact: H.H. Owen & Co, 7808 River Falls Drive, Potomac, MD 20854. Tel. (301) 469 9269.

Scenarios of the Future. This consists of creating coherent visions of future world cultures. The work is mostly performed by "graduates" of the scenario planning process of the Shell International Petroleum Co.

Contacts: Pierre Wack, "La Joannie", Curemonte, 19500 Meyssac, France. Tel. 55 25 39 66.Barbara Heinzen, 18 Wilmington Square, London WC1X 0ER. Tel. (01) 278 1175.

Peter Schwartz, 37 Poplar Road, Berkeley, Ca 94708. Tel. (415) 527 9408.

The first two are especially concerned with Asia and the Far East. Schwartz and Wack are both members of Global Business Network (see *Paradigms*.)

Story-telling. (See also *Theatrics* and *Crisis Management*.) The original emphasis on the "corporate story" comes from Alan L. Wilkins.

Contacts: Alan L. Wilkins, School of Management, Brigham Young University, Provo, Utah 84602. Harrison Owen (see *Rituals*) is also a "re-mythologizer" for corporations, creating new stories in the place of those which impede effectiveness. Will McWhinney, Enthusion Inc., 589 Grand Blvd, Venice, Ca 90211. Tel. (213) 329 1343.

Strategic Styles. Goold and Campbell isolated three "strategic cultures" in difficult companies: Strategic Planning, Strategic Control and Financial Control.

Contact: Michael Goold or Andrew Campbell, 17 Portland Place, London W1N 3AF. Tel. (01)' 323 4422.

Synergy (or Synergism). The speciality of Peter and Susan Corning, who make the elements of a business more harmonious and coherent.

Contact: Peter Corning, 310 University Ave, Palo Alto, Ca 94305.

Team Building. This is the speciality of Richard Hackman.

Contacts: Richard Hackman, Harvard Business School, Boston, Mass 02163. Tel. (617) 495 6467.Meredith Belbin (see *Appendix I*).

Theatrics. The concept of management as engaged in theatrical performances.

Contacts: Professor Iain Mangham, School of Management, University of Bath, Claverton Down, Bath BA2 7AY.Peter Vaill (see *Dilemma*).

Transformation and Transformational Leadership. (See also *Flow States*.) The term originated with the historian, James McGregor Burns, and is much overused by consultants. For a useful approach:Contact: Noel Tichy, Graduate School of Business, University of Michigan, Ann Arbor.

Transitional Objects, using magnetized boards with multicoloured hexagons, CTI Corporate Services helps managers model their own thought processes. They call this cybernovation from innovation and cybernetics.

Contact: Tony Hodgson, Eradour house, Pitlochry, Perthshire, Scotland. Tel. (0796) 3773.

Two Cultures. The term is applied especially to the UK and refers to the polarization of the arts and the sciences. For a major authority on this condition:

Contact: Liam Hudson, 34 North Park, Gerrards Cross, Bucks. Tel. (0753) 886281.

Typologies of Culture. There are several of these. Among the best known are those by Roger Harrison (see *Attunement*) and Charles Handy. Both are described in Chapter 1 (see also *Strategic Styles* and *Learning Styles*).

Contact: Charles Handy, 73 Putney Hill, London SW15 3NT. Tel. (081) 788 1610.

A famous typology is by Michael Maccoby, who distinguished the Gamesman from the Craftsman.

Contact: Michael Maccoby, 1636 Connecticut Ave, NW 400, Washington DC 20009. Tel. (202) 462 3003.

Visioning. A huge number of consultants claim to do this. A highly professional approach, using neuro-linguistics, is by PACE.

Contact: D.R. Gaster, Redvers House, 13 Fairmile, Henley, Oxon. Tel. 0491 410112, RG9 2JR.

Bibliography

Abegglen, James C. and Stalk Jr., George, *Kaisha: The Japanese Corporation*, New York: Basic Books, 1985.

Allen, Robert F., "Four Phases in Bringing about Cultural Change" in *Gaining Control of Corporate Culture*, Ralph H. Kilman, Mary J. Saxton and Roy Serpa (eds.), San Francisco: Jossey-Bass, 1986.

Argyris, Chris, *Inner Contradictions of Rigorous Research*, New York: Academic Press, 1980.

Argyris, Chris, *Strategy, Change and Defensive Routines*, Boston: Pitman, 1983.

Argyris, Chris, with Putman, R. and Smith, D. M., *Action Science*, San Francisco, Jossey-Bass, 1985.

Argyris, Chris, "Skilled incompetence", *Harvard Business Review*, Sep/Oct1986.

Argyris, Chris and Schon, Donald A., *Organizational Learning: A Theory of Action Perspective*, Reading: Addison-Wesley, 1978.

Argyris, Chris and Schon, Donald A., "Reciprocal Integrity", presented at the Symposium on Functioning of Executive Integrity, Case Western Reserve, Oct1986.

Argyris, Chris and Schon, Donald A., "Rigor or Relevance? Normal Science and Action Science Compared", Harvard University and MIT, Sep 1988.

Axelrod, Robert, *The Evolution of Cooperation*, New York: Basic Books, 1984.

Baden-Fuller, C., Nicolaides, P. and Stopford, John, "National or Global?", *Centre for Business Strategy Working Paper No. 28*, London, June 1987.

Bateson, Gregory, *Steps to an Ecology of Mind*, New York: Ballantine, 1975.

Beer, Stafford, *The Brain of the Firm*, New York: Wiley, 1981.

Belbin, R. Meredith, *Management Teams*, London: Heinemann, 1981.

Bell, Daniel, *The Coming of Post-Industrial Society*, New York: Basic Books, 1976.

Bennis, Warren and Nanus, Burt, *Leaders: The Strategies for Taking Charge*, New York: Harper and Row, 1985.

Berlin, Isaiah, *Two Concepts of Liberty*, Oxford: Clarendon, 1958.

Berlin, Isaiah, *The Hedgehog and the Fox*, New York: Mentor, 1965.

Blake, Robert R. and Mouton, Jane S., *The Managerial Grid*, Tex.: Gulf Publishing, 1965.

Boisot, Max, "Intangible Factors in Japanese Corporate Strategy", *Atlantic Papers*, 1983.

Bolman, Lee G. and Deal, Terrence E., *Modern Approaches to Understanding and Managing Organizations*, San Francisco: Jossey-Bass, 1984.

Burns, James MacGregor, *Leadership*, New York: Harper and Row, 1978.

Burns, T. and Stalker, G. M., *The Management of Innovation*, London: Tavistock, 1966.

Christopher, Robert C., *The Japanese Mind*, London: Pan Books, 1984.

Cohen, Stephen and Zysman, John, *Manufacturing Matters*, New York: Basic Books, 1987.

Corning, Peter A., *The Synergism Hypothesis: A Theory of Progressive Evolution*, New York: McGraw-Hill, 1983.

Corning, Peter A. and Corning, Susan, *Winning with Synergy*, New York: Harper and Row, 1986.

Davis, Stanley M., *Managing Corporate Culture*, Cambridge: Ballinger, 1984.

Daniels, William R., *Group Power II: A Managers Guide to Conducting Regular Meetings*, San Diego: University Associates, 1990.

De Pru, Max, *Leadership is an Art*, New York: Doubleday, 1989.

Deal, Terrence E. and Kennedy, Allan A. *Corporate Cultures: The Rites and Rituals of Corporate Life*, Reading: Addison-Wesley, 1982.

Dore, Ronald, *Taking Japan Seriously*, Stanford: Stanford University Press, 1987.

Emery, Fred, and Trist, Eric, *Towards a Social Ecology*, London: Plenun, 1973.

European Management Forum, *Annual Report on International Competitiveness*, Geneva: European Management Forum, 1987 (now IMD).

Forrester, Jay W. and Senge, Peter M., "Tests for Building Confidence in Systems Dynamics Models", *TIMS Studies in Management Sciences*, No.14, 1980.

de Geus, A. P., "Planning as Learning", *Harvard Business Review*, March/April 1988.

Goold, Michael and Campbell, Andrew, *Strategic Styles*, Oxford: Basil Blackwell, 1988.

Graves, D., *Corporate Culture: Diagnosis and Change*, N. Y.: St Martin's Press, 1986.

Halal, William E., *The New Capitalism*, New York: Wiley, 1986.

Halberstam, David, *The Reckoning*, New York: Avon, 1986.

Hampden-Turner, Charles M., *Radical Man: Towards a Theory of Psycho-social Developement*, London: Duckworth, 1973.

Hampden-Turner, Charles M., *Maps of the Mind*, New York: Macmillan, 1981.

Hampden-Turner, Charles M., *Gentlemen and Tradesmen: The Values of Economic Catastrophe*, London: Routledge and Kegan Paul, 1983.

Hampden-Turner, Charles M., "Approaching Dilemmas", *Shell Guides to Planning*, No. 3, 1985.

Hampden-Turner, Charles M., *Charting the Corporate Mind: From Dilemma to Strategy*, Oxford: Basil Blackwell, 1990.

Handy, Charles, *The Gods of Management*, London: Souvenir Press, 1978.

Handy, Charles, *The Age of Unreason*, London: Century-Hutchinson, 1989.

Harrison, Roger, "Start-up: The care and feeding of infant systems" in *Organizational Dynamics*, Sept 1981.

Harrison, Roger, "Understanding your organizations Character", *Harvard Business Review*, May-June, 1972.

Herman, Ned, *The Creative Brain*, Lake Lure, NC: Brain Books, 1988.

Hofstede, Geert, *Cultures' Consequences*, Beverly Hills: Sage, 1980.

Hurst, D. K., "Of boxes, bubbles and effective management", *Harvard Business Review*, May/June 1984.

Hurst, D. K., "Why strategic management is bankrupt", *Organizational Dynamics*, Fall, 1986.

Jaques, Elliot, *Free Enterprise Fair Employment*, New York: Crane Russak, 1982.

Jaques, Elliot, *The Form of Time*, New York: Crane Russak, 1982.

Jaques, Elliot, *Requisite Organization: The CEO's Guide to Creative Structure and Leadership*, Arlington, Va.: Cason Hall, 1989.

Kanter, Rosabeth Moss, *The Change Masters*, London: Allen and Unwin, 1984.

Kanter, Rosabeth Moss, *When Giants Learn to Dance*, New York: Simon Schuster, 1989.

Kauffman, Draper L., *Systems I: An Introduction to Systems Thinking*, Minneapolis, Minn.: Future Systems, 1980.

Keifer, Charles F. and Senge, Peter M., "Metanoic Organization" in John D. Adams (ed.), *Transforming Work*, Va.: Miles River Press, 1984.

Kilmann, Ralph H., Saxton, Mary J., Serpa, Roy and Associates, *Gaining Control of Corporate Culture*, San Francisco: Jossey-Bass, 1986.

Kilmann, Ralph H., *Beyond the Quick Fix*, San Francisco: Jossey-Bass, 1984.

Koulhaas, Jan, *Organzation Dissononce and Change*, New York: Wiley, 1982.

Kotter, John P. and Lawrence, Paul R., *Mayors in Action*, New York: Wiley, 1974.

Lawler, Edward E., *High Involvment Management*, San Francisco: Jossey-Bass, 1986.

Lawrence, Paul R. and Lorsch, Jay W., *Organization and Environment*, Boston: Harvard Division of Research, 1967.

Lebra, Takie Sugiyama, *Japanese Patterns of Behaviour*, Honolulu, Hawaii: University Press of Hawaii, 1976.

Lodge, George C., *The American Disease*, New York: Knopf, 1984.

Lodge, George C. and Vogel, Erza F. (eds), *Ideology and National Competitiveness*, Boston: Harvard Business School Press, 1987.

Mangham, Iain L., *Organizations as Theatre*, New York: Wiley, 1987.

Mangham, Iain L., *Effecting Organizational Change*, Oxford: Basil Blackwell, 1988.

Mant, Alistair, *The Rise and Fall of the British Manager*, London: Macmillan, 1977.

Martin, Joanne, and Feldman, Martha S. and Hatch, Mary Jo, "The uniqueness paradox in organizational performance", *Administrative Science Quarterly*, Vol. 28 No. 3, 1983.

Martin, Joanne, and Shiel, C., "Organizational culture and counter culture: An uneasey symbosis", *Organizational Dynamics*, 12, 1983.

McGregor, Douglas, *The Human Side of the Enterprise, New York:* McGraw-Hill, 1960.

Michael, Donald N., *On Learning to Plan and Planning to Learn*, San Francisco, Ca: Jossey-Bass, 1973.

Mintzberg, Henry, "The manager's job: Folklore or fact", *Harvard Business Review*, Jul/Aug 1976.

Mintzberg, Henry, "Planning on the left side, managing on the right', *Harvard Business Review,* Jul/Aug 1976.

Mintzberg, Henry,"Crafting strategy", *Harvard Business Review*, March/April,1987.

Mintzberg, Henry, *Mintzberg of Management: Inside our Strange World of Organizations*, New York: The Free Press, 1989.

Mitroff, Iain, *Business NOT as Usual*, San Francisco: Ca: Jossey-Bass, 1987.

Morgan, Gareth, *Images of Organization*, Beverly Hill, Ca: Sage, 1986.

Morgan, Gareth, *Riding the Waves of Change*, San Francisco, Ca: Jossey-Bass, 1988.

Ogilvy, Jay, *Many Dimensional Man*, New York: Oxford University Press, 1977.

Olins, Wally, *The Corporate Personality*, London: The Design Council, 1978.

O'Toole, James, *Vanguard Management*, New York: Doubleday, 1985.

Ouchi, William, *Theory Z: How American Business can Meet the Japanese Challenge*, Reading: Addison-Wesley, 1981.

Pascale, R. T., and Athos, A. G., *The Art of Japanese Management*, New York: Simon and Schuster, 1981.

Peters, T., and Waterman, R. H., *In Search of Excellence*, N.Y.: Harper and Row, 1982.

Porras, Jerry I., *Steam Analysis*, Reading, Mass: Addison-Wesley, 1987.

Porter, Michael E., *Competitive Strategy: Techniques for Analyzing Industries and Competitors*, New York: Free Press, 1980.

Porter, Michael E., *The Competitive Advantage of Nations, New York*: Free Press, 1990.

Quinn, J. B., "Logical incrementalism", *Sloan Management Review*, (20), Fall 1978.

Quinn, J. B., Mintzberg, Henry and James, Robert M., *The Strategy Process*, Englewood Cliffs, Prentice Hall, 1988.

Quinn, Robert E., *Beyond Rational Management,* San Francisco, Ca: Jossey-Bass, 1988.

Rapaport, Anatol, *Strategy and Conscience,* Boston: Houghton Mifflin, 1963.

Reich, Robert B., *The Next American Frontier,* New York: Times Books, 1983.

Reich, Robert B., *Tales of a New America,* New York, Times Books, 1987.

Rhodes, Jerry, and Thane, Sue, *The Colours of your Mind,* London: Collins, 1988.

Roethlisberger, Fritz, and William Dixon, *Management and the Worker,* Cambridge: Harvard University Press, 1937.

Schein, Edgar H., *Organization, Culture and Leadership,* San Francisco:Jossey-Bass, 1985.

Schon, Donald A., *Beyond the Stable State,* New York: Random House, 1971.

Schon, Donald A., "Creative Metaphor: A Perspective on Problem Setting in Social Policy" in A. Ortny (ed.), *Metaphor and Thought,* Cambridge University Press, 1979.

Schon, Donald A., *The Reflective Practitioner New York*: Basic Books, 1982.

Scott, Bruce R., and Lodge, George C, (eds), *American Competitiveness,* Boston: Harvard Business School Press, 1985.

Sculley, John, *Odessey: From Pepsi to Apple,* New York: Harper and Row, 1987.

Senge, Peter M., *The Fifth Discipline,* New York: Doubleday, 1990.

Skinner, B. F., *Beyond Freedom and Dignity,* New York: Random House, 1964.

Smircich, Linda, "Concepts of culture and organizational analysis", *Administrative Science Quarterly,* Vol. 28 No. 3, 1983.

Smith, Kerwyn K., and Simmons, Valerie M., "The Rumplestiltskin organization: metaphors on metaphors in field research", *Administration Science Quarterly,* Vol. 28 No. 3, 1983.

Thurow, Lester C., *The Zero Sum Society,* New York: McGraw-Hill, 1980.

Thurow, Lester C., (ed.), *The Management Challenge: Japanese Views,* Cambridge: MIT Press, 1985.

Thurow, Lester C., *The Zero Sum Society,* New York: Simon and Schuster, 1985.

Toffler, Alvin, *Future Shock,* New York: Bantam, 1970.

Toffler, Alvin, *The Third Wave,* New York: Bantam, 1970.

Trompenaars, Fons, "The Organization of Meaning and the Meaning of Organization", Dissertion, The Wharton School, PA.

Vogel, Ezra, *Japan as No 1,* New York: Harper and Row, 1979.

Vogel, Ezra, *Comeback: Building the Resurgence of American Business,* New York: Simon and Schuster, 1985.

Watzlawick, Paul, and Beavin, J. H. and Jackson, D. D., *Pragmatics of Human Communication,* New York: W. W. Norton, 1967.

Weisbord, Marius R., *Productive Workplace,* San Francisco: Jossey-Bass, 1987.

Wilk, James, "How Change has Changed: Organizational Culture, Justified Intervention and the Art of the Nudge", paper delivered at Sixth Conference of Education and Development in Organizations, University of Lancaster, Sept 18 1987.

Wilk, James, "Culture and Epistemology" paper delivered at One-Day Conference, London Business School, March 3 1989.

Wilk, James, "Knowledge and Know-How" paper delivered at Second Biennial Ashridge Research Conference, Jan 1987.

Wilkins, Alan L., and Ouchi, William G., Efficient Cultures: "Exploring the relationship between culture and organizational performance", *Administrative Science Quarterly,* Vol. 28 No.3, 1983.

Index